Industry AI: Applications in Healthcare, Finance, and Beyond

Gilbert Gutiérrez

Artificial Intelligence is no longer just a futuristic concept—it's here, transforming industries, streamlining processes, and redefining human-machine collaboration. From diagnosing diseases in milliseconds to predicting financial market trends with unparalleled accuracy, AI is revolutionizing every sector it touches. But how does this transformation happen, and what does it mean for businesses, professionals, and society as a whole?

In **Industry AI: Applications in Healthcare, Finance, and Beyond**, the final volume of the acclaimed **AI from Scratch series**, *Gilbert Gutiérrez* delivers a comprehensive, real-world exploration of how AI is driving unprecedented changes across multiple industries. This book serves as both a practical guide and an insightful reflection on the role of AI in modern enterprises, making it an essential read for AI practitioners, business leaders, policymakers, and enthusiasts eager to understand the next wave of AI-powered innovation.

Whether you're an AI researcher, an entrepreneur looking to leverage AI in your business, or simply fascinated by the ongoing AI revolution, this book provides a clear roadmap to understanding and implementing AI in real-world industry settings.

Why This Book?

The Final Step in Mastering Industry AI

Building upon the knowledge from the previous 15 volumes of the AI from Scratch series, this book takes a deep dive into how AI is deployed across some of the most influential industries. Unlike theoretical AI books, this volume is practical, insightful, and designed for real-world application.

- Explore AI's impact on key industries such as healthcare, finance, manufacturing, retail, education, and logistics.
- Understand cutting-edge AI technologies, from deep learning in medical imaging to AI-powered fraud detection in banking.
- Gain insight into AI-driven business transformation, automation strategies, and AI's ethical and regulatory implications.
- Learn through real-world case studies, exploring how leading companies successfully implement AI solutions.

This book is not just about understanding AI—it's about using AI to drive real impact.

What's Inside?

Part 1: Foundations of Industry AI

The book begins by examining how AI is reshaping industries, the differences between consumer AI and enterprise AI, and the regulatory and ethical challenges businesses must navigate. You'll discover how AI adoption varies across industries and the core technologies fueling these transformations, including machine learning, deep learning, natural language processing, and computer vision.

Part 2: AI in Healthcare

Few industries have experienced an AI-driven revolution quite like healthcare. Here, you'll explore how AI is:

- Enhancing medical imaging and diagnostics, enabling radiologists to detect diseases like cancer more accurately and at earlier stages.
- Accelerating drug discovery and precision medicine, allowing pharmaceutical companies to cut down research time and develop personalized treatments.
- Improving patient care with AI-powered virtual assistants and telemedicine, making healthcare more accessible across the globe.
- Optimizing hospital operations, from predictive scheduling to AI-driven medical billing, reducing inefficiencies and administrative burdens.

With a mix of real-world case studies and emerging trends, this section reveals how AI is extending human expertise rather than replacing it.

Part 3: AI in Finance

In the financial sector, AI is not just about automation—it's about intelligence. This section uncovers how AI is:

- Transforming stock trading with algorithmic and high-frequency trading, enabling real-time market analysis.
- Enhancing fraud detection and cybersecurity, using machine learning to identify suspicious financial activities before they cause damage.
- Revolutionizing banking through AI-powered chatbots, risk assessment, and personalized customer experiences.
- Driving innovation in fintech, including AI-powered lending decisions, robo-advisors, and blockchain-enhanced security.

With a deep dive into regulatory concerns, AI ethics, and real-world implementation, this section is a must-read for finance professionals and tech enthusiasts alike.

Part 4: AI Beyond Healthcare & Finance

AI's reach goes far beyond medicine and money. This section explores how AI is shaping:

- **Manufacturing & Smart Factories** – AI-driven predictive maintenance, IoT integration, and robotic automation are redefining industrial production.
- **Retail & E-Commerce** – AI recommendation engines, personalized marketing, and AI-powered supply chain management are optimizing consumer experiences.
- **Transportation & Logistics** – AI is revolutionizing route optimization, demand forecasting, and self-driving vehicle technologies.
- **Education & Learning** – AI-driven personalized learning systems, automated grading, and intelligent tutoring assistants are transforming education.

These chapters go beyond theory, providing real-life examples and case studies of how AI is actively reshaping global industries.

Part 5: The Future of Industry AI

The final section of the book looks ahead, exploring:

- The rise of quantum AI and how quantum computing could supercharge AI applications in industry.
- The importance of Explainable AI (XAI) in regulated industries like healthcare, finance, and government.
- The ethical dilemmas and societal impact of AI, including bias in AI decision-making and workforce automation.
- The future of AI regulation, compliance, and governance, ensuring AI benefits businesses and humanity responsibly.

The book concludes by reflecting on the journey of AI from theory to practice and offering key insights into the next decade of AI-driven transformation.

Who Is This Book For?

This book is written for a broad audience, from AI professionals and business leaders to students and policymakers.

- **Business executives & entrepreneurs** – Learn how to integrate AI into your industry for better efficiency, accuracy, and profitability.
- **AI developers & data scientists** – Understand the industry-specific challenges of deploying AI solutions.
- **Healthcare & finance professionals** – Gain insight into how AI is reshaping your sector and how you can leverage it for growth.
- **Researchers & academics** – Discover real-world AI applications that go beyond traditional AI theory.
- **Tech enthusiasts & AI learners** – Get a comprehensive understanding of how AI is transforming industries and where the field is headed.

If you're passionate about AI's potential to drive real-world innovation, this book is your ultimate guide to understanding industry AI.

Final Thoughts: A Legacy of AI Knowledge

As the 16th and final book in the AI from Scratch series, Industry AI serves as the capstone to an incredible journey of learning. Whether you've read the entire series or are just starting, this book will leave you with a deep appreciation for AI's impact on industry and the future it is shaping.

Are you ready to unlock the power of AI in the real world?

☞ *Get your copy of Industry AI: Applications in Healthcare, Finance, and Beyond and join the future of AI-driven industries today!*

1. Introduction: The Role of AI in Transforming Industries

Artificial Intelligence is no longer a futuristic concept—it is a present-day force driving innovation across industries. From automating complex tasks to enhancing decision-making with data-driven insights, AI is revolutionizing healthcare, finance, manufacturing, and beyond. Businesses that embrace AI gain a competitive edge, increased efficiency, and improved customer experiences, while those that resist risk falling behind. This chapter explores how AI has evolved, why industries are rapidly adopting it, and what challenges and opportunities lie ahead in this era of intelligent automation.

1.1 The Evolution of AI in Industrial Applications

Artificial Intelligence (AI) has come a long way from its conceptual origins to becoming a driving force behind modern industry. Once confined to academic research and theoretical exploration, AI has rapidly progressed into real-world applications that enhance efficiency, decision-making, and automation across multiple sectors. This evolution has been marked by key technological breakthroughs, growing computational power, and widespread industry adoption.

In this chapter, we explore the historical progression of AI in industrial applications, from early automation to today's cutting-edge innovations. Understanding AI's evolution provides critical insights into how businesses can leverage its potential for future growth.

The Early Days: AI's Industrial Foundations

AI's roots in industry date back to the mid-20th century when computer scientists began developing algorithms capable of mimicking human problem-solving. The term "Artificial Intelligence" was first coined in 1956 at the Dartmouth Conference, marking the official beginning of AI as a field of study. However, industrial applications of AI took longer to materialize due to limited computational power and the infancy of machine learning models.

During the 1960s and 1970s, AI's role in industry was largely experimental. Early systems, such as expert systems and rule-based automation, were developed to assist in decision-making for sectors like manufacturing and logistics. The first industrial robots also emerged during this time, notably Unimate, introduced in 1961 as the first programmable robotic arm used in automobile manufacturing. While these early innovations laid the groundwork for AI in industry, they were limited in intelligence and adaptability.

The Rise of Machine Learning: AI in Industry Gains Momentum (1980s-1990s)

The 1980s and 1990s saw significant advancements in AI, particularly in the development of machine learning algorithms and neural networks. These breakthroughs enabled AI systems to move beyond rule-based logic and learn from data, making them more adaptable and intelligent.

Key milestones during this period included:

- **Expert Systems in Healthcare & Finance** – AI-powered expert systems were deployed in industries like medicine (for disease diagnosis) and finance (for risk assessment and fraud detection). These systems could make rule-based decisions based on pre-programmed knowledge.
- **Industrial Robotics** – AI-powered robots became more sophisticated, improving efficiency in automotive and electronics manufacturing. Japan became a leader in AI-driven robotics, integrating intelligent automation into its factories.
- **Early AI in Supply Chains** – AI began optimizing inventory management and logistics, reducing operational costs through predictive analytics.

Despite these advancements, AI adoption remained limited due to computational constraints, high costs, and a lack of big data for training AI models. However, the groundwork for AI's future industrial applications was firmly established.

The Big Data Revolution: AI Becomes a Business Asset (2000s-2010s)

The early 2000s marked a turning point in AI's industrial evolution, driven by big data, increased computational power, and advancements in deep learning. Companies began to recognize AI as a competitive business asset, leading to widespread adoption across multiple industries.

Key developments during this period included:

AI-Powered Automation in Manufacturing

- AI-driven robots, such as those developed by Boston Dynamics and FANUC, became more intelligent and flexible, automating complex manufacturing processes.
- Predictive maintenance using AI allowed factories to reduce downtime and extend the life of equipment by analyzing sensor data for potential failures.

AI in Finance and Retail

- The finance industry leveraged AI-driven trading algorithms, fraud detection systems, and chatbots for customer service.
- Retail companies like Amazon and Walmart began using AI for demand forecasting, personalized recommendations, and dynamic pricing strategies.

AI in Healthcare and Drug Discovery

- AI-powered diagnostic tools, such as IBM Watson Health, helped doctors analyze medical records and provide treatment recommendations.
- Machine learning accelerated drug discovery by identifying potential compounds faster than traditional methods.

Self-Driving Technology and Smart Logistics

- AI-powered autonomous vehicles and drones started reshaping transportation and delivery services.
- Logistics companies like UPS and FedEx implemented AI to optimize routes and enhance delivery efficiency.

During this period, deep learning and neural networks became mainstream, allowing AI to process large volumes of unstructured data, such as images, text, and speech, with unprecedented accuracy. These advancements set the stage for the AI-driven industrial revolution of the 2020s.

The AI-Driven Industrial Revolution (2020s-Present)

Today, AI has moved from an emerging technology to a core driver of industrial transformation. AI applications are now integrated into almost every industry, reshaping how businesses operate, innovate, and compete. The key trends shaping AI's role in modern industry include:

AI and Industry 4.0

- The concept of Industry 4.0, or the Fourth Industrial Revolution, revolves around AI-driven smart factories, IoT-connected devices, and autonomous production systems.
- AI enables real-time monitoring of industrial processes, adaptive manufacturing, and intelligent automation to improve efficiency and reduce waste.

Generative AI and Autonomous Decision-Making

- AI models like GPT-4 and DALL·E have shown that AI can create new content, design innovative products, and autonomously make business decisions.
- In finance, AI-powered robo-advisors manage investments, while in healthcare, AI-assisted drug discovery is accelerating breakthroughs.

AI in Cybersecurity and Risk Management

- AI is now essential in detecting and preventing cyber threats, fraud, and supply chain vulnerabilities in real time.
- Financial institutions use AI-driven fraud detection systems, while governments deploy AI for national security and infrastructure protection.

The Future: Quantum AI and Explainable AI

- Quantum AI promises to revolutionize industries by solving complex problems beyond the reach of classical computing.
- Explainable AI (XAI) is becoming critical for ensuring transparency, ethical AI use, and compliance with global regulations.

Challenges and the Road Ahead

Despite AI's rapid evolution, industries still face challenges in its adoption, including:

- **Data Privacy and Security Risks** – As AI relies on massive datasets, concerns over data protection, bias, and ethical AI use continue to grow.
- **Integration with Legacy Systems** – Many traditional industries struggle to integrate AI with outdated infrastructure and workflows.
- **Workforce Adaptation** – AI is transforming job roles, creating the need for upskilling and reskilling the workforce to work alongside intelligent systems.

As AI continues to advance, companies must develop ethical AI strategies, invest in AI education, and adopt regulatory frameworks to ensure responsible AI deployment.

The evolution of AI in industrial applications has been a journey of innovation, adaptation, and transformation. From early rule-based systems to today's deep learning-driven automation, AI has reshaped industries by improving efficiency, reducing costs, and enabling data-driven decision-making.

1.2 Why Industry AI is Different from Consumer AI

Artificial Intelligence (AI) has transformed both industrial and consumer applications, but the way AI operates in these two domains is vastly different. While consumer AI focuses on user convenience, personalization, and engagement, industry AI is designed for efficiency, automation, precision, and large-scale decision-making.

Industrial AI powers complex systems in healthcare, finance, manufacturing, logistics, and energy, where reliability and accuracy are critical. Unlike consumer AI, which typically interacts with individuals (e.g., virtual assistants, recommendation engines, and smart devices), industry AI deals with massive datasets, mission-critical operations, and regulatory compliance. This chapter explores the key distinctions between Industry AI and Consumer AI, highlighting their unique challenges, functionalities, and impact.

1. Industrial AI vs. Consumer AI: The Core Differences

Though both forms of AI rely on machine learning, deep learning, and automation, their use cases, objectives, and deployment environments differ significantly.

1.1 Purpose & Functionality

- Consumer AI aims to enhance user experience by offering personalization, automation, and interaction. Examples include virtual assistants (Siri, Alexa), recommendation algorithms (Netflix, Spotify), and AI-powered smart home devices.
- Industry AI focuses on operational efficiency, risk management, and large-scale automation. Examples include predictive maintenance in factories, fraud detection in finance, and AI-powered medical diagnostics.

1.2 Data Complexity & Processing

- Consumer AI deals with structured data, mostly derived from user behavior, preferences, and interactions (e.g., clicks, purchases, search history).
- Industry AI processes massive, complex datasets from real-time sensors, financial transactions, supply chain logistics, and medical imaging, requiring high computational power and advanced predictive analytics.

1.3 Accuracy & Reliability

- In consumer AI, minor errors (e.g., incorrect movie recommendations) have little consequence.
- In industry AI, errors can be costly or even life-threatening, such as a misdiagnosis in AI-powered healthcare systems or an AI-driven stock market decision leading to financial losses.

1.4 Customization & Deployment

- Consumer AI solutions are often standardized and built for mass adoption, requiring minimal customization.
- Industry AI systems are highly specialized, often requiring custom-built models to fit industry-specific needs, regulations, and infrastructure.

2. Key Challenges of Industry AI

Deploying AI in an industrial environment comes with unique challenges that differ from those in the consumer space.

2.1 Regulatory and Compliance Constraints

Industries such as healthcare, finance, and defense must adhere to strict legal and ethical guidelines. AI applications in these fields require explainability, transparency, and accountability, making development and deployment far more complex than consumer AI.

2.2 Scalability and Integration

Many industries rely on legacy systems that were not built with AI in mind. Integrating AI into these environments requires custom software, advanced data pipelines, and interoperability solutions.

2.3 Data Security and Privacy

Industry AI deals with sensitive information, such as patient records, financial transactions, and proprietary business data. Unlike consumer AI, where data privacy concerns exist but are less stringent, industrial AI must ensure robust cybersecurity, compliance with data protection laws, and secure cloud or on-premise storage solutions.

3. The Future of Industry AI vs. Consumer AI

As AI continues to evolve, the gap between industry and consumer applications will become more defined. Advancements in autonomous decision-making, real-time analytics, and AI-driven automation will continue to push Industry AI toward greater precision and reliability.

Meanwhile, consumer AI will focus on more seamless user interactions, personalization, and accessibility, making everyday life more convenient. The convergence of the two—such as AI-powered personalized healthcare recommendations or AI-driven financial planning for individuals—may bridge some gaps, but the fundamental differences in scale, complexity, and purpose will remain.

By understanding these distinctions, businesses and professionals can better navigate the AI landscape, ensuring they adopt the right AI strategies for their specific needs.

1.3 Key Benefits and Challenges of AI Adoption

Artificial Intelligence (AI) has emerged as a game-changer across industries, driving efficiency, innovation, and automation. Businesses that integrate AI into their operations gain a competitive advantage, benefiting from improved decision-making, cost reduction, and enhanced customer experiences. However, AI adoption also presents significant challenges, including high implementation costs, ethical concerns, data privacy issues, and workforce disruption.

This chapter explores the key benefits and challenges of AI adoption in industries, providing a balanced perspective on how organizations can maximize AI's potential while mitigating its risks.

1. Key Benefits of AI Adoption in Industries

1.1 Increased Efficiency and Productivity

AI-powered automation streamlines operations by handling repetitive, time-consuming tasks, allowing employees to focus on higher-value work. In manufacturing, AI-driven robotics improve assembly lines, while in healthcare, AI reduces administrative burdens by automating medical record management.

1.2 Data-Driven Decision Making

AI enables organizations to analyze vast amounts of data in real time, extracting meaningful insights that enhance strategic decision-making. Businesses can leverage AI for predictive analytics, risk assessment, and market trend forecasting, improving operational planning and resource allocation.

1.3 Cost Reduction and Resource Optimization

By automating processes and minimizing errors, AI reduces operational costs. Predictive maintenance in manufacturing, for example, prevents unexpected machine failures, reducing downtime and repair costs. In finance, AI-driven fraud detection minimizes losses associated with fraudulent transactions.

1.4 Enhanced Customer Experience and Personalization

AI enhances customer engagement by offering personalized recommendations, automated support, and real-time assistance. AI-powered chatbots and virtual assistants, for example, provide 24/7 customer service, improving response times and customer satisfaction.

1.5 Improved Accuracy and Error Reduction

AI-driven systems reduce human errors by analyzing data with precision and consistency. In healthcare, AI-powered diagnostics assist doctors in detecting diseases with higher accuracy, while in finance, AI algorithms ensure accurate financial forecasting and risk assessment.

1.6 Competitive Advantage and Innovation

Industries that adopt AI early gain a significant edge over competitors. AI fosters innovation by enabling new business models, optimizing supply chains, and enhancing product development. Companies using AI for real-time market analysis and customer insights can stay ahead in rapidly evolving industries.

2. Key Challenges of AI Adoption

2.1 High Implementation Costs

AI development and deployment require substantial investment in infrastructure, skilled talent, and ongoing maintenance. Small and medium-sized enterprises (SMEs) may struggle with the costs of acquiring AI technology, training employees, and integrating AI into legacy systems.

2.2 Data Privacy and Security Risks

AI systems rely on large volumes of data, raising concerns about data security, privacy breaches, and regulatory compliance. Industries dealing with sensitive information, such as healthcare and finance, must adhere to strict data protection laws, ensuring AI systems are secure and compliant.

2.3 Workforce Displacement and Job Transformation

AI-driven automation reduces the demand for certain jobs, raising concerns about unemployment and workforce displacement. However, AI also creates new job opportunities in AI development, data science, and AI ethics governance. Organizations must focus on reskilling employees and fostering a human-AI collaborative work environment.

2.4 Bias and Ethical Concerns

AI systems can inherit biases from training data, leading to unfair decision-making in areas such as hiring, lending, and law enforcement. Ethical AI development requires transparent algorithms, fairness audits, and bias mitigation strategies to ensure AI-driven decisions are fair and unbiased.

2.5 Lack of Explainability and Trust in AI

Many AI models, particularly deep learning algorithms, function as black boxes, making it difficult to interpret their decision-making processes. Industries such as healthcare and finance require explainable AI (XAI) to ensure transparency, accountability, and regulatory compliance.

2.6 Integration with Legacy Systems

Many industries rely on outdated IT infrastructure that is not AI-ready. Integrating AI with existing systems requires custom solutions, API development, and significant IT investments, posing a challenge for organizations with limited technological resources.

2.7 Ethical and Regulatory Compliance

AI adoption must align with industry regulations, data protection laws, and ethical guidelines. Industries such as healthcare, finance, and autonomous vehicles must navigate strict compliance requirements, ensuring AI systems operate safely, transparently, and responsibly.

3. Balancing AI's Benefits and Challenges

To maximize AI's advantages while mitigating risks, businesses must adopt a strategic approach to AI implementation. This includes:

- Investing in AI literacy and workforce training to prepare employees for AI-driven job roles.
- Developing ethical AI frameworks to ensure fairness, transparency, and accountability.
- Ensuring strong cybersecurity and data protection to safeguard sensitive information.
- Gradually integrating AI into existing workflows to minimize disruption and optimize productivity.

By addressing these challenges proactively, industries can harness the full potential of AI while ensuring responsible and ethical deployment.

1.4 AI Trends Across Major Industries

Artificial Intelligence (AI) is reshaping industries by enhancing efficiency, automation, and decision-making. From healthcare and finance to manufacturing and retail, AI is driving innovation and competitive advantages across diverse sectors. Understanding these trends helps businesses and professionals anticipate AI's impact and adapt to the evolving landscape.

This chapter explores the latest AI trends in key industries, highlighting how organizations leverage AI for transformation, the challenges they face, and the future of AI-driven solutions.

1. AI in Healthcare: Revolutionizing Diagnostics and Treatment

1.1 AI-Powered Medical Imaging & Diagnostics

- AI-driven computer vision algorithms are improving disease detection in X-rays, MRIs, and CT scans.
- AI models, such as DeepMind's AlphaFold, are transforming drug discovery by predicting protein structures with high accuracy.

1.2 Personalized Medicine & AI-Driven Drug Discovery

- AI analyzes genomic data and patient history to recommend personalized treatments.
- AI is accelerating drug discovery by identifying potential compounds and optimizing clinical trials.

1.3 Virtual Health Assistants & Remote Monitoring

- AI-powered chatbots and voice assistants provide 24/7 virtual health consultations.
- Wearable devices powered by AI monitor heart rate, glucose levels, and early disease symptoms.

2. AI in Finance: Enhancing Security & Automation

2.1 Algorithmic Trading & AI-Driven Investment Strategies

- AI models analyze market trends and trading patterns to execute high-frequency trades.
- AI-based robo-advisors provide personalized investment recommendations.

2.2 Fraud Detection & Risk Management

- AI detects anomalies in transactions to prevent fraud in real-time.
- Financial institutions use AI for credit scoring, risk assessment, and compliance monitoring.

2.3 AI-Powered Chatbots & Personalized Banking

- AI-driven chatbots handle customer queries, process transactions, and provide financial advice.
- AI personalizes banking services based on user spending habits and financial goals.

3. AI in Manufacturing: Smart Factories & Automation

3.1 Predictive Maintenance & AI-Driven Quality Control

- AI detects early signs of machine failure, reducing downtime and maintenance costs.
- AI-powered visual inspection ensures product quality and defect detection.

3.2 Robotics & AI-Powered Assembly Lines

- AI-driven robots automate assembly, welding, and packaging.
- AI improves supply chain management with demand forecasting and inventory optimization.

4. AI in Retail: Personalized Shopping & Customer Engagement

4.1 AI-Powered Recommendation Engines

- AI analyzes purchase history and browsing behavior to provide personalized recommendations.
- Retail giants like Amazon and Netflix use AI for dynamic pricing and targeted advertising.

4.2 AI in Supply Chain & Inventory Management

- AI optimizes inventory levels by predicting demand trends.
- AI automates warehouse operations with autonomous robots and smart logistics.

5. AI in Transportation & Logistics: Autonomous Vehicles & Smart Routing

5.1 Self-Driving Cars & AI-Powered Traffic Management

- AI is advancing autonomous vehicle technology with real-time decision-making.
- AI-powered systems optimize traffic flow and route planning to reduce congestion.

5.2 AI in Logistics & Supply Chain Optimization

- AI automates last-mile delivery, warehouse management, and demand forecasting.
- AI-driven drones and autonomous delivery bots improve supply chain efficiency.

6. AI in Education: Smart Learning & Automated Assessments

6.1 Personalized Learning with AI

- AI-powered platforms like Khan Academy and Coursera customize learning paths based on student progress.
- AI tutors provide real-time assistance and adaptive learning recommendations.

6.2 AI-Driven Grading & Administrative Automation

- AI automates exam grading, plagiarism detection, and administrative workflows.
- AI chatbots assist students with academic guidance and career counseling.

The Future of AI Across Industries

AI will continue to reshape industries with advancements in quantum computing, edge AI, and explainable AI. While AI adoption presents challenges, including ethical concerns, job displacement, and regulatory compliance, its benefits far outweigh its risks when implemented responsibly. Businesses that embrace AI will gain a competitive advantage, improved efficiency, and new growth opportunities.

2. Industry-Specific AI: Understanding the Landscape

AI is not a one-size-fits-all solution; its impact varies across industries, adapting to unique challenges and demands. While healthcare leverages AI for diagnostics and personalized medicine, finance uses it for fraud detection and risk management, and manufacturing integrates AI-driven automation for efficiency. Understanding these diverse applications is key to recognizing how AI transforms each sector differently. This chapter provides an overview of AI's role across various industries, highlighting key trends, technologies, and adoption strategies that define the modern AI landscape.

2.1 AI's Role in Regulated vs. Non-Regulated Industries

Artificial Intelligence (AI) is transforming industries worldwide, but its adoption and implementation vary significantly depending on whether an industry is regulated or non-regulated. Regulated industries—such as healthcare, finance, and defense—operate under strict government policies, compliance requirements, and ethical guidelines. On the other hand, non-regulated industries—such as entertainment, e-commerce, and hospitality—have more flexibility in how they leverage AI, often focusing on customer experience, automation, and innovation.

Understanding the role of AI in these different environments helps businesses navigate compliance challenges, risk management, and innovation strategies while ensuring responsible AI deployment.

1. AI in Regulated Industries: Challenges and Opportunities

Regulated industries must adhere to strict laws, compliance standards, and ethical considerations, which impact how AI can be developed, deployed, and monitored.

1.1 AI in Healthcare: Ensuring Safety & Compliance

- AI is revolutionizing healthcare with AI-powered diagnostics, robotic surgeries, and personalized medicine.
- Compliance with HIPAA (Health Insurance Portability and Accountability Act), GDPR (General Data Protection Regulation), and FDA (Food and Drug Administration) regulations ensures patient data privacy and AI system reliability.

- AI models must be explainable and transparent to ensure ethical decision-making in medical diagnoses and treatment plans.

1.2 AI in Finance: Risk Management & Fraud Prevention

- AI helps financial institutions with fraud detection, algorithmic trading, and credit scoring.
- Compliance with KYC (Know Your Customer), AML (Anti-Money Laundering), and SEC (Securities and Exchange Commission) regulations prevents financial crimes.
- AI-powered risk assessment models must be free from bias to avoid discrimination in loan approvals and credit ratings.

1.3 AI in Defense & Law Enforcement: Security & Surveillance

- AI enhances national security through facial recognition, predictive analytics, and cybersecurity measures.
- Compliance with ethics in AI warfare, data protection laws, and public privacy rights is critical.
- AI in policing raises concerns about racial bias, mass surveillance, and civil rights violations.

1.4 AI in Legal & Compliance: Automating Decision-Making

- AI-powered tools assist in contract analysis, legal research, and case prediction.
- Compliance with legal ethics and privacy laws ensures fair use of AI in legal decision-making.
- Explainable AI is crucial in preventing bias in judicial AI models.

2. AI in Non-Regulated Industries: Innovation & Agility

Unlike regulated industries, non-regulated sectors have greater flexibility in adopting AI, enabling faster innovation and experimentation.

2.1 AI in E-Commerce & Retail: Personalization & Automation

- AI optimizes product recommendations, demand forecasting, and chatbots for customer service.
- AI-driven dynamic pricing adjusts prices based on consumer behavior and market demand.

- Unlike healthcare or finance, AI in e-commerce faces fewer legal restrictions, allowing rapid deployment.

2.2 AI in Entertainment & Media: Content Creation & Curation

- AI powers recommendation engines for Netflix, Spotify, and YouTube, enhancing user engagement.
- AI-generated content (e.g., deepfake videos, AI-written articles) raises ethical concerns but faces fewer regulations.
- AI assists in automated video editing, music composition, and gaming AI for immersive experiences.

2.3 AI in Marketing & Advertising: Data-Driven Insights

- AI-driven marketing tools analyze consumer behavior, optimize ad targeting, and personalize campaigns.
- Ethical concerns arise regarding data privacy, surveillance capitalism, and misinformation spread.
- AI automates A/B testing, sentiment analysis, and customer segmentation for improved ROI.

2.4 AI in Hospitality & Tourism: Enhancing Customer Experience

- AI chatbots and virtual assistants provide 24/7 customer support for travel and hospitality businesses.
- AI-driven hotel pricing algorithms and smart booking systems optimize occupancy rates.
- AI in tourism enhances personalized travel recommendations and real-time language translation.

3. Key Differences Between AI in Regulated vs. Non-Regulated Industries

Aspect	Regulated Industries (Healthcare, Finance, Defense)	Non-Regulated Industries (Retail, Entertainment, Marketing)
Compliance & Regulation	Strict compliance with laws (e.g., HIPAA, SEC, GDPR)	Fewer restrictions, more flexibility
Risk & Liability	High-risk (human lives, financial security, privacy)	Lower risk, focus on innovation
AI Transparency	Explainability required for decision-making	Less emphasis on explainability
Ethical Concerns	Bias, discrimination, fairness, security risks	Data privacy, misinformation, AI-generated content
Adoption Speed	Slower due to regulatory hurdles	Faster due to fewer legal constraints

4. The Future of AI in Regulated & Non-Regulated Sectors

As AI evolves, governments and regulatory bodies are introducing AI governance frameworks to balance innovation with responsibility. Key future trends include:

- **AI Regulation Expansion**: More industries will face AI-specific regulations to address bias, transparency, and accountability.
- **Self-Regulation in Non-Regulated Sectors**: Companies will adopt AI ethics guidelines to maintain public trust.
- **AI Compliance Automation**: AI will assist in automating compliance monitoring, ensuring adherence to evolving regulations.
- **Cross-Industry AI Ethics Standards**: Global organizations may establish universal AI ethics guidelines for responsible AI adoption.

By understanding the differences in AI's role across industries, businesses can develop strategic AI adoption plans that align with their regulatory landscape while driving innovation and competitive advantage.

2.2 Industry AI Adoption: A Comparative Study

Artificial Intelligence (AI) adoption varies significantly across industries, depending on factors such as regulatory constraints, data availability, technological infrastructure, and financial investment. While some industries, like finance and healthcare, have rapidly integrated AI for mission-critical applications, others, such as manufacturing and retail, are leveraging AI primarily for automation and optimization. This chapter provides a comparative study of AI adoption across different industries, highlighting key trends, challenges, and success factors.

1. AI Adoption Across Key Industries

1.1 AI in Healthcare: Revolutionizing Patient Care

Key Use Cases:

- AI-powered medical imaging and diagnostics (e.g., detecting cancer through deep learning).
- Predictive analytics for disease outbreak forecasting.
- AI-driven virtual health assistants and chatbots for patient support.
- Drug discovery and personalized medicine using AI-based genomic analysis.

Adoption Challenges:

- Regulatory barriers (HIPAA, GDPR, FDA approvals).
- High costs of AI deployment and integration with legacy healthcare systems.
- AI transparency and ethical concerns in patient treatment.

1.2 AI in Finance: Enhancing Security & Efficiency

Key Use Cases:

- Algorithmic trading for high-speed, data-driven investments.
- Fraud detection and cybersecurity using AI-based anomaly detection.
- AI-powered risk assessment models for loan approvals and credit scoring.
- AI-driven chatbots for banking customer support and automated transactions.

Adoption Challenges:

- Bias in AI-driven financial decisions (credit scoring, lending models).
- Regulatory compliance (AML, SEC, KYC).
- Data privacy and cybersecurity risks.

1.3 AI in Manufacturing: Smart Factories & Automation

Key Use Cases:

- Predictive maintenance to prevent machine breakdowns.
- AI-powered robotic process automation (RPA) for assembly lines.
- Supply chain optimization with AI-driven demand forecasting.
- Quality control through AI-based defect detection in production.

Adoption Challenges:

- High initial costs of AI-powered robotics and infrastructure.
- Need for skilled workforce to manage AI-driven systems.
- Integration with legacy industrial systems.

1.4 AI in Retail: Personalization & Customer Insights

Key Use Cases:

- AI recommendation engines (e.g., Amazon, Netflix, and Spotify).
- Automated inventory management using AI-driven demand forecasting.
- AI-powered chatbots and virtual assistants for 24/7 customer service.
- Dynamic pricing algorithms that adjust product prices based on demand.

Adoption Challenges:

- Customer data privacy concerns (GDPR, CCPA compliance).
- Balancing AI automation with human-driven customer interactions.
- AI bias in personalized marketing and product recommendations.

1.5 AI in Transportation & Logistics: Efficiency & Automation

Key Use Cases:

- Autonomous vehicles for self-driving transportation.
- AI-driven route optimization to reduce fuel consumption.
- AI-powered logistics management for efficient deliveries.
- Traffic prediction and smart city planning with AI-driven models.

Adoption Challenges:

- Regulatory restrictions on autonomous vehicle deployment.
- High cost of AI-driven fleet management.

- Safety concerns and ethical issues in AI-based traffic control.

2. Comparative Analysis of AI Adoption Levels

2.1 AI Maturity Levels by Industry

Industries adopt AI at different speeds based on technological readiness, regulatory environment, and investment levels. The table below categorizes AI adoption into three stages:

Industry	AI Adoption Level	Key Drivers	Key Barriers
Healthcare	Moderate to High	Data-driven diagnostics, predictive analytics	Regulatory compliance, data privacy
Finance	High	Fraud detection, automated trading, risk analysis	Bias in AI models, security risks
Manufacturing	Moderate	Predictive maintenance, automation, robotics	High initial costs, integration with legacy systems
Retail	High	AI-driven recommendations, customer engagement	AI bias, data privacy concerns
Transportation	Moderate	Self-driving tech, logistics automation	Regulation, safety risks

3. Key Factors Influencing AI Adoption

3.1 Regulatory Landscape

- **Highly regulated industries** (e.g., healthcare, finance) face compliance hurdles, slowing AI adoption.
- **Non-regulated industries** (e.g., retail, entertainment) adopt AI more freely, focusing on customer engagement and revenue growth.

3.2 Data Availability & Quality

- AI thrives on large datasets; industries with structured, high-quality data (e.g., finance, healthcare) benefit the most.
- Data-driven AI models in sectors like manufacturing and logistics require advanced IoT integration to improve accuracy.

3.3 Cost of Implementation

- AI adoption requires investment in infrastructure, cloud computing, and skilled workforce.
- Industries with lower AI expertise (e.g., small-scale manufacturing, traditional retail) struggle with AI deployment.

3.4 Workforce Adaptation & Skill Development

- AI implementation demands retraining of employees to work alongside AI-driven systems.
- Resistance to AI adoption is higher in traditional industries where automation threatens job roles.

4. The Future of Industry AI Adoption

4.1 AI Standardization & Ethical AI Frameworks

- Governments and organizations are pushing for AI governance models to ensure transparency and fairness.
- Explainable AI (XAI) will become essential in regulated industries to ensure compliance.

4.2 AI-Driven Cross-Industry Collaboration

AI adoption will enable cross-industry innovation, such as:

- AI-driven healthcare-fintech partnerships for AI-powered insurance underwriting.
- AI-powered smart cities integrating AI in transportation, security, and energy management.

4.3 AI Democratization: Making AI Accessible

- Advancements in low-code/no-code AI platforms will enable smaller businesses to adopt AI without large technical teams.
- AI-powered cloud solutions will make AI adoption more cost-effective and scalable across industries.

AI adoption is advancing rapidly across industries, but the pace, challenges, and benefits differ based on industry-specific factors. While healthcare and finance must navigate strict regulatory landscapes, industries like retail and e-commerce enjoy more freedom to leverage AI for personalization and automation. The future of AI adoption will depend on responsible AI governance, improved data accessibility, and advancements in AI technology, making AI a critical driver of industrial transformation in the coming decades.

2.3 Ethics and Compliance: Navigating AI Regulations

As artificial intelligence (AI) continues to transform industries, the need for ethical AI development and regulatory compliance has become more critical than ever. Governments, policymakers, and industry leaders are working to establish clear AI governance frameworks that ensure AI systems operate fairly, transparently, and responsibly. However, navigating AI regulations is a complex challenge, as different industries face varying levels of oversight. This chapter explores AI ethics principles, major compliance frameworks, and the key challenges organizations face in implementing ethical AI practices.

1. The Importance of AI Ethics & Compliance

AI-driven decisions impact human lives, financial systems, healthcare, and security, making ethical and compliant AI systems a necessity. A lack of regulation or ethical oversight can lead to biased decision-making, privacy violations, and misuse of AI technologies. Industries such as healthcare, finance, and law enforcement require strict AI regulations, while others, such as retail and entertainment, face fewer restrictions but must still address consumer privacy and data security concerns.

1.1 Why AI Ethics Matters

- **Fairness & Bias Mitigation**: AI models trained on biased data can lead to discriminatory outcomes, such as biased hiring decisions or unfair loan approvals.
- **Transparency & Explainability**: Organizations must ensure AI decisions are understandable and interpretable to build trust.
- **Data Privacy & Security**: AI systems process vast amounts of sensitive data, making cybersecurity and compliance with privacy laws critical.
- **Accountability & Governance**: Companies must ensure AI accountability, with clear policies on who is responsible for AI-driven decisions.

2. Key AI Ethics Principles

Several organizations, including the European Commission, the U.S. National Institute of Standards and Technology (NIST), and the IEEE, have developed AI ethics frameworks. Below are five core AI ethics principles:

2.1 Transparency & Explainability

- AI models should provide clear reasoning for decisions, ensuring users understand how outcomes are generated.
- **Example**: In finance, AI-driven credit scoring systems must justify loan approvals or rejections.

2.2 Fairness & Non-Discrimination

- AI systems should eliminate bias and promote fairness across different demographics.
- **Example**: AI-driven hiring algorithms must ensure equal opportunities regardless of gender, race, or socioeconomic status.

2.3 Privacy & Data Protection

- AI models must comply with privacy laws such as GDPR, CCPA, and HIPAA.
- **Example**: Healthcare AI must protect patient data under HIPAA regulations.

2.4 Accountability & Human Oversight

- Organizations must implement AI governance structures to audit AI decisions and ensure human oversight.
- **Example**: AI-powered facial recognition systems used in law enforcement must have strict human intervention policies.

2.5 Security & Robustness

- AI systems should be secure, resilient, and free from adversarial attacks.
- Example: AI-powered fraud detection in banking must prevent financial cyberattacks.

3. Major AI Regulations & Compliance Frameworks

Different regions and industries have specific AI compliance frameworks to govern AI development and deployment.

3.1 Global AI Regulatory Frameworks

Regulation	Region	Key Provisions	Industry Impact
GDPR (General Data Protection Regulation)	EU	Data privacy, user consent, right to be forgotten	Affects finance, healthcare, and retail
CCPA (California Consumer Privacy Act)	USA	Data privacy, consumer rights	Impacts big tech, marketing, and e-commerce
AI Act (EU Proposal)	EU	Risk-based AI regulation, bans on high-risk AI	Affects healthcare, finance, law enforcement
HIPAA (Health Insurance Portability and Accountability Act)	USA	Healthcare data protection	Affects AI in healthcare & telemedicine
AML/KYC (Anti-Money Laundering & Know Your Customer)	Global	Prevents financial fraud and identity theft	Impacts banks & fintech companies

4. Industry-Specific AI Compliance Challenges

4.1 AI in Healthcare: Balancing Innovation & Patient Privacy

Key Compliance Issues:

- HIPAA (USA) and GDPR (Europe) restrict how AI can access and process patient data.
- AI-driven diagnostics must be clinically validated and FDA-approved before real-world use.
- Lack of explainability in AI-driven diagnoses raises ethical concerns.

4.2 AI in Finance: Preventing Fraud & Bias

Key Compliance Issues:

- Fair lending laws require that AI-driven credit scoring models avoid racial or gender bias.
- AML/KYC regulations demand that AI fraud detection systems identify suspicious activities.
- High-frequency trading algorithms must comply with SEC (U.S. Securities and Exchange Commission) regulations.

4.3 AI in Retail & Marketing: Ethical Consumer Targeting

Key Compliance Issues:

- GDPR & CCPA restrict consumer data collection for AI-powered advertising.
- Ethical concerns around AI-driven price discrimination and personalized recommendations.
- AI chatbots must disclose when consumers are interacting with AI vs. humans.

4.4 AI in Law Enforcement: Balancing Public Safety & Privacy

Key Compliance Issues:

- AI-powered facial recognition systems face bans in some cities due to bias concerns.
- Governments are debating regulations around predictive policing AI.
- AI surveillance systems must comply with civil rights and data privacy laws.

5. Best Practices for AI Compliance & Ethical AI Deployment

To ensure AI compliance and ethical responsibility, organizations should follow best practices:

5.1 Conduct AI Ethics Audits

- Regularly assess AI systems for bias, fairness, and transparency.
- **Example**: Google & Microsoft conduct AI audits to detect algorithmic bias.

5.2 Implement Explainable AI (XAI) Frameworks

- AI-driven decisions must be interpretable and justifiable.
- **Example**: IBM's AI Fairness 360 toolkit helps businesses assess AI bias.

5.3 Ensure Cross-Industry Compliance Collaboration

- Organizations should collaborate with regulators and policymakers to align AI with legal standards.
- **Example**: Partnership on AI (PAI) is a consortium of AI leaders promoting ethical AI research.

5.4 Establish AI Governance Boards

- Companies should create internal AI ethics teams to oversee compliance.
- **Example**: Facebook and OpenAI have AI ethics review boards.

6. The Future of AI Ethics & Compliance

As AI continues to advance, AI regulations will become more standardized globally, with increased focus on:

- **AI Transparency Laws**: Governments will mandate explainability in high-risk AI applications.
- **Stronger AI Bias Prevention Measures**: Companies will be required to audit AI systems for fairness.
- **More Cross-Border AI Regulations**: Countries will collaborate on global AI governance frameworks.
- **AI for Compliance Automation**: AI itself will be used to monitor and enforce compliance in industries.

AI's impact on society depends on how ethically and responsibly it is deployed. While AI offers immense benefits, it also poses risks related to bias, privacy, and accountability. Businesses must navigate the complex landscape of AI regulations by adopting best practices, ensuring transparency, and complying with ethical standards. In the future, AI governance frameworks will become more robust, ensuring that AI continues to be a force for innovation while respecting human rights and ethical principles.

2.4 AI Infrastructure: Cloud, Edge, and On-Premise AI

The success of AI adoption in industries relies heavily on the underlying infrastructure used to process, store, and analyze data. AI infrastructure determines how quickly businesses can deploy AI models, scale operations, and ensure security and compliance. The three primary deployment models—Cloud AI, Edge AI, and On-Premise AI—each offer distinct advantages and challenges depending on industry needs. This chapter explores the key characteristics, use cases, and trade-offs of these AI infrastructure models, helping businesses choose the right approach for their AI-driven transformation.

1. Understanding AI Infrastructure Models

AI infrastructure encompasses hardware, software, and network resources needed to run machine learning (ML) models efficiently. The choice between cloud-based, edge-based, or on-premise AI depends on factors like data sensitivity, latency requirements, computational power, and regulatory constraints.

1.1 Cloud AI: Scalable and Cost-Effective AI Deployment

Cloud AI refers to AI models running on cloud platforms like AWS, Google Cloud, and Microsoft Azure, where companies can access AI services on demand without maintaining their own hardware.

Key Features of Cloud AI:

- **Scalability** – Easily scale AI workloads up or down as needed.
- **Cost-Effective** – Pay-as-you-go model eliminates the need for large upfront investments.
- **High Computational Power** – Cloud providers offer GPUs and TPUs optimized for AI training.
- **Collaboration & Accessibility** – Enables remote teams to collaborate and access AI models globally.

Use Cases of Cloud AI:

- AI-Powered Chatbots & Virtual Assistants (e.g., Amazon Lex, Google Dialogflow).
- Fraud Detection in Finance using AI-powered anomaly detection.
- Healthcare Diagnostics with AI-driven medical image analysis on cloud platforms.
- Retail AI Recommendations powered by cloud-based ML models.

Challenges of Cloud AI:

- **Data Privacy Concerns** – Sensitive data stored on the cloud may violate compliance regulations (e.g., GDPR, HIPAA).
- **Latency Issues** – Cloud processing introduces delays for real-time AI applications.
- **Internet Dependency** – AI models require stable network connectivity for cloud access.

1.2 Edge AI: Real-Time AI Processing at the Source

Edge AI enables AI models to run on local devices and sensors rather than relying on the cloud. This reduces latency and enhances real-time decision-making, making it ideal for autonomous systems, IoT devices, and critical infrastructure.

Key Features of Edge AI:

- **Low Latency** – AI inference happens instantly at the data source.
- **Improved Security & Privacy** – Sensitive data remains on the device, reducing compliance risks.
- **Reduced Cloud Dependency** – AI can function offline or with limited connectivity.

Use Cases of Edge AI:

- **Autonomous Vehicles** – Self-driving cars use Edge AI for real-time object detection and navigation.
- **Industrial IoT (IIoT) & Predictive Maintenance** – AI-powered sensors in factories detect equipment failures before they happen.
- **AI-Powered Surveillance & Security** – Edge AI enables real-time facial recognition and threat detection.
- **Healthcare Wearables** – AI-driven smartwatches and medical devices monitor heart rate, glucose levels, and vitals in real time.

Challenges of Edge AI:

- **Limited Computational Power** – Edge devices have lower processing capacity compared to cloud AI.
- **Hardware Constraints** – Requires custom AI chips like NVIDIA Jetson, Google Edge TPU, or Intel Movidius.
- **Higher Initial Costs** – Deploying Edge AI infrastructure can be expensive due to specialized hardware.

1.3 On-Premise AI: Secure & Customized AI Infrastructure

On-Premise AI involves running AI models on an organization's own servers and data centers, ensuring full control over data and infrastructure. This model is preferred in industries with strict compliance requirements, such as finance, defense, and healthcare.

Key Features of On-Premise AI:

- **Data Security & Compliance** – Organizations retain full ownership of their AI data, ensuring GDPR, HIPAA, and SOC 2 compliance.
- **High Performance** – Dedicated AI servers and GPUs offer powerful computational capabilities.
- **Customization & Control** – Companies can fine-tune AI infrastructure based on business needs.

Use Cases of On-Premise AI:

- **Banking & Financial Institutions** – AI-driven risk management, fraud detection, and algorithmic trading.
- **Healthcare & Biotech** – AI-powered drug discovery, medical research, and hospital management.
- **Government & Defense AI** – AI used for cybersecurity, surveillance, and military intelligence.

Challenges of On-Premise AI:

- **High Infrastructure Costs** – Requires expensive AI hardware (e.g., NVIDIA A100, Google TPUs) and maintenance.
- **Scalability Limitations** – Scaling on-premise AI requires purchasing additional servers.
- **IT & Security Expertise** – Requires in-house AI and cybersecurity teams to manage AI workloads.

2. Cloud vs. Edge vs. On-Premise AI: A Comparative Analysis

Feature	Cloud AI	Edge AI	On-Premise AI
Scalability	High	Low	Medium
Latency	High (dependent on internet)	Low (real-time processing)	Medium (in-house servers)
Data Security & Compliance	Medium (depends on provider)	High (local processing)	High (full control)
Computational Power	High (GPUs & TPUs)	Medium (AI chips)	Very High (dedicated servers)
Cost Efficiency	High (pay-as-you-go)	High (low cloud costs)	Low (high initial investment)
Ideal Use Cases	AI services, chatbots, fraud detection	IoT, autonomous systems, smart devices	Banking, government, research

3. Choosing the Right AI Infrastructure for Your Industry

3.1 Factors to Consider When Selecting AI Infrastructure

- **Data Sensitivity & Compliance**: Industries handling sensitive data (e.g., finance, healthcare) benefit from On-Premise or Edge AI for greater security.
- **Latency Requirements**: Applications needing real-time AI (e.g., autonomous driving, industrial automation) require Edge AI.
- **Computational Needs & Budget**: AI models requiring high-performance computing (e.g., AI research, deep learning) are better suited for Cloud or On-Premise AI.

3.2 Hybrid AI: Combining Cloud, Edge, and On-Premise AI

Many organizations adopt a hybrid approach, leveraging the strengths of multiple AI infrastructure models.

- **Example 1**: Smart Hospitals use On-Premise AI for patient data storage while utilizing Cloud AI for AI-powered diagnostics.
- **Example 2:** Autonomous Vehicles rely on Edge AI for real-time navigation while sending data to the cloud for long-term analysis.

4. The Future of AI Infrastructure

4.1 AI at the Edge: Expanding AI's Reach

- Edge AI is expected to grow, with AI-powered IoT devices becoming more widespread.
- AI chip advancements (e.g., Apple Neural Engine, NVIDIA Jetson) will enhance Edge AI capabilities.

4.2 AI Cloud Evolution: More Accessible & Cost-Effective AI

- AI-as-a-Service (AIaaS) will make AI cheaper and more accessible for startups and small businesses.
- Serverless AI models will allow businesses to run AI without managing infrastructure.

4.3 On-Premise AI for Regulated Industries

- Financial institutions and healthcare providers will continue investing in on-premise AI for compliance.
- AI data centers will become more energy-efficient, improving sustainability.

Choosing the right AI infrastructure—Cloud AI, Edge AI, or On-Premise AI—is critical for maximizing performance, ensuring security, and optimizing costs. As AI adoption grows across industries, businesses must strategically integrate AI infrastructure to balance scalability, security, and efficiency while embracing emerging AI trends.

3. Medical Imaging and AI Diagnostics

AI is revolutionizing medical imaging by enhancing accuracy, speed, and early disease detection. With deep learning algorithms analyzing X-rays, MRIs, and CT scans, AI-powered diagnostics assist radiologists in identifying conditions such as cancer, neurological disorders, and cardiovascular diseases with unprecedented precision. These systems not only reduce human error but also streamline workflows, lower costs, and improve patient outcomes. This chapter explores the cutting-edge AI technologies behind medical imaging, real-world applications, and the challenges of integrating AI into clinical practice.

3.1 How Deep Learning is Revolutionizing Radiology

Radiology has always been at the forefront of medical innovation, and with the advent of deep learning, it is undergoing a transformational shift. Traditionally, radiologists have relied on years of expertise and manual image interpretation to diagnose diseases from X-rays, CT scans, MRIs, and ultrasounds. However, deep learning—a subset of AI that mimics the human brain's ability to recognize patterns—has introduced unprecedented accuracy, speed, and efficiency in medical imaging and diagnostics. By leveraging convolutional neural networks (CNNs), deep learning models can detect anomalies, classify diseases, and even predict patient outcomes with human-level or superior performance. This chapter explores the role of deep learning in radiology, its key breakthroughs, real-world applications, and the challenges that come with integrating AI into clinical workflows.

1. The Evolution of AI in Radiology

1.1 From Traditional Image Processing to AI-Driven Insights

For decades, radiologists have used computer-aided detection (CAD) systems to assist in identifying abnormalities in medical images. However, traditional CAD relied on rule-based algorithms and handcrafted features, which were often inflexible and required constant updates. With the rise of deep learning, AI can now automatically learn complex features from medical images without human intervention, significantly improving diagnostic accuracy.

1.2 The Rise of Convolutional Neural Networks (CNNs) in Medical Imaging

CNNs have become the backbone of modern AI-driven radiology. Unlike traditional CAD systems, CNNs can:

- Extract features autonomously from raw medical images.
- Recognize subtle patterns that may be undetectable to the human eye.
- Adapt and improve with more data over time.

2. Key Applications of Deep Learning in Radiology

2.1 AI-Powered Disease Detection & Classification

Deep learning models are now capable of detecting various diseases with remarkable accuracy. Some key breakthroughs include:

- **Lung Cancer Detection**: AI models like Google's DeepMind have outperformed radiologists in detecting lung nodules in CT scans.
- **Breast Cancer Screening**: AI-driven mammography tools (e.g., MIT CSAIL's deep learning model) have reduced false positives and false negatives.
- **Brain Tumor Diagnosis**: CNNs can identify tumors in MRI scans and classify them by type (e.g., gliomas, meningiomas, pituitary tumors).

2.2 Automated Image Segmentation & Feature Extraction

AI models can segment and highlight abnormal regions in medical images, reducing the manual workload of radiologists.

- **Example**: AI-based segmentation tools for cardiac MRI help cardiologists measure ventricular volume, ejection fraction, and myocardial thickness.
- **Example**: Deep learning in ophthalmology can detect diabetic retinopathy and macular degeneration from retinal scans.

2.3 AI-Assisted Radiology Workflows & Decision Support Systems

AI is not replacing radiologists—it is augmenting their capabilities. AI-driven clinical decision support systems (CDSS) help radiologists:

- Prioritize high-risk cases in imaging queues.
- Reduce reading time by pre-annotating scans.
- Provide second opinions by comparing images with extensive AI-trained databases.

3. Real-World Case Studies in AI-Powered Radiology

3.1 AI for Lung Disease Detection in COVID-19

During the COVID-19 pandemic, AI models were rapidly developed to analyze chest X-rays and CT scans to detect COVID-induced pneumonia. Hospitals worldwide deployed AI-powered radiology tools for early diagnosis, severity assessment, and treatment monitoring.

3.2 AI-Driven Stroke Detection in Emergency Settings

Time is critical in stroke diagnosis. AI-powered tools like Viz.ai analyze CT angiograms to detect strokes in real time, alerting neurologists instantly and reducing treatment delays.

3.3 AI in Oncology: Enhancing Cancer Screening & Prognosis

AI models like IBM Watson for Oncology assist oncologists in diagnosing and treating cancer by analyzing histopathology slides, genomic data, and imaging results to provide personalized treatment recommendations.

4. Challenges & Ethical Considerations in AI Radiology

4.1 Data Privacy & Security Concerns

Medical images contain sensitive patient information. AI-driven radiology systems must comply with HIPAA, GDPR, and other healthcare regulations to ensure patient data remains secure.

4.2 AI Bias & Fairness Issues

AI models trained on biased datasets may underperform for certain populations, leading to healthcare disparities. Ensuring diverse, well-represented training data is crucial.

4.3 Radiologists' Resistance to AI Adoption

Many radiologists fear AI will replace their roles. However, AI is designed to work alongside radiologists, reducing fatigue and enhancing diagnostic confidence.

5. The Future of Deep Learning in Radiology

5.1 Explainable AI (XAI) for Better Interpretability

AI models must provide transparent explanations of their diagnoses to build trust among radiologists. Explainable AI (XAI) techniques, such as heatmaps and attention mechanisms, highlight how AI arrives at its decisions.

5.2 AI-Powered Radiology Training & Education

AI is also being integrated into medical education. Trainee radiologists can use AI-powered simulation platforms to learn image interpretation skills faster and more efficiently.

5.3 AI-Driven Precision Medicine & Predictive Analytics

Future AI models will not just diagnose diseases but also predict patient outcomes, helping doctors design personalized treatment plans based on genomics, imaging, and clinical data.

Deep learning is revolutionizing radiology by enhancing disease detection, improving workflow efficiency, and enabling faster, more accurate diagnoses. While challenges remain—such as data privacy, bias, and AI interpretability—the future of AI-powered radiology is promising. As deep learning models become more sophisticated, radiologists and AI will work hand-in-hand to deliver better, faster, and more precise healthcare solutions worldwide.

3.2 AI for X-rays, MRIs, and CT Scan Analysis

Medical imaging is one of the most critical areas where artificial intelligence (AI) is making a transformative impact. The ability of AI to analyze X-rays, MRIs, and CT scans with high accuracy and speed is revolutionizing diagnostic radiology, assisting radiologists in detecting diseases earlier, reducing workload, and improving patient outcomes. With the power of deep learning, convolutional neural networks (CNNs), and reinforcement learning, AI-driven medical imaging solutions are reshaping how doctors interpret images, identify abnormalities, and make clinical decisions. This chapter explores AI's role in automating, enhancing, and accelerating medical image analysis across different imaging modalities.

1. AI-Powered X-ray Analysis

X-rays are one of the most widely used imaging techniques in healthcare, often serving as the first step in diagnosing conditions ranging from fractures to lung diseases. AI-driven X-ray analysis is enhancing radiology workflows, improving accuracy, and reducing misdiagnoses.

1.1 AI in Chest X-ray Interpretation

Chest X-rays are used to diagnose pneumonia, tuberculosis, lung cancer, and COVID-19-related lung infections. AI models trained on large datasets can:

- Detect abnormal lung opacities indicative of infections or malignancies.
- Identify early signs of pulmonary diseases that may not be immediately visible to the human eye.
- Prioritize critical cases, ensuring faster diagnosis in emergency settings.

Example: Google's DeepMind AI developed a model capable of detecting tuberculosis (TB) from X-rays with radiologist-level accuracy, significantly improving TB screening in underdeveloped regions.

1.2 AI for Musculoskeletal X-rays

Orthopedic AI solutions analyze fractures, joint dislocations, and bone abnormalities in X-ray images. AI-powered tools assist in:

- Automating fracture detection in emergency departments.
- Identifying early-stage arthritis in knee and hip joints.
- Guiding orthopedic surgeries through AI-assisted image processing.

Example: The AI model BoneXpert accurately assesses bone age in pediatric X-rays, helping in diagnosing growth disorders.

2. AI in MRI Analysis: Advancing Neurology & Oncology

MRI (Magnetic Resonance Imaging) provides detailed soft-tissue imaging, making it crucial for diagnosing neurological disorders, tumors, and musculoskeletal conditions. AI-powered MRI analysis is speeding up scan interpretation, reducing human errors, and enabling precision medicine.

2.1 AI in Brain MRI for Neurological Disorders

Deep learning models help in detecting conditions such as:

- **Alzheimer's Disease & Dementia**: AI can track brain atrophy in MRI scans, detecting early signs of neurodegeneration.
- **Stroke Detection**: AI-powered MRI analysis can quickly differentiate between ischemic and hemorrhagic strokes, allowing for timely treatment interventions.
- **Multiple Sclerosis (MS) Monitoring**: AI can segment and quantify MS lesions, aiding in disease progression tracking.

Example: The AI tool qMRI developed by MIT enhances the detection of early-stage Alzheimer's by analyzing hippocampal volume loss.

2.2 AI for Cancer Detection in MRI Scans

AI-powered MRI analysis is playing a significant role in early cancer detection and treatment planning.

- **Breast Cancer**: AI assists radiologists in detecting subtle tumors that are often missed by traditional MRI interpretation.
- **Prostate Cancer**: AI models segment prostate tumors with high precision, improving biopsy accuracy.
- **Brain Tumors**: AI-driven MRI analysis helps classify tumors into categories like gliomas, meningiomas, and metastatic tumors.

Example: IBM Watson developed an AI-assisted MRI interpretation tool that predicts the aggressiveness of prostate cancer, guiding treatment decisions.

3. AI in CT Scan Analysis: Speeding Up Emergency Diagnoses

Computed Tomography (CT) scans provide high-resolution, cross-sectional images that are essential in emergency medicine, oncology, and cardiology. AI-driven CT analysis is improving diagnostic accuracy, reducing scan-to-diagnosis time, and assisting in life-saving interventions.

3.1 AI for Lung CT Scans in Cancer & COVID-19 Detection

CT scans are widely used for lung cancer screening and COVID-19 pneumonia detection. AI tools:

- Identify early-stage lung nodules that might indicate lung cancer.
- Assess COVID-19 pneumonia severity by segmenting infected lung regions.
- Differentiate between benign and malignant lung lesions, reducing unnecessary biopsies.

Example: Google's Lung-RADS AI tool improved lung nodule classification in CT scans, reducing false positives and unnecessary interventions.

3.2 AI for Cardiovascular CT Imaging

AI is significantly improving cardiac CT angiography, which is crucial for detecting coronary artery disease (CAD). AI applications include:

- Automated coronary artery calcium (CAC) scoring, predicting heart attack risk.
- Identifying plaque buildup in arteries, aiding in early intervention.
- Enhancing 3D reconstruction of heart structures for personalized surgery planning.

Example: The AI tool HeartFlow Analysis uses deep learning to create 3D models of coronary arteries, helping doctors assess blood flow restrictions and cardiac risks.

3.3 AI in Trauma & Emergency CT Analysis

In trauma cases, time is critical. AI-powered CT analysis enables:

- Automated hemorrhage detection in brain CT scans, reducing diagnosis time for stroke and traumatic brain injuries.
- Bone fracture detection in trauma patients, assisting emergency teams.
- Internal organ injury assessment, improving surgical planning.

Example: The Viz.ai Stroke Detection AI automatically detects large vessel occlusions (LVOs) in stroke patients, alerting neurologists in real-time for faster intervention.

4. Benefits & Challenges of AI in Medical Imaging

4.1 Key Benefits of AI in Radiology

✓ **Faster Diagnoses** – AI reduces image interpretation time from hours to minutes.
✓ **Higher Accuracy** – AI models detect subtle patterns that radiologists might miss.

✓ **Workload Reduction** – AI automates repetitive tasks, allowing radiologists to focus on complex cases.

✓ **Early Disease Detection** – AI identifies early-stage abnormalities, improving patient survival rates.

✓ **Personalized Treatment** – AI models help tailor treatments based on image-derived biomarkers.

4.2 Challenges & Ethical Considerations

⚠ **Data Privacy Issues** – AI must comply with HIPAA, GDPR, and patient confidentiality laws.

⚠ **Bias in AI Models** – AI models trained on limited or biased datasets may lead to disparities in diagnosis.

⚠ **Regulatory Approvals** – AI-based imaging tools require FDA & CE clearances before clinical use.

⚠ **Radiologist-AI Collaboration** – AI should support rather than replace human expertise.

5. The Future of AI in Medical Imaging

AI is evolving rapidly, and future advancements in medical imaging AI will focus on:

- **Explainable AI** (XAI): Making AI models more transparent for radiologists.
- **Self-Learning AI**: Models that continuously learn and adapt from new imaging data.
- **AI-Integrated PACS**: Seamless integration of AI into hospital imaging systems.
- **3D & 4D Imaging AI**: AI-driven real-time 4D medical imaging for dynamic organ analysis.

Conclusion: AI is revolutionizing X-ray, MRI, and CT scan analysis, making medical imaging faster, more precise, and highly efficient. As AI adoption grows, radiologists and AI will work hand in hand to create a future where diseases are diagnosed earlier and treated more effectively.

3.3 Challenges in AI-Driven Medical Diagnosis

Artificial intelligence is transforming medical diagnosis, offering faster, more accurate, and highly efficient methods for detecting diseases. However, despite its incredible potential,

AI-driven diagnostics face significant challenges that must be addressed before widespread adoption in healthcare. From data privacy concerns and regulatory hurdles to bias in AI models and the need for clinician trust, overcoming these barriers is essential for ensuring safe, ethical, and effective AI deployment. This chapter explores the key challenges in AI-driven medical diagnosis, along with possible solutions to mitigate risks and maximize AI's benefits in clinical practice.

1. Data-Related Challenges in AI Diagnosis

1.1 Data Privacy & Security Concerns

Medical data is highly sensitive, requiring strict adherence to HIPAA (Health Insurance Portability and Accountability Act), GDPR (General Data Protection Regulation), and other data protection laws. AI models require large amounts of patient data to learn and improve, but:

- Data breaches and cyberattacks pose significant risks to patient confidentiality.
- Unauthorized AI access to medical records could lead to misuse or unethical exploitation.
- Patient consent and data sharing regulations vary across countries, complicating global AI deployment.

Solution: Implement secure encryption, anonymization techniques, and blockchain-based health records to ensure data security while complying with regulations.

1.2 Limited and Imbalanced Datasets

AI models require diverse and high-quality datasets to make accurate diagnoses. However, challenges include:

- Insufficient labeled data for rare diseases, limiting AI's ability to learn from limited cases.
- Imbalanced datasets, where AI is trained on mostly healthy patients or specific ethnic groups, leading to biased outcomes.
- Data variability across hospitals, as different imaging machines, techniques, and protocols affect AI model generalization.

Solution: Improve dataset diversity by collaborating with multiple hospitals, implementing federated learning, and using synthetic data augmentation techniques.

2. Algorithmic Challenges in AI Medical Diagnosis

2.1 Bias and Fairness Issues in AI Models

AI models can inherit biases from the data they are trained on, leading to unequal healthcare outcomes. Bias in medical AI can result in:

- Underdiagnosis in certain demographics (e.g., AI models trained on predominantly Caucasian datasets may underperform for Black or Asian patients).
- Gender disparities, where some AI models fail to detect heart disease symptoms in women due to historical underrepresentation in medical studies.
- False positives or false negatives, where AI misclassifies diseases due to a skewed dataset distribution.

Solution: Ensure balanced and diverse datasets, implement bias detection algorithms, and conduct regular audits of AI performance across different demographic groups.

2.2 AI Explainability & the "Black Box" Problem

Most AI models, especially deep learning algorithms, function as black boxes, meaning their decision-making process is not transparent. In medical settings, lack of explainability can lead to:

- Clinician distrust, as doctors may be hesitant to rely on AI diagnoses they cannot interpret.
- Legal and ethical concerns, especially if AI-based misdiagnoses lead to medical errors or malpractice claims.
- Difficulty in regulatory approval, as healthcare authorities require AI models to provide clear reasoning for their decisions.

Solution: Develop Explainable AI (XAI) models that highlight which features in medical images or lab tests led to the diagnosis, allowing clinicians to understand and verify AI-driven insights.

3. Regulatory & Compliance Barriers

3.1 Complex Regulatory Approvals for AI in Healthcare

AI-driven diagnostics must meet stringent regulatory requirements before being deployed in clinical settings. Challenges include:

- **Lengthy approval processes**: AI-powered medical devices must receive FDA, CE, or other regulatory approvals, which can take years.
- **Changing AI behavior over time**: Unlike static medical devices, AI models continue learning, raising concerns about how to regulate AI updates.
- Lack of universal AI healthcare standards, making it difficult to ensure AI safety and effectiveness across different countries.

Solution: Establish adaptive regulatory frameworks that allow for continuous AI validation, and implement AI version control to monitor updates in real time.

3.2 Legal & Ethical Liability in AI Misdiagnosis

Who is responsible if an AI-powered diagnosis is incorrect and leads to patient harm—the hospital, the software developer, or the doctor? Legal challenges include:

- AI liability gaps, where existing laws do not clearly define who is accountable for AI-generated decisions.
- Doctor vs. AI conflicts, as human experts and AI systems may provide conflicting diagnoses, creating uncertainty.
- Ethical dilemmas in AI-assisted decision-making, particularly in life-and-death situations where AI recommendations could influence critical medical choices.

Solution: Develop clear liability frameworks, ensure clinicians have the final decision-making authority, and mandate human-AI collaboration rather than full AI autonomy in medical diagnosis.

4. Technical & Operational Challenges in AI Deployment

4.1 Integration of AI with Existing Healthcare Systems

Hospitals and clinics operate on legacy electronic health record (EHR) systems that may not be compatible with modern AI tools. Challenges include:

- High implementation costs, as AI requires expensive infrastructure and specialized hardware.
- Interoperability issues, where AI platforms do not integrate well with existing PACS (Picture Archiving and Communication Systems) or EHR software.
- Lack of technical expertise, as many healthcare providers lack AI-trained personnel to manage and interpret AI-driven diagnostics.

Solution: Develop modular AI tools that can be easily integrated into existing hospital systems, provide AI training for healthcare professionals, and encourage government funding for AI adoption.

4.2 AI Model Generalization Across Different Hospitals

An AI model trained in one hospital or country may not perform well when used in another region due to variations in:

- Imaging protocols and equipment settings.
- Medical terminology and diagnosis criteria.
- Patient demographics and disease prevalence.

Solution: Use transfer learning, where AI models pre-trained on one dataset are fine-tuned with local hospital data before full deployment.

5. The Future of AI in Medical Diagnosis: Overcoming These Challenges

Despite these challenges, AI will continue to play an increasing role in healthcare diagnostics. Steps to ensure AI's responsible and effective use include:

✅ **Developing Transparent AI Models** – Explainable AI will improve clinician trust and regulatory approval.
✅ **Creating Ethical AI Frameworks** – AI governance policies will ensure fairness, privacy, and accountability.
✅ **Enhancing Data Sharing & Collaboration** – Federated learning will enable hospitals to share AI insights without compromising patient privacy.
✅ **Investing in AI Education for Clinicians** – Doctors and radiologists will receive specialized AI training to work alongside AI tools.

Conclusion: AI has the potential to revolutionize medical diagnosis, but overcoming these challenges is crucial to ensure safe, ethical, and effective AI integration. By addressing data privacy, algorithmic bias, regulatory hurdles, and interoperability issues, AI can truly become a trusted partner in modern healthcare.

3.4 Regulatory Approvals and Ethical Concerns

Artificial intelligence (AI) is transforming healthcare by enhancing diagnostic accuracy, reducing human error, and optimizing medical workflows. However, the integration of AI into medical diagnostics requires strict regulatory oversight and ethical considerations to ensure patient safety, fairness, and transparency. Without proper regulation, AI-driven medical tools risk misdiagnosis, biased predictions, and violations of patient privacy. This chapter explores the regulatory landscape, ethical dilemmas, and the challenges AI developers and healthcare providers face in ensuring compliance with global standards.

1. Regulatory Landscape for AI in Healthcare

Before an AI-powered diagnostic tool can be deployed in a hospital or clinic, it must receive approval from regulatory agencies that evaluate its safety, effectiveness, and reliability. The approval process varies across different countries, with major regulators including:

1.1 U.S. Food and Drug Administration (FDA) Approval

The FDA is responsible for regulating AI-driven medical devices under the 21st Century Cures Act and the Medical Device Regulation (MDR) framework. AI in healthcare is categorized into:

- **Software as a Medical Device (SaMD):** AI-driven applications that assist in diagnosing diseases.
- **AI-assisted Imaging Tools**: AI models used for analyzing MRIs, CT scans, and X-rays.
- **Adaptive AI Systems**: AI that continuously learns from new patient data, posing additional regulatory challenges.

Challenges with FDA Approval:

- Lengthy approval processes delay AI implementation in hospitals.
- Lack of standardized guidelines for continuously evolving AI models.
- Balancing AI innovation with patient safety while ensuring real-world performance matches clinical trials.

1.2 European Medicines Agency (EMA) & CE Marking in Europe

In the European Union, AI-based healthcare tools must comply with the Medical Devices Regulation (MDR) and In Vitro Diagnostic Regulation (IVDR) to obtain CE marking for commercial use.

- AI models must demonstrate clinical validity, safety, and risk mitigation strategies.
- General Data Protection Regulation (GDPR) enforces strict rules on AI's access and usage of patient data.
- EMA encourages the development of Explainable AI (XAI) to ensure medical professionals understand AI-based decisions.

1.3 Global AI Regulations: China, India & Beyond

- China's National Medical Products Administration (NMPA) has introduced AI-specific guidelines, requiring real-world validation of AI models before approval.
- India's Medical Device Rules, 2017, regulate AI-driven medical software, with a focus on data localization and privacy.
- Canada's Health Canada mandates AI models undergo pre-market approval and post-market surveillance to ensure reliability.

Common Global Regulatory Challenges:

- Different approval criteria across countries create obstacles for AI developers expanding globally.
- Unclear regulations for self-learning AI systems, which update over time based on new data.
- Lack of AI-specific regulatory bodies dedicated to healthcare innovation.

2. Ethical Concerns in AI-Driven Medical Diagnosis

2.1 AI Bias & Fairness in Diagnosis

AI models can inherit biases from their training data, leading to disparities in medical diagnosis.

- AI trained on Western patient datasets may misdiagnose conditions in non-Western populations.
- Gender biases exist in AI models detecting heart disease, as historical studies focused on male patients.
- Socioeconomic disparities arise when AI tools are inaccessible to low-income populations.

Ethical Solution:

- Ensure diverse and representative datasets.
- Conduct bias audits before AI deployment.
- Implement regulatory guidelines requiring AI fairness testing.

2.2 Patient Privacy & Data Protection

AI-powered diagnostics rely on massive amounts of patient data, raising concerns about:

- Unauthorized AI access to sensitive medical records.
- AI models storing patient information beyond regulatory limits.
- Cybersecurity threats, including data breaches and AI-driven fraud.

Ethical Solution:

- Use privacy-preserving AI techniques like federated learning (where AI learns from decentralized patient data without transferring it).
- Strengthen encryption and access controls for AI-driven healthcare systems.
- Enforce strict data retention policies to prevent misuse.

2.3 The "Black Box" Problem & Lack of Explainability

Most AI models operate as black boxes, meaning their decision-making processes are not easily interpretable by doctors or regulators.

- Physicians hesitate to trust AI recommendations they cannot explain to patients.
- Lack of transparency in AI undermines accountability in misdiagnosis cases.
- Regulatory agencies struggle to evaluate opaque AI models for safety compliance.

Ethical Solution:

- Promote Explainable AI (XAI) to make AI decisions more transparent.
- Require AI models to provide human-readable explanations alongside their predictions.
- Develop regulatory standards that mandate interpretability before approval.

3. Liability & Legal Challenges in AI Misdiagnosis

3.1 Who is Responsible for an AI Misdiagnosis?

If an AI system misdiagnoses a disease, leading to improper treatment, who is legally responsible?

- **Doctors**? If they relied on AI recommendations without verifying results.
- **Hospitals**? If they implemented AI without ensuring accuracy.
- **AI Developers**? If the algorithm contained flaws or biases.

Solution:

- Establish clear liability frameworks for AI-powered medical devices.
- Require AI-generated diagnoses to be verified by human doctors before clinical decisions.
- Introduce "AI malpractice insurance" for healthcare providers using AI tools.

3.2 Informed Consent for AI Diagnosis

Patients have the right to know if AI is involved in their medical diagnosis and decision-making. However:

- Many hospitals fail to disclose AI usage to patients.
- AI decisions lack transparency, making informed consent difficult.
- Ethical concerns arise when AI-based decisions override human judgment.

Solution:

- Implement policies requiring patient consent before AI-based diagnosis.
- Provide explainable AI reports to ensure patients understand AI-driven recommendations.
- Encourage shared decision-making between AI, doctors, and patients.

4. The Future of AI Regulation & Ethics in Healthcare

As AI continues to evolve, new regulatory frameworks and ethical standards will be necessary. Future developments may include:

✅ Real-time AI auditing to detect and prevent biases in medical AI models.

✅ Global AI healthcare regulations, ensuring unified compliance across countries.

✅ AI liability insurance, protecting both patients and healthcare providers.

✅ Stronger Explainable AI guidelines, ensuring AI-driven diagnoses are interpretable.

✅ Secure AI data-sharing models, enabling hospitals to share AI insights while protecting patient privacy.

AI-driven medical diagnosis has enormous potential to save lives, improve efficiency, and reduce healthcare costs. However, regulatory approvals, ethical concerns, and legal challenges must be addressed to ensure AI's responsible and safe adoption. By implementing fair, explainable, and privacy-conscious AI systems, the healthcare industry can fully harness AI's capabilities while protecting patients and medical professionals alike.

4. AI in Drug Discovery and Personalized Medicine

AI is transforming drug discovery and personalized medicine by accelerating research, reducing costs, and enabling targeted treatments. Traditional drug development can take years, but AI-driven algorithms analyze vast datasets to identify potential drug candidates, predict molecular interactions, and optimize clinical trials in a fraction of the time. In personalized medicine, AI tailors treatments based on an individual's genetic profile, lifestyle, and medical history, leading to more effective and precise healthcare solutions. This chapter explores how AI is reshaping pharmaceutical research, improving patient outcomes, and overcoming challenges in regulatory approval and ethical considerations.

4.1 AI's Role in Accelerating Drug Development

The process of drug development is notoriously time-consuming, expensive, and complex, often taking 10–15 years and costing billions of dollars before a new drug reaches the market. However, artificial intelligence (AI) is revolutionizing this process by reducing research time, enhancing accuracy, and lowering costs. AI-driven drug discovery enables faster identification of potential drug candidates, prediction of molecular interactions, and optimization of clinical trials, ultimately accelerating the journey from lab to patient.

This chapter explores how AI is transforming drug development through advanced algorithms, deep learning models, and data-driven insights, highlighting key breakthroughs and ongoing challenges.

1. The Traditional Drug Development Process: Slow & Expensive

Before understanding AI's role, it's important to recognize the traditional steps involved in drug discovery:

- **Target Identification** – Finding the biological molecule (protein, gene, etc.) linked to a disease.
- **Drug Screening** – Testing thousands of chemical compounds to identify potential drugs.
- **Preclinical Testing** – Conducting lab and animal tests to assess safety.

- **Clinical Trials** – Testing on humans in three phases, ensuring safety and effectiveness.
- **Regulatory Approval** – Submitting data to agencies like the FDA, EMA, or MHRA for approval.

Each stage is lengthy, costly, and has a high failure rate, often due to:

- Incomplete understanding of diseases at the molecular level.
- Trial-and-error drug screening methods.
- Expensive and slow clinical trials with high dropout rates.

AI is reshaping these challenges by making drug discovery smarter, faster, and more precise.

2. AI-Driven Drug Discovery: Transforming Early-Stage Research

2.1 AI in Target Identification & Biomarker Discovery

Finding the right biological target (protein or gene) is the first and most crucial step in drug development. AI enhances this process by:

✓ Analyzing vast amounts of genomic and proteomic data to identify new disease-related targets.

✓ Using natural language processing (NLP) to extract insights from scientific literature.

✓ Predicting gene-disease associations using deep learning models.

♦ **Example**: DeepMind's AlphaFold AI accurately predicts protein structures, helping researchers understand diseases at a molecular level.

2.2 AI-Powered Drug Screening & Molecular Simulation

Traditional drug screening involves testing millions of compounds to find potential drug candidates, which is costly and time-intensive. AI speeds up this process through:

✓ **Virtual screening** – AI models predict how molecules interact with biological targets.
✓ **Generative AI for drug design** – Algorithms like DeepChem generate novel drug candidates.

✅ **Quantum simulations** – AI-enhanced simulations predict molecular behavior, reducing reliance on lab experiments.

◆ **Example**: AI-driven company Insilico Medicine identified a new fibrosis drug in just 46 days—a process that typically takes years.

3. AI in Preclinical & Clinical Trials: Faster and More Efficient Testing

3.1 AI-Enhanced Preclinical Testing

Before human trials, drugs must be tested in cell cultures and animal models to assess safety. AI enhances this step by:

✅ Predicting toxicity and side effects before lab testing.

✅ Using computer models ("in silico" trials) to simulate drug effects, reducing animal testing.

✅ Automating drug-repurposing, finding new uses for existing drugs.

◆ **Example**: AI helped repurpose Remdesivir as a COVID-19 treatment by analyzing viral interaction patterns.

3.2 AI in Clinical Trials: Optimizing Human Testing

Clinical trials are the most expensive and time-consuming phase, often failing due to poor patient selection or high dropout rates. AI improves trials by:

✅ **Patient recruitment optimization** – Identifying ideal participants based on EHRs and genetic profiles.
✅ **Adaptive trial designs** – AI monitors real-time data to adjust dosages, reducing trial failure.
✅ **Predictive analytics** – AI forecasts trial outcomes, saving costs on unsuccessful drugs.

◆ **Example**: AI-driven platform IBM Watson Health accelerates clinical trial matching, improving recruitment efficiency.

4. AI & Personalized Medicine: The Future of Drug Development

4.1 AI for Precision Drug Development

Traditional drug development follows a one-size-fits-all approach, but AI enables personalized medicine by:

✅ Analyzing genomic data to create customized treatments.

✅ Predicting how different patients respond to drugs based on biomarkers.

✅ Tailoring dosages and drug combinations to individual needs.

◆ **Example**: AI helps oncologists select targeted cancer therapies based on a patient's genetic mutations.

4.2 AI & mRNA Drug Discovery

AI is playing a crucial role in developing mRNA-based drugs and vaccines, such as:

✅ Designing customized mRNA vaccines for infectious diseases.

✅ Optimizing mRNA sequences for higher stability and effectiveness.

✅ Accelerating COVID-19 and cancer vaccine development.

◆ **Example**: AI helped Moderna and BioNTech develop COVID-19 vaccines in record time.

5. Challenges & Ethical Concerns in AI-Driven Drug Discovery

While AI offers immense benefits, several challenges must be addressed:

5.1 Data Privacy & Security

- AI models require massive amounts of patient data, raising concerns about data security.
- Regulations like HIPAA & GDPR restrict AI access to sensitive health information.
- Risk of AI-driven data leaks or cyberattacks in drug research.

Solution: Implement secure AI algorithms, ensure data anonymization, and enforce regulatory compliance.

5.2 AI Bias & Drug Accessibility

- AI models may be trained on biased datasets, leading to inequitable drug development.
- Drugs discovered by AI may be more accessible to wealthy nations while neglecting low-income populations.

Solution: Use diverse, global datasets and promote ethical AI drug policies to ensure fairness.

5.3 Regulatory Approval for AI-Designed Drugs

- Traditional FDA and EMA guidelines are not built for AI-generated drugs.
- AI's ability to create novel molecules at scale raises concerns about quality control and safety validation.

Solution: Develop AI-specific regulatory frameworks that ensure AI-driven drug discovery meets clinical safety standards.

6. The Future of AI in Drug Development

AI is rapidly revolutionizing drug discovery, paving the way for:

✓ AI-powered "automated labs" for high-speed drug testing.

✓ Blockchain-based drug development to improve transparency and security.

✓ Quantum AI models that simulate molecular behavior with near-perfect accuracy.

✓ AI-driven "biological twins" – virtual simulations of human bodies for testing drug effects.

AI is accelerating drug development, reducing costs, and improving treatment precision. While challenges remain in data privacy, regulation, and fairness, continued innovation and ethical AI deployment will reshape the pharmaceutical industry and revolutionize modern medicine.

4.2 Predictive Modeling for Drug Discovery

The integration of predictive modeling in drug discovery has transformed the pharmaceutical industry by making drug research faster, more cost-effective, and more precise. Traditional drug discovery relies on extensive trial-and-error methods, but AI-driven predictive models can analyze massive datasets, simulate molecular interactions, and predict drug efficacy with unprecedented accuracy. This chapter explores how predictive modeling is revolutionizing drug discovery, from identifying drug candidates to optimizing clinical trials, while also addressing challenges and ethical considerations.

1. Understanding Predictive Modeling in Drug Discovery

Predictive modeling uses AI, machine learning (ML), and deep learning algorithms to forecast outcomes in drug research. These models analyze chemical structures, biological interactions, and patient data to:

✓ Identify promising drug candidates before lab testing.

✓ Predict how molecules interact with disease targets.

✓ Reduce costly experimental failures by screening compounds virtually.

✓ Optimize dosages, toxicity levels, and side effects before clinical trials.

◆ **Example**: AI-driven predictive models helped develop COVID-19 treatments in record time by identifying antiviral compounds rapidly.

2. How AI-Based Predictive Models Work in Drug Discovery

2.1 Drug Target Identification & Validation

Predictive modeling analyzes genomic, proteomic, and biochemical data to:

✓ Discover new disease-associated targets (e.g., proteins, enzymes).

✓ Validate whether a target can be modified by a drug.

✓ Predict the biological pathways involved in disease progression.

◆ **Example**: DeepMind's AlphaFold AI predicts 3D protein structures, helping scientists understand disease mechanisms faster.

2.2 Virtual Screening & Molecular Docking

Instead of testing millions of compounds in the lab, AI-driven virtual screening predicts which molecules will bind effectively to a drug target.

✅ Machine learning algorithms screen massive chemical libraries to shortlist potential drugs.

✅ Molecular docking simulations predict how well a drug binds to a target.

✅ Deep learning models assess the stability of drug-target interactions.

◆ **Example**: AI models helped BenevolentAI identify Baricitinib, an FDA-approved drug repurposed for treating COVID-19.

2.3 Predicting Drug Toxicity & Side Effects

AI models analyze chemical structures and patient data to predict:

✅ Toxicity levels before human trials.

✅ Side effect probabilities based on past drug failures.

✅ Metabolic interactions, ensuring drugs don't cause adverse reactions.

◆ **Example**: MIT's AI-based model predicts which drugs may cause liver toxicity, reducing clinical trial failures.

2.4 Predicting Drug Absorption & Pharmacokinetics

AI-driven predictive modeling assesses how a drug behaves in the body, including:

✅ Absorption (how quickly it enters the bloodstream).

✅ Distribution (which organs it affects).

✅ Metabolism (how the body processes it).

✅ Excretion (how long it stays in the system).

◆ **Example**: AI predicts drug half-life, ensuring optimal dosage levels and minimizing overdose risks.

3. AI-Powered Predictive Models in Clinical Trials

Clinical trials are the most expensive and time-consuming phase of drug development. AI-based predictive models optimize patient recruitment, predict trial outcomes, and improve efficiency.

3.1 Patient Selection & Recruitment

Predictive modeling analyzes electronic health records (EHRs) and genetic data to:

✅ Identify ideal clinical trial candidates.

✅ Predict which patients will respond best to a drug.

✅ Reduce dropout rates by selecting engaged participants.

◆ **Example**: AI-driven platforms like Deep 6 AI analyze millions of patient records to match participants with trials in minutes instead of months.

3.2 Adaptive Trial Design & Real-Time Monitoring

Predictive models continuously analyze real-time trial data to:

✅ Adjust drug dosages based on patient responses.

✅ Detect adverse effects early, preventing trial failures.

✅ Improve overall trial success rates.

◆ **Example**: AI-driven adaptive clinical trials helped optimize COVID-19 vaccine dosages efficiently.

4. The Role of Deep Learning in Drug Discovery

Deep learning (DL) takes predictive modeling to the next level by analyzing high-dimensional biological and chemical data.

4.1 Neural Networks for Drug Design

Deep learning models use neural networks to:

✅ Recognize complex molecular patterns in drug compounds.

✅ Generate new drug candidates using generative adversarial networks (GANs).

✅ Improve drug-target binding predictions.

◆ **Example**: AI-generated drugs like DSP-1181, a potential OCD treatment, were designed in months instead of years.

4.2 Natural Language Processing (NLP) in Drug Discovery

NLP helps pharmaceutical companies extract insights from millions of research papers and clinical reports by:

✅ Identifying new drug-disease relationships from scientific literature.

✅ Predicting potential drug repurposing opportunities.

✅ Automating clinical trial documentation for efficiency.

◆ **Example**: IBM Watson Health uses NLP to analyze medical research and accelerate drug discovery.

5. Challenges & Ethical Considerations in AI-Powered Predictive Modeling

Despite its advantages, AI-driven predictive modeling faces several challenges:

5.1 Data Quality & Bias in AI Models

- AI models depend on high-quality, diverse datasets to make accurate predictions.
- Bias in training data can lead to incorrect drug recommendations.
- Limited data availability for rare diseases affects prediction accuracy.

Solution: Use balanced, global datasets and conduct AI bias audits.

5.2 Regulatory & Compliance Issues

- AI-driven predictions must meet FDA, EMA, and HIPAA regulations.

- Lack of clear AI guidelines in pharmaceutical research creates barriers to adoption.

Solution: Implement AI-specific regulatory frameworks to ensure compliance and patient safety.

5.3 Ethical AI & Drug Accessibility

- AI-driven drug discovery may lead to high-cost patented drugs, limiting accessibility.
- Developing countries may struggle to benefit from AI-driven advancements due to economic barriers.

Solution: Promote open-source AI drug models to make treatments more accessible.

6. The Future of Predictive Modeling in Drug Discovery

Predictive modeling is rapidly evolving, paving the way for:

✓ AI-powered "self-learning" drug discovery platforms.

✓ Quantum AI models to simulate ultra-precise molecular interactions.

✓ Blockchain integration for secure AI-driven clinical trials.

✓ AI-generated personalized drugs, tailored to individual genetic profiles.

AI-powered predictive modeling is revolutionizing how drugs are discovered, tested, and brought to market. By harnessing big data, deep learning, and real-time simulations, predictive models reduce costs, enhance accuracy, and accelerate life-saving drug development. Despite challenges in data quality, regulation, and accessibility, the future of AI-driven drug discovery holds enormous potential for global healthcare.

4.3 AI and Genomics: The Future of Precision Medicine

The integration of AI and genomics is revolutionizing precision medicine, allowing treatments to be tailored to individual genetic profiles. Traditional medicine follows a one-size-fits-all approach, often leading to varying responses to the same treatment. However, AI-driven genomic analysis enables the identification of disease risks, drug responses, and personalized therapies, transforming patient care.

This chapter explores how AI is reshaping genomic research, personalized treatments, and drug development, while also addressing key challenges and ethical considerations in precision medicine.

1. The Role of AI in Genomics and Precision Medicine

Genomics is the study of DNA, genes, and their functions. AI enhances genomic research by:

✅ Identifying genetic mutations linked to diseases (e.g., cancer, Alzheimer's).

✅ Predicting disease susceptibility based on genetic variations.

✅ Optimizing drug treatments for individual patients.

✅ Enabling gene editing for disease prevention and treatment.

◆ **Example**: AI models can analyze a patient's DNA to predict their risk of inherited diseases and recommend preventive strategies.

2. AI-Powered Genomic Sequencing: Accelerating DNA Analysis

2.1 The Evolution of Genome Sequencing

The Human Genome Project (2003) took nearly 13 years and cost $3 billion to map the human genome. Today, AI-driven genome sequencing:

✅ Reduces sequencing time to hours instead of years.

✅ Lowers costs to under $1,000 per genome.

✅ Improves accuracy in identifying genetic mutations and disease risks.

◆ **Example**: Google's DeepVariant AI can identify genetic mutations with 99.9% accuracy, enhancing diagnostic precision.

2.2 AI in Whole Genome & Exome Sequencing

AI improves whole genome sequencing (WGS) and whole exome sequencing (WES) by:

✅ Filtering millions of genetic variants to detect disease-related mutations.

✓ Identifying rare genetic disorders through deep learning models.

✓ Enhancing CRISPR gene-editing by targeting faulty genes more precisely.

◆ **Example**: AI-based genomic analysis helped diagnose rare diseases in children by rapidly sequencing their DNA.

3. AI-Driven Personalized Medicine: Tailoring Treatments to DNA

3.1 AI for Cancer Treatment & Oncology

AI is transforming cancer genomics by:

✓ Identifying tumor-specific mutations for targeted therapies.

✓ Predicting which chemotherapy or immunotherapy will work best.

✓ Developing personalized cancer vaccines based on a patient's DNA.

◆ **Example**: AI-driven platforms like IBM Watson for Oncology recommend custom cancer treatments based on genetic markers.

3.2 AI in Pharmacogenomics (Drug Response Prediction)

Pharmacogenomics studies how genes affect drug responses. AI enhances this by:

✓ Predicting which medications will work best for an individual.

✓ Reducing adverse drug reactions by analyzing genetic variations.

✓ Optimizing dosages for personalized treatment plans.

◆ **Example**: AI predicts whether a patient metabolizes drugs too fast or too slow, helping doctors adjust prescriptions accordingly.

3.3 AI in Neurological & Cardiovascular Genomics

AI is advancing genomics in brain and heart diseases by:

✓ Detecting genetic markers for Alzheimer's and Parkinson's.

✅ Predicting stroke and heart disease risk based on DNA.

✅ Enabling gene therapy research for inherited disorders.

◆ **Example**: AI-driven genomics identified genetic risk factors for atrial fibrillation, helping cardiologists prevent strokes.

4. AI & Gene Editing: The Future of Disease Prevention

4.1 AI in CRISPR Gene Editing

CRISPR technology allows scientists to edit defective genes to cure genetic disorders. AI improves CRISPR by:

✅ Identifying gene-editing targets more accurately.

✅ Predicting off-target effects to avoid harmful mutations.

✅ Designing personalized gene therapies for rare diseases.

◆ **Example**: AI is helping researchers develop gene therapies for sickle cell anemia and cystic fibrosis.

4.2 AI in Stem Cell & Regenerative Medicine

AI enhances stem cell therapy by:

✅ Identifying optimal stem cell donors based on genetic compatibility.

✅ Predicting stem cell differentiation patterns for regenerative medicine.

✅ Enhancing 3D bioprinting of tissues and organs.

◆ **Example**: AI-driven stem cell research is advancing customized organ transplants.

5. Ethical & Privacy Challenges in AI-Driven Genomics

Despite its promise, AI-powered genomics faces critical ethical challenges:

5.1 Data Privacy & Genetic Discrimination

- Genomic data is highly personal and sensitive.
- Companies and insurers could misuse DNA data for discrimination.
- Regulations like GDPR & HIPAA must protect patient genetic data.
- **Solution**: Implement secure AI encryption and strict data-sharing policies.

5.2 AI Bias & Genetic Inequality

- Most genomic databases are Eurocentric, leading to biases.
- Minority populations may receive less accurate predictions.
- AI-based treatments must be inclusive of all ethnic groups.
- **Solution**: Train AI on diverse global genomic datasets.

5.3 Gene Editing Ethics: Playing with Human DNA

- Should we allow AI-driven human gene modification?
- Where is the line between curing diseases and genetic enhancement?
- Do we risk creating "designer babies"?
- **Solution**: Establish global ethical guidelines for AI in genomics.

6. The Future of AI & Genomics in Precision Medicine

AI-driven genomics is paving the way for:

✓ AI-based disease risk prediction apps for consumers.

✓ Fully personalized AI-designed medications.

✓ Genome-editing therapies for incurable genetic disorders.

✓ AI-powered regenerative medicine for growing replacement organs.

AI and genomics are unlocking the full potential of precision medicine, offering targeted treatments, early disease detection, and personalized therapies. Despite ethical challenges, AI's ability to decode the human genome will redefine the future of healthcare.

4.4 Ethical and Safety Concerns in AI-Driven Medicine

As AI continues to revolutionize medicine, its potential to enhance diagnosis, treatment, drug discovery, and patient care is undeniable. However, these advancements come with ethical, safety, and regulatory concerns that must be addressed to ensure that AI-driven healthcare remains trustworthy, fair, and safe for all.

This chapter explores the key ethical dilemmas, safety challenges, and regulatory considerations in AI-driven medicine, focusing on areas like patient privacy, algorithmic bias, medical accountability, and the future of AI governance in healthcare.

1. Patient Privacy & Data Security in AI Healthcare

AI in medicine depends on massive datasets from electronic health records (EHRs), genetic information, and real-time patient monitoring systems. While this data is essential for training AI models, it also raises serious privacy risks.

1.1 The Risk of Data Breaches & Cybersecurity Threats

✅ Medical records are prime targets for cybercriminals.

✅ AI-driven health platforms store highly sensitive patient information.

✅ A single data breach can expose millions of patient records.

◆ **Example**: The 2015 Anthem data breach exposed 80 million patient records, highlighting the vulnerabilities of digital healthcare.

Solution:

◆ Implement blockchain-based medical records for secure data storage.
◆ Use AI-powered cybersecurity tools to detect hacking attempts.
◆ Strengthen HIPAA, GDPR, and AI-specific data protection laws.

1.2 AI's Role in Data Collection & Informed Consent

AI systems collect patient data from wearables, EHRs, and genetic testing. The challenge? Many patients aren't fully aware of how their data is used.

Key Concerns:

✖ Patients may unknowingly consent to AI-driven data usage.

✖ AI models can be trained on health data without explicit approval.

✗ Companies may sell or misuse genetic and medical data.

Solution:

◆ Ensure transparent consent forms with clear AI usage details.
◆ Implement patient-controlled data access, allowing users to choose how AI utilizes their data.

2. Bias in AI: The Risk of Unequal Healthcare

AI models learn from historical medical data, but if this data is biased, AI can exacerbate existing healthcare inequalities.

2.1 Racial & Gender Bias in AI-Driven Diagnoses

✓ AI models trained on Western-centric datasets may misdiagnose patients from different ethnic backgrounds.

✓ Medical AI tools often underperform for women and minorities due to biased training data.

✓ Some AI-based skin cancer detection systems struggle to diagnose darker skin tones.

◆ **Example**: An AI system designed for detecting lung cancer showed lower accuracy for Black patients, highlighting racial disparities in medical data.

Solution:

◆ Train AI models on diverse, global datasets.
◆ Conduct bias audits to detect and correct AI discrimination.
◆ Develop AI fairness regulations to ensure equal healthcare access.

3. AI Accountability: Who is Responsible for AI Errors?

3.1 AI Malpractice & Medical Errors

If an AI system misdiagnoses a patient or recommends the wrong treatment, who is responsible—the doctor, the AI developer, or the hospital?

✗ AI systems lack legal accountability for incorrect medical decisions.

✗ Physicians may over-rely on AI, leading to misdiagnoses.

✗ The "black box" problem makes it difficult to explain AI's decisions in court.

◆ **Example**: An AI-powered radiology system misclassified tumors, leading to delayed cancer treatments for some patients.

Solution:

◆ Implement human-AI collaboration, where AI supports—but doesn't replace—doctors.
◆ Require AI explainability, ensuring physicians understand how AI makes decisions.
◆ Develop clear legal frameworks for AI-related medical errors.

3.2 The Risk of Over-Automation in Healthcare

✓ AI can process millions of patient cases faster than doctors.

✓ Hospitals may over-automate patient diagnostics, reducing human oversight.

✓ The loss of human empathy and judgment could negatively impact patient care.

Solution:

◆ Keep doctors in control of AI-assisted decisions.
◆ Ensure AI complements human expertise rather than replacing it.

4. Ethical Challenges in AI-Driven Drug Discovery

AI accelerates drug development, but it also raises serious ethical concerns.

4.1 AI and Experimental Drug Testing

✓ AI helps discover new drugs faster than traditional methods.

✓ Pharmaceutical companies might rush clinical trials due to AI predictions.

✓ AI-driven trials may bypass ethical safeguards, risking patient safety.

◆ **Example**: AI discovered a potential Alzheimer's drug, but its rushed human trials led to severe side effects in some patients.

Solution:

◆ Ensure rigorous clinical trial validation, even for AI-discovered drugs.
◆ Enforce strict AI ethics guidelines in pharmaceutical research.

4.2 The Risk of AI-Generated Bioweapons

✗ AI models can design powerful new drugs, but they could also create deadly biological weapons.

✗ In 2022, a study showed that AI designed 40,000 toxic molecules in less than 6 hours.

Solution:

◆ Strengthen AI security protocols in drug research.
◆ Implement AI regulations to prevent misuse of biotechnology.

5. AI Regulation & The Future of AI in Medicine

5.1 The Need for Global AI Healthcare Regulations

AI in medicine currently lacks universal regulations, leading to:

✗ Different AI safety standards across countries.

✗ Unregulated AI medical devices entering the market.

✗ The potential for AI-driven healthcare monopolies.

◆ **Example**: Some AI medical tools approved in the U.S. have been banned in the EU due to stricter regulations.

Solution:

◆ Develop a global AI medical governance framework.
◆ Enforce AI-specific FDA & EMA approval processes.

5.2 Explainable AI (XAI): The Key to Trustworthy AI

✖ Many AI models operate as "black boxes", meaning their decision-making process is not transparent.

✓ Explainable AI (XAI) helps doctors and regulators understand AI decisions.

✓ Patients must be able to question AI-based diagnoses.

Solution:

◆ Require all medical AI tools to provide clear, interpretable outputs.
◆ Develop AI systems that justify their recommendations.

6. The Future of Ethical AI in Medicine

AI in medicine will continue to evolve, but ethical safeguards must keep pace. The future will involve:

✓ Stronger AI governance laws to protect patients.

✓ Ethical AI frameworks ensuring fair, bias-free healthcare.

✓ AI-human collaboration, where AI supports, but never replaces, doctors.

✓ Secure patient data protocols, preventing medical privacy breaches.

AI has the potential to revolutionize medicine, but without ethical oversight, it can also create risks. Addressing privacy, bias, accountability, and regulation challenges is essential to ensure that AI-driven medicine remains safe, fair, and beneficial for all patients.

5. AI-Powered Virtual Health Assistants & Remote Care

AI-driven virtual health assistants and remote care solutions are redefining patient engagement, accessibility, and healthcare delivery. From AI chatbots that provide medical guidance to voice-enabled virtual nurses monitoring chronic conditions, these technologies are improving patient outcomes while reducing the burden on healthcare professionals. Telemedicine, powered by AI, enables remote diagnostics, personalized treatment recommendations, and real-time health monitoring, making quality care more accessible worldwide. This chapter explores the role of AI in virtual healthcare, the benefits of remote patient management, and the challenges of privacy, security, and ethical considerations in digital health.

5.1 AI-Powered Chatbots in Telemedicine

The integration of AI-powered chatbots in telemedicine is transforming the way patients interact with healthcare providers. These chatbots serve as virtual health assistants, capable of providing 24/7 medical guidance, appointment scheduling, symptom analysis, and even mental health support. As telemedicine grows, AI chatbots are playing a critical role in bridging gaps in healthcare accessibility, reducing hospital workload, and enhancing patient engagement.

In this chapter, we explore how AI-driven chatbots are revolutionizing telemedicine, their benefits and limitations, and the future of AI-assisted virtual healthcare.

1. The Role of AI Chatbots in Telemedicine

Telemedicine relies on remote consultations, digital diagnostics, and virtual health monitoring. AI chatbots enhance telemedicine by:

✓ Providing instant medical advice based on symptom analysis.

✓ Reducing wait times for non-emergency healthcare inquiries.

✓ Automating appointment booking and prescription reminders.

✓ Offering mental health support through conversational AI.

◆ **Example**: AI chatbots like Babylon Health, Ada Health, and Buoy Health assist patients by evaluating symptoms and recommending the next steps.

2. How AI Chatbots Work in Virtual Healthcare

AI chatbots use Natural Language Processing (NLP), Machine Learning (ML), and medical databases to provide accurate responses. Their core functions include:

2.1 Symptom Checkers & Triage Bots

✓ Patients describe their symptoms, and AI assesses possible conditions.

✓ The chatbot provides self-care advice or refers the patient to a doctor.

✓ AI-based triage reduces emergency room overcrowding.

◆ **Example**: Infermedica's AI chatbot helps users identify illness risks before seeing a doctor.

2.2 Appointment Scheduling & Medication Reminders

✓ AI chatbots integrate with hospital systems to book appointments.

✓ They remind patients to take medications on time.

✓ Chatbots help reduce missed doctor visits by sending alerts.

◆ **Example**: AI chatbots used by hospitals reduce patient no-show rates by 40%.

2.3 AI Chatbots for Mental Health & Therapy

✓ Conversational AI provides emotional support for anxiety & depression.

✓ AI therapy bots like Woebot use cognitive behavioral therapy (CBT) techniques.

✓ AI-driven mental health tools help those with limited access to therapists.

◆ **Example**: Woebot AI engages in text-based therapy to help patients manage mental health.

3. Benefits of AI Chatbots in Telemedicine

3.1 Increased Accessibility to Healthcare

✅ AI chatbots provide 24/7 medical guidance, especially in rural areas.

✅ They bridge language barriers by supporting multilingual communication.

✅ Chatbots reduce dependency on overburdened healthcare systems.

3.2 Cost Savings & Efficiency

✅ AI chatbots cut down healthcare costs by automating routine consultations.

✅ They reduce administrative workload for doctors and nurses.

✅ AI reduces the need for unnecessary doctor visits.

◈ **Example**: AI chatbots saved $3 billion in healthcare costs in 2023 alone.

3.3 Personalized & Data-Driven Healthcare

✅ AI chatbots learn patient history to provide personalized responses.

✅ They analyze medical data to detect health patterns and risks.

✅ Chatbots can predict disease outbreaks based on symptom reports.

4. Challenges & Ethical Concerns in AI Chatbots for Healthcare

4.1 Accuracy & Reliability Issues

✖ AI chatbots are not 100% accurate in diagnosing medical conditions.

✖ Patients may misinterpret chatbot recommendations as professional advice.

✖ Some AI models lack real-time updates on medical research.

4.2 Data Privacy & Security Risks

✖ AI chatbots collect sensitive patient data, leading to privacy concerns.

✖ There's a risk of cyberattacks and data breaches.

✘ AI healthcare systems must comply with HIPAA & GDPR regulations.

◆ **Solution**: Implement blockchain encryption to secure patient records.

4.3 Ethical Concerns & AI Bias

✘ AI chatbots may exhibit biases in diagnosis, based on training data limitations.

✘ Chatbots cannot replace human empathy and personalized doctor-patient interactions.

✘ Over-reliance on AI may lead to misdiagnosis or delayed human intervention.

◆ **Solution**: Ensure AI-human collaboration, where doctors validate chatbot recommendations.

5. The Future of AI-Powered Chatbots in Telemedicine

5.1 AI + IoT for Remote Patient Monitoring

✓ AI chatbots will integrate with wearable health devices.

✓ Real-time monitoring of heart rate, blood pressure, and glucose levels.

✓ AI chatbots will alert doctors in case of critical health issues.

◆ **Example**: AI-powered telehealth systems will automatically notify doctors if a patient's vitals reach dangerous levels.

5.2 AI Chatbots & Virtual Hospitals

✓ The future of healthcare includes AI-driven virtual hospitals.

✓ Chatbots will handle initial patient consultations before doctor appointments.

✓ AI will assist in post-surgery recovery tracking.

◆ **Example**: AI-driven "digital hospitals" will reduce physical hospital visits by 50%.

AI-powered chatbots are revolutionizing telemedicine by enhancing accessibility, improving efficiency, and personalizing healthcare. Despite challenges in accuracy, privacy, and ethical concerns, their potential to automate patient care, reduce healthcare costs, and integrate with IoT devices makes them a game-changer in modern medicine. The future of telemedicine will see smarter AI chatbots working alongside doctors, ensuring better patient outcomes worldwide.

5.2 AI for Remote Patient Monitoring & Predictive Healthcare

The rise of Artificial Intelligence (AI) in remote patient monitoring (RPM) and predictive healthcare is transforming the way medical professionals track, diagnose, and treat patients. With AI-driven wearable devices, smart sensors, and real-time analytics, healthcare providers can monitor patients' health remotely and predict potential health risks before they become critical. This innovation is especially valuable for chronic disease management, post-surgical care, elderly healthcare, and emergency prevention.

In this chapter, we explore how AI-powered RPM systems work, their benefits, challenges, and how predictive healthcare is shaping the future of preventive medicine and personalized treatment.

1. Understanding AI-Driven Remote Patient Monitoring (RPM)

Remote Patient Monitoring (RPM) refers to the use of wearables, IoT devices, and AI-driven analytics to track patient health outside of traditional clinical settings.

1.1 How AI Enhances Remote Monitoring

✅ AI algorithms process real-time patient data to detect early warning signs.

✅ Machine learning models identify patterns and predict potential health risks.

✅ AI-powered systems alert doctors and patients when intervention is needed.

◆ **Example**: AI-based RPM systems help diabetes patients by continuously tracking blood glucose levels and predicting potential hypoglycemia or hyperglycemia episodes.

1.2 Key AI Technologies in RPM

✔ **Wearable Sensors** – Smartwatches & fitness trackers monitor heart rate, ECG, oxygen levels, sleep, and more.

✓ **AI-Based Data Analytics** – Predicts health trends and identifies potential complications.

✓ **Telehealth Integration** – Syncs with doctors and healthcare systems for remote consultations.

✓ **Smart Medication Adherence Systems** – Reminds patients to take medications and alerts doctors in case of non-compliance.

◆ **Example**: Apple Watch, Fitbit, and Garmin use AI to analyze heart rhythms and detect atrial fibrillation (AFib), preventing stroke risks.

2. Predictive Healthcare: AI's Role in Preventing Medical Crises

Predictive healthcare uses AI and big data analytics to anticipate medical conditions before symptoms appear.

2.1 AI-Based Disease Prediction Models

✓ AI models analyze historical health data to predict disease risks.

✓ Machine learning helps doctors identify high-risk patients before they experience serious symptoms.

✓ AI predicts chronic disease progression for diabetes, heart disease, and cancer.

◆ **Example**: Google's DeepMind AI predicts kidney failure 48 hours before symptoms appear, giving doctors time to act.

2.2 AI in Early Detection of Life-Threatening Conditions

✓ **AI for Heart Attack Prediction** – Monitors heart patterns and alerts patients before a cardiac event.

✓ **AI for Sepsis Detection** – Identifies early signs of infection in ICU patients.

✓ **AI in Oncology** – Detects early-stage cancer through pattern recognition in scans & blood tests.

◆ **Example**: MIT's AI model predicts breast cancer up to five years before traditional screenings.

3. Benefits of AI in Remote Patient Monitoring & Predictive Healthcare

3.1 Enhanced Patient Outcomes

✔ AI identifies potential health risks early, preventing complications.

✔ Patients receive personalized health alerts, allowing them to take proactive measures.

✔ AI-driven RPM reduces hospital admissions and emergency visits.

3.2 Reduced Healthcare Costs & Hospital Burden

✔ AI-based remote monitoring reduces unnecessary doctor visits.

✔ Predictive healthcare prevents costly hospitalizations by detecting issues early.

✔ AI helps optimize hospital resource allocation, reducing patient congestion.

◆ **Example**: AI-driven RPM has cut hospital readmissions by 38% in chronic disease management.

3.3 Better Chronic Disease Management

✔ AI-powered wearables continuously monitor diabetes, hypertension, and heart disease.

✔ AI models adjust treatment plans based on real-time patient data.

✔ AI reduces emergency episodes for chronic patients.

◆ **Example**: AI-driven glucose monitors adjust insulin levels automatically for diabetic patients.

4. Challenges & Risks of AI in Remote Healthcare

4.1 Data Privacy & Security Concerns

✘ AI-based RPM devices collect vast amounts of personal health data.

✘ Cybersecurity threats can lead to data breaches and hacking risks.

✘ Not all AI healthcare tools comply with HIPAA, GDPR, or global data protection regulations.

◆ **Solution**: Implement blockchain encryption and multi-layered security for AI-driven health data.

4.2 Accuracy & Reliability of AI Predictions

✘ AI models can misinterpret data, leading to false alarms or missed diagnoses.

✘ Over-reliance on AI may cause doctors to overlook traditional diagnosis methods.

✘ AI's effectiveness depends on high-quality, unbiased training data.

◆ **Solution**: Ensure continuous AI model training with diverse, real-world patient datasets.

4.3 Patient Compliance & Trust Issues

✘ Some patients may distrust AI-driven health recommendations.

✘ Elderly patients may struggle to use AI-based monitoring devices.

✘ AI needs human supervision to prevent errors and ensure patient-centered care.

◆ **Solution**: Improve AI-human collaboration where doctors validate AI-generated insights.

5. The Future of AI in Remote Healthcare

5.1 AI-Powered Virtual Health Assistants

✓ Future AI chatbots will interpret patient health data in real-time.

✓ AI assistants will provide personalized diet, exercise, and medication guidance.

✓ Patients will receive real-time AI-driven health coaching.

◆ **Example**: Future AI-powered Siri-like healthcare assistants will guide patients through daily health monitoring.

5.2 AI + IoT for Real-Time Emergency Response

✓ AI-driven wearables will instantly alert emergency services in case of a stroke or cardiac arrest.

✓ AI-integrated smart homes will monitor elderly patients and detect falls, seizures, or unconsciousness.

✓ AI will automate emergency response systems for faster medical intervention.

◆ **Example**: AI-based fall detection in smart homes will automatically notify ambulance services within seconds.

5.3 AI-Driven Precision Medicine & Genomics

✓ AI will analyze genomic data to create personalized disease prevention plans.

✓ Predictive healthcare will shift focus from treatment to proactive prevention.

✓ AI-driven gene therapy will help cure inherited diseases before symptoms develop.

◆ **Example**: AI-powered genomics tools will predict Alzheimer's or cancer risks decades in advance.

AI-powered Remote Patient Monitoring (RPM) and Predictive Healthcare are reshaping modern medicine. By leveraging AI-driven wearables, machine learning analytics, and predictive diagnostics, healthcare providers can detect early warning signs, prevent medical crises, and improve patient outcomes. While challenges like data privacy, AI accuracy, and patient trust remain, the future of AI in telemedicine will focus on seamless AI-human collaboration, real-time emergency interventions, and AI-driven precision medicine—paving the way for a healthier, smarter future.

5.3 Speech and NLP in AI Healthcare Assistants

The integration of Speech Recognition and Natural Language Processing (NLP) in AI-powered healthcare assistants is revolutionizing the way patients interact with medical professionals and digital health services. These AI-driven systems can interpret voice commands, process natural language, and provide intelligent responses to medical queries, significantly improving patient engagement, telemedicine efficiency, and healthcare accessibility. From voice-enabled virtual assistants to AI-driven transcription services for doctors, Speech and NLP technologies are playing a critical role in automating administrative tasks, improving diagnostics, and personalizing patient care.

In this chapter, we explore how Speech and NLP enhance AI healthcare assistants, their key applications, challenges, and the future of voice-driven AI in the medical field.

1. How Speech Recognition and NLP Work in Healthcare

Speech and NLP technologies allow AI healthcare assistants to:

✅ Recognize and process spoken language through advanced speech-to-text models.

✅ Analyze patient conversations to extract medical insights.

✅ Convert spoken words into structured medical records for doctors.

✅ Provide voice-enabled support for hands-free healthcare interactions.

◆ **Example**: AI-driven voice assistants like Amazon Alexa, Google Assistant, and Apple Siri are now being integrated into healthcare applications for voice-based patient interactions.

1.1 Key Components of AI Speech & NLP in Healthcare

✔ **Speech-to-Text (STT):** Converts spoken words into written text for documentation.

✔ **Natural Language Understanding (NLU):** Analyzes patient speech to extract medical intent.

✔ **Conversational AI**: Enables real-time, intelligent dialogue between patients and AI.

✔ **Text-to-Speech (TTS):** AI converts medical text responses into natural-sounding voice output.

◆ **Example**: Nuance's Dragon Medical One uses AI-driven voice transcription to automatically document patient records during doctor visits.

2. Applications of Speech and NLP in AI Healthcare Assistants

2.1 AI-Powered Virtual Health Assistants

✓ AI chatbots and voice assistants interact with patients using spoken language.

✓ They help in scheduling appointments, medication reminders, and answering medical FAQs.

✓ Patients can receive real-time symptom analysis and triage support through voice-based systems.

◆ **Example**: Babylon Health's AI assistant uses NLP to analyze patient speech and provide AI-driven health recommendations.

2.2 Voice-Enabled Doctor-Patient Consultations

✓ AI-driven speech-to-text transcription services assist doctors in real-time.

✓ Doctors can dictate patient history, prescriptions, and notes, reducing paperwork.

✓ Voice-powered telehealth platforms allow remote consultations without typing.

◆ **Example**: Microsoft's Nuance AI automates clinical documentation through voice recognition, saving doctors over 30% of their time.

2.3 AI in Elderly & Accessibility Healthcare

✓ AI-powered voice assistants help seniors manage medications and receive health updates.

✓ NLP technology assists visually impaired patients with voice-based health navigation.

✓ AI-driven voice recognition helps patients with speech impairments communicate effectively.

◆ **Example**: Google's Euphonia Project uses AI-powered NLP to understand and transcribe speech for patients with speech disorders like ALS or Parkinson's.

2.4 Speech Analytics for Mental Health Monitoring

☑ AI analyzes tone, pitch, and speech patterns to detect mental health conditions.

☑ NLP can detect signs of depression, anxiety, or cognitive decline based on speech.

☑ AI voice assistants provide mental health support via conversational therapy bots.

◆ **Example**: AI-powered Ellipsis Health analyzes voice tone and word choice to assess mental well-being and provide early depression detection.

3. Benefits of Speech and NLP in Healthcare AI

3.1 Increased Efficiency for Doctors & Hospitals

☑ AI-powered speech recognition automates medical documentation, reducing administrative burden.

☑ NLP-driven virtual assistants handle patient inquiries, freeing up healthcare staff.

☑ Doctors can dictate notes hands-free, improving consultation speed.

◆ **Example**: AI voice transcription reduces medical note-taking time by 45%.

3.2 Enhanced Patient Engagement & Accessibility

☑ Voice AI allows patients to interact naturally, improving healthcare accessibility.

☑ NLP-driven chatbots provide personalized health guidance in multiple languages.

☑ AI voice assistants improve healthcare access for disabled or elderly patients.

◆ **Example**: Voice-enabled AI chatbots improve patient response times by up to 80%.

3.3 Improved Accuracy in Medical Transcription & Diagnosis

☑ AI reduces human errors in medical documentation through real-time transcription.

☑ NLP-driven systems ensure structured, accurate, and HIPAA-compliant medical records.

☑ AI-powered voice analytics help detect early signs of neurological disorders.

◈ **Example**: AI speech analytics detect Alzheimer's symptoms by analyzing speech patterns years before diagnosis.

4. Challenges & Ethical Concerns in Speech and NLP for Healthcare

4.1 Data Privacy & Security Risks

✕ AI voice assistants collect and store sensitive patient conversations.

✕ Risks of hacking and unauthorized access to speech-based health data exist.

✕ AI voice models must comply with HIPAA, GDPR, and global privacy laws.

◈ **Solution**: Implement end-to-end encryption for AI-driven voice interactions.

4.2 Accuracy & Bias in AI Speech Recognition

✕ AI speech models may struggle with diverse accents and speech impairments.

✕ NLP-based healthcare AI can exhibit biases based on training data limitations.

✕ Incorrect AI interpretations can lead to misdiagnosis or patient misinformation.

◈ **Solution**: Use inclusive and diverse speech datasets for AI model training.

4.3 Ethical Concerns & AI's Role in Healthcare Decisions

✕ Patients may over-rely on AI healthcare assistants instead of consulting doctors.

✕ Ethical concerns arise when AI makes health decisions without human oversight.

✕ AI voice assistants should complement doctors, not replace them.

◈ **Solution**: Ensure human-AI collaboration where doctors validate AI-driven insights.

5. The Future of Speech and NLP in AI Healthcare Assistants

5.1 AI-Powered Voice Assistants for Real-Time Health Monitoring

✅ AI-driven wearables will integrate speech recognition for health tracking.

✅ Voice-based AI will detect breathing irregularities for respiratory diseases.

✅ AI voice analytics will monitor cognitive decline in neurodegenerative diseases.

◆ **Example**: AI-driven voice biomarkers will predict Parkinson's and Alzheimer's through speech analysis.

5.2 Multilingual & Emotionally Intelligent AI Assistants

✅ AI healthcare chatbots will support multiple languages for global healthcare accessibility.

✅ NLP-driven AI will recognize patient emotions and stress levels.

✅ AI voice assistants will provide empathetic, human-like health interactions.

◆ **Example**: AI chatbots with emotional recognition will improve mental health therapy.

5.3 AI-Powered Virtual Doctors & Smart Homes

✅ AI voice assistants will integrate with smart homes for real-time health monitoring.

✅ AI-driven virtual doctors will provide speech-based medical consultations.

✅ Voice-enabled healthcare AI will work alongside human physicians for better patient outcomes.

◆ **Example**: Future voice AI in smart homes will monitor elderly patients' health in real time.

AI-driven Speech Recognition and NLP are transforming healthcare by enabling voice-powered medical interactions, automating documentation, and improving patient engagement. Despite privacy, accuracy, and ethical challenges, the future of AI in healthcare lies in advanced voice analytics, multilingual support, and empathetic conversational AI—paving the way for a more accessible, intelligent, and human-centered healthcare system.

5.4 Overcoming Trust Issues in AI-Based Patient Care

As artificial intelligence (AI) becomes more prevalent in healthcare, building trust between patients, doctors, and AI-driven systems is a critical challenge. While AI offers enhanced diagnostics, predictive analytics, and virtual health assistants, skepticism persists due to data privacy concerns, potential biases, and fears of dehumanized care. Patients often worry about misdiagnosis, lack of transparency, and the ethical implications of AI making medical decisions. Healthcare professionals, too, may be hesitant to fully trust AI recommendations, fearing errors and liability issues.

To overcome these trust barriers, AI developers and healthcare providers must focus on transparency, explainability, data security, and ethical AI implementation. This chapter explores the root causes of AI mistrust in healthcare, strategies to enhance confidence in AI-driven patient care, and how the future of AI can foster a collaborative human-AI relationship for better medical outcomes.

1. Why Patients & Doctors Distrust AI in Healthcare

1.1 Lack of Transparency in AI Decision-Making

✘ Many AI models function as "black boxes," where the decision-making process is unclear.

✘ Patients and doctors find it hard to verify AI-generated diagnoses and recommendations.

✘ Without clear explanations, AI loses credibility as a reliable medical tool.

◆ **Solution**: Implement Explainable AI (XAI) to provide clear, interpretable insights into how AI reaches medical conclusions.

1.2 Fear of AI Replacing Human Doctors

✘ Some patients fear AI will replace human doctors, leading to less personalized care.

✘ AI chatbots or virtual assistants may lack the emotional intelligence needed for patient interactions.

✘ Healthcare professionals worry about job displacement and reduced human oversight.

✦ **Solution**: Position AI as a supportive tool, not a replacement—enhancing rather than eliminating human doctors.

1.3 Data Privacy & Security Concerns

✗ AI systems require access to vast amounts of patient data, raising security risks.

✗ Cyberattacks on AI-driven healthcare platforms could lead to sensitive data breaches.

✗ Patients are often unaware of how their data is collected, stored, and shared.

✦ **Solution**: Enforce strict encryption, HIPAA/GDPR compliance, and patient consent protocols for AI-driven healthcare systems.

1.4 Bias in AI Medical Models

✗ AI models trained on biased datasets may produce inaccurate diagnoses for certain demographics.

✗ If AI lacks diverse medical data, it can lead to healthcare disparities.

✗ Bias in AI can result in misdiagnosis for underrepresented groups.

✦ **Solution**: Train AI on inclusive, diverse datasets to ensure fair, bias-free healthcare outcomes.

2. Strategies to Build Trust in AI-Based Healthcare

2.1 Explainable & Transparent AI (XAI)

✓ AI should provide clear explanations for medical diagnoses and treatment recommendations.

✓ Patients and doctors should have access to AI-generated reports with reasoning behind decisions.

✓ Healthcare AI systems must incorporate interpretable models to gain user confidence.

◆ **Example**: IBM Watson Health provides transparent AI insights for doctors, ensuring medical decisions are backed by explainable data.

2.2 Human-AI Collaboration in Patient Care

✓ AI should function as a decision-support tool rather than a replacement for doctors.

✓ Healthcare professionals must validate AI recommendations before implementing treatments.

✓ Hybrid models (AI + human oversight) improve accuracy and boost patient confidence in AI.

◆ **Example**: AI-assisted radiology helps doctors detect anomalies in scans faster, but final diagnoses remain human-led.

2.3 Ethical AI Development & Regulatory Compliance

✓ AI in healthcare must adhere to strict ethical guidelines and global regulations (HIPAA, GDPR, FDA, etc.).

✓ Developers must ensure AI fairness, accountability, and bias mitigation.

✓ Patients should have control over how their data is used in AI-driven systems.

◆ **Example**: The FDA's AI regulatory framework ensures that AI-driven medical tools meet safety, efficacy, and ethical standards.

2.4 Strengthening AI Cybersecurity & Patient Data Protection

✓ AI-driven healthcare platforms should use blockchain encryption for secure patient data storage.

✓ Multi-layered authentication should protect medical AI systems from cyber threats.

✓ Patients should be given clear consent options regarding data sharing with AI.

◆ **Example**: AI-powered privacy-preserving technologies like federated learning allow medical AI to train on decentralized patient data without storing it in one central location.

3. The Future of AI Trust in Healthcare

3.1 Emotionally Intelligent AI for Patient Interaction

✓ AI assistants will become more empathetic and context-aware, improving patient trust.

✓ NLP advancements will enable emotion recognition in AI healthcare chatbots.

✓ AI will adapt its tone and responses based on patient emotions and concerns.

◆ **Example**: AI-powered mental health chatbots like Woebot use emotion-sensitive NLP to provide personalized therapy.

3.2 AI-Driven Second Opinions for Patients

✓ Patients will receive AI-generated second opinions on medical diagnoses.

✓ AI will compare millions of medical cases to suggest alternative diagnoses or treatments.

✓ AI-assisted second opinions will enhance trust and reduce misdiagnosis risks.

◆ **Example**: Google's DeepMind AI can detect eye diseases from retinal scans with 95% accuracy, aiding doctors in second-opinion assessments.

3.3 AI in Medical Ethics Committees & Policy Making

✓ AI systems will become part of healthcare ethics boards to provide unbiased risk assessments.

✓ AI-powered auditing tools will monitor compliance with medical ethics.

✓ AI governance models will enhance transparency and patient trust in AI-driven treatments.

◆ **Example**: AI-driven compliance tools help hospitals ensure adherence to global healthcare regulations.

Conclusion: The Path to Trusted AI in Healthcare

Trust in AI-based patient care must be built through transparency, ethical development, and patient-centered implementation. Addressing data privacy concerns, algorithmic biases, and AI explainability will be crucial in gaining both patient and doctor confidence in AI-driven healthcare systems. As emotionally intelligent AI, explainable models, and human-AI collaboration become more advanced, AI will no longer be seen as a mysterious black box but as a trusted partner in medical care. By taking a responsible and ethical approach, the future of AI in healthcare can be both transformative and trustworthy.

6. Operational AI: AI in Hospital Management & Administration

AI is not only transforming patient care but also optimizing hospital operations and administration. From predictive scheduling and AI-driven resource allocation to automated medical billing and patient flow optimization, AI enhances efficiency and reduces operational costs. Smart hospital management systems leverage machine learning to streamline administrative tasks, minimize wait times, and improve staff productivity, allowing healthcare professionals to focus more on patient care. This chapter explores how AI is revolutionizing hospital management, reducing inefficiencies, and addressing challenges in data security, interoperability, and regulatory compliance.

6.1 AI for Patient Flow Optimization & Predictive Scheduling

Efficient patient flow management is a critical factor in hospital operations, resource utilization, and patient satisfaction. Delays in admissions, diagnostics, treatments, and discharges can lead to overcrowding, increased costs, and negative patient experiences. AI-powered predictive scheduling and patient flow optimization leverage machine learning (ML), real-time analytics, and automation to improve hospital efficiency. These technologies analyze historical data, predict patient demand, and optimize resource allocation, ensuring that beds, staff, and medical equipment are utilized effectively.

This chapter explores how AI-driven predictive scheduling, automated triage, and real-time bed management are transforming hospital administration. We will also examine the challenges, ethical considerations, and future advancements in AI-powered patient flow optimization.

1. The Challenges of Traditional Patient Flow Management

Before AI integration, hospitals relied on manual scheduling, administrative estimations, and static resource planning. These conventional methods presented several challenges:

✗ Overcrowded waiting rooms due to unpredictable patient demand.

✗ Inefficient staff scheduling, leading to burnout or understaffing.

✗ Delayed patient discharges, causing bed shortages and ER congestion.

✘ Underutilization or overutilization of resources, affecting hospital efficiency.

✘ Emergency department (ED) bottlenecks, increasing patient wait times.

AI addresses these challenges by providing data-driven insights, automation, and real-time decision-making, ensuring seamless patient flow and optimal hospital operations.

2. How AI Enhances Patient Flow & Scheduling

2.1 Predictive Patient Volume Forecasting

✓ AI analyzes historical hospital data, seasonal trends, and external factors (flu outbreaks, weather, holidays).

✓ Machine learning models predict patient inflow, allowing hospitals to prepare in advance.

✓ AI-driven forecasts help adjust staffing levels and resource allocation accordingly.

◆ **Example**: AI algorithms predict ER visit spikes during flu season, enabling hospitals to allocate more staff and beds proactively.

2.2 AI-Driven Appointment & Scheduling Optimization

✓ AI reduces patient no-shows by predicting likelihood based on past behavior.

✓ Automated scheduling systems suggest optimal appointment slots, reducing idle time.

✓ AI-based scheduling adjusts real-time based on cancellations and emergency cases.

◆ **Example**: AI-powered appointment scheduling platforms reduce no-show rates by up to 30% by sending personalized reminders and rescheduling options.

2.3 Real-Time Bed Management & Patient Discharge Planning

✓ AI predicts when beds will become available based on patient recovery trends.

✓ Hospitals can pre-plan patient transfers and discharges, minimizing waiting times.

✓ AI integrates with electronic health records (EHRs) to provide real-time patient status updates.

◆ **Example**: AI-powered bed management systems help hospitals reduce ER wait times by up to 40% through proactive patient discharge planning.

2.4 AI-Powered Triage & Emergency Department Optimization

✓ AI-driven triage tools assess patient symptoms and prioritize critical cases.

✓ Predictive models suggest the best departments for patient transfers to avoid bottlenecks.

✓ NLP-based AI chatbots assist in pre-screening patients, directing them to the right care level.

◆ **Example**: AI-assisted triage in emergency rooms reduces non-urgent ER visits by up to 50%, ensuring that critical patients receive faster care.

3. Benefits of AI in Patient Flow Optimization

3.1 Reduced Wait Times & Faster Patient Processing

✓ AI optimizes appointment scheduling and triage, reducing unnecessary delays.

✓ Predictive analytics help allocate beds and staff more efficiently.

✓ AI-driven automation reduces administrative bottlenecks in hospitals.

◆ **Impact**: Hospitals using AI-driven scheduling experience 30-50% faster patient processing times.

3.2 Improved Hospital Resource Utilization

✓ AI ensures efficient use of hospital beds, equipment, and medical staff.

✓ Machine learning algorithms analyze peak demand times, helping hospitals plan efficient staffing shifts.

✓ AI helps reduce wasteful overbooking or underutilization of hospital assets.

⬥ **Impact**: AI-powered scheduling can reduce hospital operating costs by 10-20% through optimized resource allocation.

3.3 Enhanced Patient Experience & Satisfaction

✓ AI-powered triage systems provide faster diagnosis and referral.

✓ Patients spend less time waiting and receive quicker, more personalized care.

✓ AI-powered virtual assistants reduce patient frustration by offering real-time updates.

⬥ **Impact**: AI-driven scheduling leads to higher patient satisfaction scores due to shorter wait times and seamless hospital experiences.

3.4 Increased Staff Productivity & Reduced Burnout

✓ AI-powered predictive scheduling balances workload among medical staff.

✓ Hospitals can automate repetitive administrative tasks, allowing doctors to focus on care.

✓ AI-driven decision support systems assist healthcare professionals in managing high patient volumes efficiently.

⬥ **Impact**: AI-driven hospital management can reduce staff burnout rates by 25%, leading to better healthcare outcomes.

4. Challenges & Considerations in AI-Driven Patient Flow Optimization

4.1 Data Privacy & Security Risks

✗ AI systems require access to sensitive patient data, raising privacy concerns.

✗ Cybersecurity risks may expose patient records to data breaches or unauthorized access.

✗ AI-based scheduling tools must comply with HIPAA, GDPR, and healthcare data protection laws.

♦ **Solution**: Implement robust encryption, secure cloud storage, and strict patient consent policies for AI-driven scheduling systems.

4.2 Algorithm Bias & Fairness Issues

✗ AI predictions may unintentionally favor certain patient groups based on biased training data.

✗ Underrepresented communities might receive less accurate predictions from AI-driven triage systems.

♦ **Solution**: Ensure AI models are trained on diverse, unbiased datasets and continuously monitored for fair decision-making.

4.3 Integration with Legacy Hospital Systems

✗ Many hospitals still rely on outdated scheduling and EHR systems that may not integrate well with AI solutions.

✗ Implementing AI requires staff training and infrastructure upgrades, which can be costly.

♦ **Solution**: Hospitals should adopt scalable, cloud-based AI solutions that integrate with existing healthcare IT systems.

5. Future of AI in Patient Flow Optimization

5.1 AI-Powered Digital Twins for Hospital Management

✓ AI will create "digital twins" of hospitals, simulating patient flow scenarios.

✓ Hospitals can test different patient flow strategies in a virtual AI model before real-world implementation.

◆ **Example**: AI-driven hospital simulation platforms predict how different scheduling adjustments impact overall efficiency.

5.2 AI-Integrated Wearable Devices for Real-Time Patient Monitoring

✅ AI-powered wearables will track patient vitals, sending real-time alerts for early intervention.

✅ Data from wearables will integrate with AI-based predictive hospital scheduling systems.

◆ **Example**: Smartwatches detecting early signs of heart failure can alert hospitals to prepare resources in advance.

5.3 AI Chatbots for Real-Time Patient Scheduling & Updates

✅ AI-driven chatbots will interact with patients, adjusting appointment schedules dynamically.

✅ Patients will receive real-time status updates about their expected wait times and next steps.

◆ **Example**: AI chatbots in hospitals will enable real-time self-check-in, scheduling changes, and estimated wait-time notifications.

Conclusion: The AI-Powered Future of Hospital Operations

AI-driven patient flow optimization and predictive scheduling are revolutionizing hospital management, patient care, and resource utilization. By leveraging machine learning, real-time analytics, and automation, AI can reduce wait times, optimize hospital resources, enhance staff productivity, and improve patient experiences. While challenges such as data privacy, algorithmic bias, and IT integration exist, the future of AI in healthcare operations is promising, paving the way for smarter, more efficient hospitals that provide seamless, patient-centered care.

6.2 AI in Resource Allocation & Supply Chain Management

Efficient resource allocation and supply chain management are critical for healthcare institutions to provide high-quality patient care while minimizing costs. Hospitals and healthcare providers rely on vast networks of suppliers, medical equipment, pharmaceuticals, and human resources to operate effectively. However, traditional supply chain models and resource planning methods are often reactive, leading to inefficiencies such as overstocking, supply shortages, equipment underutilization, and operational bottlenecks.

AI-driven resource allocation and supply chain optimization use machine learning (ML), predictive analytics, automation, and real-time monitoring to ensure that hospitals and healthcare organizations have the right resources, at the right time, in the right place. This chapter explores how AI is transforming healthcare logistics, from inventory management and predictive demand forecasting to automated procurement and supply chain risk mitigation.

1. Challenges in Traditional Healthcare Resource Allocation

The healthcare industry has long struggled with supply chain inefficiencies due to manual inventory tracking, reactive ordering systems, and fragmented logistics networks. Some key challenges include:

1.1 Inventory Mismanagement

✗ Overstocking of medical supplies increases storage costs and wastage (especially for perishable items like vaccines).

✗ Shortages of critical drugs and medical equipment lead to delayed patient care and operational disruptions.

✗ Manual tracking methods cause inaccuracies in inventory levels, resulting in inefficient supply chain decisions.

◆ **Solution**: AI-driven inventory management ensures optimal stock levels, minimizes waste, and automates restocking.

1.2 Unpredictable Demand Fluctuations

✖ Healthcare demand varies due to seasonal illnesses, pandemics, and unpredictable patient inflows.

✖ Poor demand forecasting leads to supply shortages or excessive procurement of unnecessary items.

◆ **Solution**: Predictive AI models analyze historical patient trends, disease outbreaks, and external factors to optimize demand forecasting.

1.3 Inefficient Procurement & Supplier Management

✖ Hospitals often struggle with supply chain bottlenecks, causing delays in medical deliveries.

✖ Traditional procurement processes rely on manual contract negotiations, supplier coordination, and invoice processing.

◆ **Solution**: AI-driven procurement platforms automate supplier selection, contract management, and order processing for faster, cost-effective purchasing.

2. AI Applications in Resource Allocation & Supply Chain Optimization

2.1 AI-Powered Inventory Management

✓ AI continuously monitors stock levels and predicts depletion rates in real time.

✓ Automated ordering systems replenish supplies proactively, avoiding stockouts and reducing excess inventory.

✓ Computer vision technology tracks medical supply usage via RFID tags, IoT sensors, and smart shelves.

◆ **Example**: AI-powered inventory platforms like IBM Watson Supply Chain predict stock needs and automate hospital restocking processes, reducing wastage and storage costs.

2.2 Predictive Analytics for Demand Forecasting

✓ Machine learning models analyze historical hospital data, seasonal trends, and patient admissions to predict supply needs.

✓ AI considers external factors such as flu outbreaks, regional disease trends, and emergency situations for proactive planning.

✓ AI-driven demand forecasting helps hospitals optimize budgets and prevent last-minute shortages.

♦ **Example**: AI-driven demand forecasting helped hospitals prepare for COVID-19 surges, ensuring adequate ventilator and PPE supplies ahead of peak cases.

2.3 AI-Driven Supplier & Procurement Optimization

✓ AI-based procurement platforms analyze supplier performance, pricing trends, and delivery reliability.

✓ NLP-powered AI chatbots automate contract negotiations and order placements with suppliers.

✓ AI-driven procurement platforms compare supplier bids and select the most cost-effective, high-quality option.

♦ **Example**: AI-powered procurement systems like Coupa AI Supply Chain enable automated supplier bidding, cost forecasting, and contract management.

2.4 Smart Routing & Logistics Optimization

✓ AI-powered logistics platforms use real-time GPS tracking and route optimization for medical deliveries.

✓ Machine learning predicts potential delays (weather disruptions, supplier backlogs) and suggests alternate solutions.

✓ AI helps hospitals consolidate shipments to minimize transportation costs and delivery times.

◆ **Example**: AI-driven route optimization reduced emergency medical supply delivery times by 30% in disaster-hit areas.

3. Benefits of AI in Healthcare Supply Chain Management

3.1 Cost Reduction & Waste Minimization

✓ AI reduces excess inventory costs by maintaining optimal stock levels.

✓ Predictive analytics prevent overordering of perishable medical supplies, reducing waste and financial losses.

✓ AI-driven automation lowers procurement costs and administrative overhead.

◆ **Impact**: Hospitals using AI-based inventory management reduce operational costs by 15-25%.

3.2 Improved Supply Chain Resilience

✓ AI identifies supply chain risks early, helping hospitals find alternative suppliers when needed.

✓ Machine learning detects market disruptions and suggests contingency plans.

✓ AI enables faster decision-making during medical crises, ensuring continuity of care.

◆ **Impact**: AI-based supply chain systems reduce disruptions by 40%, ensuring uninterrupted access to essential medical supplies.

3.3 Enhanced Patient Care & Faster Response Times

✓ AI ensures critical medical supplies are available exactly when needed, reducing patient wait times.

✓ Automated scheduling ensures efficient allocation of medical equipment such as MRI machines and ventilators.

✓ AI-powered resource planning prevents hospital overcrowding and ER delays.

◆ **Impact**: AI-based hospital resource planning improves patient care efficiency by 30%.

4. Challenges in AI-Driven Supply Chain Management

4.1 Data Integration & Compatibility Issues

✗ Many hospitals still use legacy systems that don't integrate well with AI-driven platforms.

✗ Data silos prevent AI from accessing real-time supply chain insights across multiple locations.

◆ **Solution**: Implement cloud-based AI supply chain platforms that integrate with existing hospital IT infrastructure.

4.2 Ethical & Compliance Concerns

✗ AI-driven procurement must ensure fair supplier selection without biases.

✗ Automated decision-making in procurement must comply with hospital ethics policies and regulatory guidelines.

◆ **Solution**: Hospitals must ensure human oversight in AI-driven procurement and decision-making processes.

4.3 Cybersecurity Risks in AI Supply Chain Systems

✗ AI-driven procurement platforms may be vulnerable to cyberattacks and data breaches.

✗ Hacking of medical supply chain networks can disrupt critical hospital operations.

◆ **Solution**: Implement AI-powered cybersecurity measures like blockchain for secure procurement transactions.

5. The Future of AI in Healthcare Resource Management

5.1 AI-Powered Blockchain for Transparent Medical Supply Chains

✅ Blockchain combined with AI ensures end-to-end visibility in healthcare logistics.

✅ Hospitals can track medical shipments securely and verify authenticity of pharmaceuticals.

♦ **Example**: AI-blockchain integration prevents counterfeit drug supply chains by verifying medicine authenticity.

5.2 AI Digital Twins for Hospital Resource Planning

✅ AI-powered digital twins simulate hospital supply chain operations in a virtual environment.

✅ Hospitals can test different inventory strategies in simulations before implementing them in real-time.

♦ **Example**: AI-powered hospital digital twins predict how supply chain adjustments impact hospital efficiency.

Conclusion: AI's Role in Smarter, More Efficient Healthcare Logistics

AI-driven resource allocation and supply chain management are revolutionizing hospital logistics, procurement, and inventory management. By leveraging predictive analytics, automation, and real-time monitoring, AI ensures optimal resource distribution, prevents shortages, and enhances cost efficiency. While challenges such as data integration, cybersecurity, and ethical AI procurement remain, the future of AI in healthcare supply chains is poised to enhance efficiency, resilience, and patient care quality.

6.3 AI-Powered Medical Billing & Insurance Processing

Medical billing and insurance processing are among the most complex and time-consuming aspects of the healthcare industry. Traditional billing systems often involve manual data entry, complex coding procedures, and lengthy insurance claim approvals, leading to errors, delays, and financial losses for both healthcare providers and patients. Artificial Intelligence (AI) is transforming medical billing and insurance workflows by automating claims processing, fraud detection, and revenue cycle management, significantly improving efficiency and accuracy.

This chapter explores how AI-driven billing systems are streamlining healthcare payments, reducing administrative burdens, minimizing fraud, and enhancing patient experience.

1. Challenges in Traditional Medical Billing & Insurance Processing

Medical billing involves multiple stakeholders—hospitals, insurance companies, government agencies, and patients. The complexity of insurance policies, claim approvals, and coding errors creates bottlenecks that delay payments and increase healthcare costs.

1.1 High Error Rates & Claim Denials

✘ Manual coding errors lead to insurance claim denials and delayed reimbursements.

✘ Complex insurance policies make it difficult for patients to understand out-of-pocket costs.

✘ Billing discrepancies increase administrative overhead for hospitals and clinics.

◆ **Solution**: AI-driven coding systems ensure accurate billing and error-free claim submissions.

1.2 Slow & Inefficient Claim Approvals

✘ Traditional insurance claim processing takes weeks or months due to paper-based reviews.

✘ Insurance companies manually verify claims, leading to delays and inefficiencies.

◆ **Solution**: AI automates insurance verification and claim approvals, reducing processing time from weeks to days.

1.3 Healthcare Fraud & Revenue Leakage

✗ Fraudulent claims, upcoding, and duplicate billing cost healthcare systems billions of dollars annually.

✗ Medical billing fraud increases insurance premiums and financial losses for patients.

◆ **Solution**: AI detects anomalies in billing patterns, identifying potential fraud in real time.

2. How AI is Transforming Medical Billing & Insurance Processing

2.1 AI-Powered Medical Coding & Automated Billing

✓ AI automates ICD-10, CPT, and HCPCS medical coding, reducing errors in claim submissions.

✓ Natural Language Processing (NLP) extracts diagnoses, procedures, and treatment details from medical records.

✓ AI ensures real-time claim validation, reducing denials and rework costs.

◆ **Example**: AI-driven medical coding platforms like 3M M*Modal and nThrive improve billing accuracy, reducing claim rejection rates by 30%.

2.2 AI-Based Insurance Verification & Claims Processing

✓ AI verifies patient insurance coverage, copays, and deductibles instantly.

✓ Machine learning models analyze past claims to predict approval probabilities.

✓ AI chatbots assist patients in understanding their insurance benefits.

◆ **Example**: Olive AI automates insurance eligibility verification, reducing verification time by 90%.

2.3 AI in Fraud Detection & Revenue Protection

✓ AI detects billing anomalies, duplicate charges, and fraudulent claims.

✓ Machine learning models flag suspicious billing patterns in real time.

✓ AI prevents upcoding (billing for more expensive procedures) and phantom billing (billing for services never provided).

◆ **Example**: AI-driven fraud detection in insurance processing has reduced healthcare fraud losses by 20%.

2.4 AI-Powered Revenue Cycle Management (RCM)

✓ AI optimizes hospital revenue cycles by automating payment tracking and collections.

✓ Predictive analytics forecast cash flow, helping hospitals manage finances efficiently.

✓ AI identifies unpaid claims and accelerates follow-ups to improve revenue collection.

◆ **Example**: AI-powered RCM platforms reduce claim denial rates, increasing hospital revenue by 15-25%.

3. Benefits of AI in Medical Billing & Insurance Processing

3.1 Faster Claims Processing & Reduced Administrative Burden

✓ AI eliminates manual claim processing, reducing claim turnaround times from weeks to days.

✓ Hospitals can process higher claim volumes with fewer administrative staff, cutting costs.

✓ Automated claim approvals improve patient access to timely medical care.

◆ **Impact**: AI-driven claim processing increases efficiency by 40-60%, reducing administrative workloads.

3.2 Enhanced Billing Accuracy & Fewer Claim Denials

✓ AI reduces human errors in medical coding, insurance verification, and billing.

✓ Predictive analytics flag incorrect codes before claim submission, minimizing denials.

✓ AI automatically updates billing codes based on insurance policy changes, ensuring compliance.

✦ **Impact**: Hospitals using AI-powered billing experience a 30-50% reduction in claim rejections.

3.3 Improved Fraud Detection & Revenue Protection

✓ AI detects fraudulent claims, duplicate charges, and unnecessary procedures.
✓ AI-driven anomaly detection prevents revenue loss by flagging suspicious claims in real time.
✓ Insurance companies benefit from reduced fraud-related losses, lowering premium costs for patients.

✦ **Impact**: AI-driven fraud detection reduces healthcare fraud losses by billions of dollars annually.

3.4 Better Patient Experience & Transparency

✓ AI chatbots assist patients in understanding medical bills and insurance policies.
✓ Patients receive real-time cost estimates and breakdowns of out-of-pocket expenses.
✓ AI-powered self-service portals allow faster payments, claim tracking, and financial assistance.

✦ **Impact**: AI-based billing systems improve patient satisfaction by 35% due to greater billing transparency.

4. Challenges & Ethical Considerations in AI-Based Medical Billing

4.1 Data Privacy & Security Risks

✗ AI-driven billing systems handle sensitive financial and medical data, increasing cybersecurity risks.

✗ Data breaches could expose patient insurance records, leading to identity theft.

◆ **Solution**: AI billing platforms must follow HIPAA, GDPR, and healthcare cybersecurity standards.

4.2 Bias & Fairness in AI Billing Systems

✗ AI models trained on biased data may discriminate against certain patients in billing approvals.

✗ Automated billing algorithms could unintentionally favor insurance companies over patients.

◆ **Solution**: AI systems should be continuously audited for fairness and bias reduction.

4.3 Integration with Legacy Systems

✗ Many hospitals still use outdated electronic health record (EHR) and billing systems, making AI adoption difficult.

✗ Integrating AI with existing hospital IT systems requires significant investment and staff training.

◆ **Solution**: Cloud-based AI billing platforms offer scalable integration options for hospitals and insurance companies.

5. The Future of AI in Medical Billing & Insurance Processing

5.1 AI & Blockchain for Secure Billing Transactions

✓ AI + blockchain ensures transparent, tamper-proof billing records.
✓ Hospitals, insurers, and patients can track billing histories securely.

◆ **Example**: AI-blockchain integration prevents fraudulent billing by verifying the authenticity of each transaction.

5.2 AI-Powered Predictive Billing for Personalized Payment Plans

✅ AI analyzes patient financial history and insurance coverage to suggest personalized payment plans.

✅ Predictive analytics help hospitals estimate patient payment capabilities and reduce bad debt.

◆ **Example**: AI-powered billing assistants help hospitals optimize revenue collection without burdening patients.

5.3 AI Chatbots for Real-Time Billing Assistance

✅ AI-powered chatbots answer billing-related patient inquiries instantly.

✅ Patients can check claim statuses, resolve disputes, and make payments through AI assistants.

◆ **Example**: AI-driven chatbots reduce patient billing inquiries by 50%, improving customer service.

Conclusion: AI's Role in Smarter, Faster, and More Transparent Healthcare Billing

AI-driven medical billing and insurance processing are revolutionizing healthcare financial workflows, making billing faster, more accurate, and transparent. By leveraging machine learning, automation, and predictive analytics, AI ensures error-free claim submissions, faster insurance approvals, and fraud prevention. While challenges like data privacy, bias, and system integration exist, the future of AI-powered billing promises greater efficiency, cost savings, and improved patient experiences.

6.4 Case Studies: AI in Real-World Hospital Systems

AI is revolutionizing hospital operations worldwide, improving efficiency, reducing costs, and enhancing patient care. Leading healthcare institutions have adopted AI-powered medical billing, resource allocation, and insurance processing solutions to optimize their workflows. This chapter explores real-world case studies showcasing how hospitals have successfully implemented AI-driven technologies to address challenges in administration, financial management, and patient care delivery.

Case Study 1: Mayo Clinic – AI in Predictive Resource Allocation

Challenge

Mayo Clinic, one of the world's leading healthcare institutions, struggled with patient flow inefficiencies and resource allocation issues. With thousands of daily patient visits, managing hospital beds, staff scheduling, and medical equipment distribution was a major challenge. Overcrowding in emergency rooms and inefficient supply chain management often resulted in long patient wait times and higher operational costs.

AI Solution

Mayo Clinic implemented an AI-powered predictive analytics system to optimize resource allocation and hospital workflow management. Key AI applications included:

✔ **Predictive Scheduling**: AI analyzed historical patient data to forecast hospital bed occupancy rates and adjust staffing needs accordingly.
✔ **AI-Driven Supply Chain Management**: Machine learning models predicted demand for medical supplies, ensuring optimal stock levels without overordering.
✔ **Patient Flow Optimization**: AI algorithms analyzed patient admission trends and recommended real-time adjustments to reduce ER congestion.

Results

✔ Reduced ER wait times by 30% through optimized patient flow management.

✔ Decreased hospital supply wastage by 25%, lowering overall operational costs.

✔ Improved staff scheduling efficiency, reducing physician burnout and ensuring better patient care.

Case Study 2: Mount Sinai Health System – AI in Medical Billing & Revenue Cycle Management

Challenge

Mount Sinai Health System, a leading hospital network in New York, faced challenges in medical billing inefficiencies, high claim rejection rates, and revenue cycle bottlenecks. Billing errors and delayed insurance claim approvals resulted in millions of dollars in lost revenue annually.

AI Solution

Mount Sinai adopted an AI-powered medical billing platform with the following features:

✅ **Automated Medical Coding**: AI extracted ICD-10 and CPT codes from patient records with 98% accuracy, reducing manual errors.

✅ **AI-Powered Insurance Verification**: The system instantly verified insurance eligibility and predicted claim approval likelihood.

✅ **Fraud Detection & Revenue Optimization**: AI flagged suspicious billing patterns, reducing fraudulent claims and revenue leakage.

Results

✓ Reduced medical coding errors by 45%, minimizing claim rejections.

✓ Increased revenue collection by 20%, optimizing cash flow.

✓ Decreased billing processing time from 2 weeks to 48 hours, expediting claim approvals.

Case Study 3: Cleveland Clinic – AI in AI-Powered Virtual Assistants & Patient Billing Transparency

Challenge

Cleveland Clinic faced difficulties in managing patient billing inquiries and improving transparency in healthcare costs. Many patients struggled to understand their medical bills, leading to delayed payments and frequent disputes. The hospital needed a way to provide real-time billing support and improve patient experience.

AI Solution

Cleveland Clinic deployed an AI-driven virtual assistant to handle patient billing inquiries and insurance-related questions. Key AI functionalities included:

✓ **AI Chatbot for Billing Assistance**: A 24/7 virtual assistant helped patients understand medical bills, insurance claims, and payment options.

✓ **Real-Time Cost Estimation**: AI predicted out-of-pocket costs based on insurance coverage, allowing patients to plan payments.

✓ **Automated Dispute Resolution**: NLP-based AI analyzed patient disputes and provided automated resolutions for common billing issues.

Results

✓ Patient satisfaction scores increased by 40%, thanks to faster billing assistance.

✓ Reduced billing disputes by 35%, improving hospital-patient trust.

✓ Improved bill payment collection rates, reducing outstanding patient debts.

Case Study 4: Apollo Hospitals – AI in Insurance Fraud Detection & Claims Processing

Challenge

Apollo Hospitals, one of India's largest healthcare providers, faced rising cases of fraudulent insurance claims and slow claim approvals. Manual fraud detection methods were inefficient, causing delays in legitimate insurance claims and increased financial risks for both patients and insurance companies.

AI Solution

Apollo Hospitals integrated an AI-based fraud detection system into their insurance processing workflow. The AI solution included:

✓ **Anomaly Detection Algorithms**: AI analyzed historical billing data to detect fraudulent claims and overbilling patterns.

✓ **Real-Time Claim Validation**: AI flagged high-risk claims for human review, reducing fraudulent reimbursements.

✓ **Automated Claim Processing**: AI expedited legitimate insurance claims, cutting down approval time.

Results

✓ Fraudulent claims reduced by 50%, saving millions in financial losses.

✓ Insurance approval times improved by 60%, benefiting both hospitals and patients.

✓ Increased trust between hospitals, insurers, and patients, reducing billing disputes.

Case Study 5: Kaiser Permanente – AI in Predictive Healthcare Billing & Revenue Optimization

Challenge

Kaiser Permanente, one of the largest healthcare providers in the U.S., needed a solution to predict and manage patient billing issues before they arose. Many patients faced unexpected medical bills, leading to delayed payments and financial stress.

AI Solution

Kaiser Permanente implemented an AI-powered predictive billing system with the following capabilities:

✓ **Personalized Payment Plans**: AI analyzed patient financial history and insurance coverage to recommend customized payment options.
✓ **Predictive Billing Alerts**: Patients received real-time notifications about expected costs before treatments.
✓ **Automated Payment Assistance**: AI chatbots assisted patients in setting up payment plans and applying for financial aid.

Results

✓ 70% of patients enrolled in AI-recommended payment plans, reducing unpaid bills.

✓ Billing transparency improved by 50%, increasing patient satisfaction.

✓ Reduced hospital revenue loss from unpaid medical bills, optimizing financial stability.

Conclusion: AI is the Future of Hospital Operations

These real-world case studies demonstrate how AI-powered solutions are transforming hospital systems by improving resource allocation, billing efficiency, fraud detection, and patient financial experiences. From reducing medical coding errors to predicting patient billing issues, AI is reshaping hospital administration and financial management.

As AI continues to evolve, its role in automating and optimizing hospital workflows will expand, leading to smarter, faster, and more efficient healthcare systems.

7. Algorithmic Trading and AI in Financial Markets

AI is revolutionizing financial markets through algorithmic trading, predictive analytics, and real-time decision-making. With machine learning models analyzing vast amounts of market data, AI-powered trading systems can identify patterns, predict price movements, and execute trades within milliseconds, far beyond human capabilities. Hedge funds, investment banks, and retail traders leverage AI to optimize portfolios, manage risk, and gain a competitive edge. This chapter explores the role of AI in algorithmic trading, the advantages of automation in financial markets, and the challenges of market volatility, regulatory compliance, and ethical AI trading practices.

7.1 How AI is Disrupting Stock Market Predictions

The stock market has always been a complex, high-stakes environment where investors seek to gain an edge through data analysis, financial modeling, and market intuition. Traditional trading strategies rely on fundamental and technical analysis, requiring human expertise to interpret economic indicators, corporate earnings, and historical price trends. However, with the rise of Artificial Intelligence (AI), stock market predictions have undergone a significant transformation.

AI is disrupting financial markets by leveraging machine learning, deep learning, and natural language processing (NLP) to analyze vast amounts of data, detect market patterns, and predict price movements with greater accuracy. From high-frequency trading (HFT) to sentiment analysis and portfolio optimization, AI-driven models are reshaping investment strategies, reducing human biases, and providing traders with real-time insights.

In this chapter, we explore how AI is revolutionizing stock market predictions, its impact on trading strategies, and the challenges associated with AI-driven market forecasting.

1. The Role of AI in Stock Market Prediction

Traditional stock market prediction methods relied on technical analysis (chart patterns, indicators) and fundamental analysis (economic factors, earnings reports). While these approaches remain relevant, AI-driven systems offer faster, more accurate, and data-driven insights by analyzing a broader range of market variables in real time.

1.1 Machine Learning & Predictive Analytics

✓ **Supervised Learning**: AI models trained on historical stock price data identify patterns in market fluctuations.

✓ **Unsupervised Learning**: Clustering techniques help discover hidden market correlations and anomalies.

✓ **Reinforcement Learning**: AI-powered agents optimize trading strategies by continuously learning from market rewards and penalties.

◆ **Example**: Hedge funds use random forest models and neural networks to predict stock price movements based on past data trends.

1.2 Sentiment Analysis & NLP in Market Forecasting

✓ AI analyzes news articles, earnings reports, and social media sentiment to predict market movements.

✓ NLP-driven models detect bullish or bearish sentiment from financial statements and investor opinions.

✓ AI bots scan Reddit (WallStreetBets), Twitter, and financial news to identify market-moving events.

◆ **Example**: AI-powered sentiment analysis predicted Tesla's stock surge following Elon Musk's tweets.

1.3 High-Frequency Trading (HFT) & Algorithmic Trading

✓ AI algorithms execute trades within microseconds, capitalizing on small price inefficiencies.

✓ Machine learning detects market patterns invisible to human traders, ensuring optimal entry and exit points.

✓ AI-driven trading bots continuously adjust positions based on real-time market data.

◆ **Example**: Citadel Securities and Renaissance Technologies use AI-powered HFT algorithms to trade billions of dollars daily.

2. Key AI Techniques in Stock Market Predictions

2.1 Deep Learning & Neural Networks

✓ AI models like Long Short-Term Memory (LSTM) networks process historical stock prices to predict future trends.

✓ Convolutional Neural Networks (CNNs) analyze financial charts and time-series data to detect trading signals.

◆ **Example**: AI-driven hedge funds leverage deep learning models to generate alpha (excess returns above the market benchmark).

2.2 Reinforcement Learning for Trading Strategies

✓ AI agents use trial-and-error techniques to develop optimal trading strategies.

✓ Reinforcement learning helps hedge funds and trading firms optimize risk-adjusted returns.

◆ **Example**: Deep Q Networks (DQN) and Proximal Policy Optimization (PPO) are used for portfolio management and stock allocation.

2.3 AI in Portfolio Optimization

✓ AI algorithms allocate assets based on historical returns, risk tolerance, and market conditions.

✓ Portfolio managers use AI to diversify holdings, minimize volatility, and maximize returns.

◆ **Example**: Robo-advisors like Wealthfront and Betterment use AI-driven Modern Portfolio Theory (MPT) for investment optimization.

3. The Benefits of AI in Stock Market Predictions

✓ **Higher Accuracy**: AI-driven forecasts outperform traditional models by detecting hidden market patterns.

✓ **Speed & Efficiency**: AI executes trades in milliseconds, outperforming human traders.

✓ **Risk Management**: AI models identify market risks and anomalies, preventing financial losses.

✓ **Data-Driven Decision-Making**: AI removes human biases, relying purely on statistical models and real-time data.

◆ **Example**: AI-based trading systems generated 20% higher annualized returns compared to traditional trading methods.

4. Challenges & Risks of AI in Stock Market Predictions

4.1 Market Volatility & AI Biases

✗ AI models trained on historical data may fail to predict black swan events (e.g., COVID-19 crash, 2008 financial crisis).

✗ Algorithmic biases may lead to overfitting, where AI relies too heavily on past trends.

◆ **Solution**: AI models should incorporate adaptive learning techniques to adjust to real-world market shocks.

4.2 AI & Flash Crashes

✗ High-frequency trading algorithms can trigger market-wide flash crashes, leading to sudden stock price drops.

✗ The 2010 Flash Crash saw AI-driven trades erase $1 trillion in market value within minutes.

◆ **Solution**: Regulators implement circuit breakers to prevent AI-induced extreme volatility.

4.3 Ethical & Regulatory Concerns

✗ AI-driven insider trading risks market manipulation and unethical trading practices.

✗ AI trading firms must comply with SEC, FINRA, and MiFID II regulations to ensure market transparency.

◆ **Solution**: Governments are introducing AI governance frameworks to prevent algorithmic abuses.

5. Future Trends in AI-Powered Stock Market Predictions

5.1 Quantum AI in Stock Trading

✓ Quantum computing will revolutionize stock market simulations, predicting market trends with near-perfect accuracy.

✓ AI + quantum models will process millions of stock variables simultaneously, outperforming traditional trading models.

◆ **Example**: Google and IBM are developing quantum trading algorithms for institutional investors.

5.2 AI-Driven Decentralized Finance (DeFi)

✓ AI will power blockchain-based financial trading, eliminating intermediaries in stock markets.

✓ AI-powered smart contracts will enable autonomous stock trades without human intervention.

◆ **Example**: AI is being integrated into DeFi protocols like Uniswap and Aave to optimize trading.

5.3 Explainable AI (XAI) in Trading Decisions

✓ Investors demand transparent AI-driven investment strategies to build trust in algorithmic trading.

✓ Explainable AI (XAI) will provide clear reasoning for stock picks, trade execution, and risk assessments.

◆ **Example**: AI-powered hedge funds are adopting XAI frameworks to comply with regulatory transparency requirements.

Conclusion: The AI Revolution in Stock Trading

AI is disrupting stock market predictions, making trading faster, more efficient, and data-driven. By leveraging machine learning, deep learning, and NLP, AI-powered trading systems can analyze vast amounts of financial data, predict market trends, and execute trades with unmatched precision.

However, challenges such as market volatility, regulatory concerns, and AI biases must be addressed to ensure fair and ethical trading practices. As quantum computing, decentralized finance, and explainable AI continue to evolve, the future of stock market prediction will be smarter, more transparent, and driven by advanced AI technologies.

◆ The era of human-dominated investing is fading, and AI-powered trading is shaping the future of global financial markets. 🚀

7.2 Machine Learning in High-Frequency Trading

High-Frequency Trading (HFT) is a fast-paced, algorithm-driven trading strategy that relies on executing a large number of trades in milliseconds. HFT firms leverage machine learning (ML) algorithms to identify profitable trading opportunities, predict market movements, and execute orders at ultra-high speeds. Unlike traditional trading, where humans analyze charts and make decisions, HFT uses AI-driven models that react faster than any human trader—taking advantage of microsecond price fluctuations.

With the rise of machine learning, deep learning, and reinforcement learning, HFT has become even more sophisticated. Today, ML-powered HFT systems can detect arbitrage opportunities, optimize trade execution, and mitigate risks in real time. This chapter explores how machine learning is transforming HFT, the different ML techniques used, and the challenges associated with AI-driven trading.

1. Understanding High-Frequency Trading (HFT) and its Evolution

HFT has grown significantly over the past two decades, with major trading firms like Citadel Securities, Renaissance Technologies, and Virtu Financial using AI-driven strategies to dominate the market. HFT firms use co-location services (placing servers near stock exchange data centers) and low-latency networks to execute trades faster than competitors.

1.1 How HFT Works

✅ **Ultra-Fast Trade Execution**: HFT firms use AI models to analyze market data in milliseconds and place trades instantly.

✅ **Market-Making Strategies**: AI identifies liquidity gaps and executes buy/sell orders to profit from bid-ask spreads.

✅ **Arbitrage Trading**: ML-powered systems exploit price differences between exchanges before humans can react.

◆ **Example**: If a stock is priced at $100 on the NYSE and $100.05 on the NASDAQ, an AI algorithm can instantly buy on the NYSE and sell on the NASDAQ to pocket the profit.

1.2 Evolution of AI in HFT

◆ **Early 2000s** – Simple rule-based trading algorithms.

◆ **2010s** – Introduction of machine learning models for adaptive trading.

◆ **Today** – Deep learning, reinforcement learning, and NLP drive AI-powered HFT systems.

2. Machine Learning Techniques in High-Frequency Trading

HFT firms deploy multiple ML models to analyze market patterns, predict price movements, and execute trades at lightning speed.

2.1 Supervised Learning in HFT

✔ **Regression Models**: Predict stock price movements based on historical data.

✔ **Classification Models**: Categorize stocks into buy/sell signals using past trends.

✔ **Gradient Boosting (XGBoost, LightGBM):** Identify profitable trade setups in real time.

◆ **Example**: AI models trained on past stock price movements predict the probability of price changes in the next 10 milliseconds.

2.2 Deep Learning & Neural Networks for HFT

✓ **Long Short-Term Memory (LSTM) Networks**: Process time-series data to forecast stock price fluctuations.

✓ **Convolutional Neural Networks (CNNs):** Detect trading patterns from financial charts.

✓ **Autoencoders**: Reduce noise from raw market data to enhance prediction accuracy.

◆ **Example**: Deep learning models can detect hidden market signals that traditional statistical models miss.

2.3 Reinforcement Learning for HFT Strategies

✓ AI trading agents learn through trial and error to maximize profitability.

✓ Deep Q Networks (DQN) and Proximal Policy Optimization (PPO) help AI adapt to real-time market conditions.

✓ AI continuously adjusts its buy/sell decisions based on market feedback.

◆ **Example**: Reinforcement learning agents optimize trade execution to minimize slippage and maximize returns.

2.4 Natural Language Processing (NLP) for Market Sentiment Analysis

✓ AI processes news articles, social media posts, and earnings reports to detect market sentiment.

✓ NLP models classify text as bullish, bearish, or neutral, influencing HFT trading strategies.

◆ **Example**: If Elon Musk tweets about Tesla, NLP-based AI detects positive sentiment and instantly buys Tesla stock.

3. Benefits of Machine Learning in High-Frequency Trading

✅ **Faster Decision-Making** – AI analyzes vast amounts of data and executes trades in milliseconds.

✅ **Higher Accuracy** – ML models detect market inefficiencies that human traders miss.

✅ **Reduced Trading Costs** – AI optimizes order execution to minimize transaction fees and slippage.

✅ **Adaptive Strategies** – ML-powered HFT continuously learns and adjusts to changing market conditions.

◆ **Example**: AI-driven HFT firms consistently outperform human traders in speed, precision, and profit generation.

4. Challenges & Risks of AI in High-Frequency Trading

Despite its advantages, AI-powered HFT comes with risks and challenges that can destabilize financial markets.

4.1 Market Volatility & Flash Crashes

✖ AI-driven HFT has been responsible for flash crashes, where stocks plummet due to automated trading errors.

✖ In 2010, the Flash Crash wiped out $1 trillion in market value in minutes, caused by HFT algorithms overreacting to market signals.

◆ **Solution**: Regulators use circuit breakers to halt AI-induced crashes and prevent excessive volatility.

4.2 AI Model Bias & Overfitting

✖ AI models trained on historical data may fail to predict black swan events (e.g., COVID-19 market crash).

✖ Overfitting to past trends can lead to AI misinterpreting new market conditions.

◆ **Solution**: AI models should incorporate adaptive learning techniques and real-world stress testing.

4.3 Regulatory Scrutiny & Ethical Concerns

✘ Governments are tightening HFT regulations due to concerns over market manipulation.

✘ AI-driven insider trading and market exploitation raise ethical and legal issues.

◆ **Solution**: Compliance with SEC, FINRA, and MiFID II regulations ensures fair AI-driven trading practices.

5. The Future of AI in High-Frequency Trading

5.1 Quantum Computing for HFT

✓ Quantum AI will process millions of market signals in nanoseconds, outperforming classical AI models.

✓ Quantum trading algorithms will identify arbitrage opportunities faster than traditional HFT models.

◆ **Example**: Goldman Sachs and IBM are exploring quantum-powered HFT strategies.

5.2 AI-Powered Decentralized Finance (DeFi) Trading

✓ AI will optimize crypto HFT strategies, executing trades on decentralized exchanges (DEXs).

✓ Machine learning will enhance liquidity pooling and automated market-making (AMM) strategies.

◆ **Example**: AI is being integrated into Uniswap, Aave, and other DeFi protocols for algorithmic trading.

5.3 Explainable AI (XAI) in Algorithmic Trading

✓ Regulators and investors demand transparent AI trading decisions.

✓ Explainable AI (XAI) will ensure traders understand why AI executes certain trades.

♦ **Example**: Hedge funds are adopting XAI frameworks to comply with financial regulations.

Conclusion: AI is Redefining High-Frequency Trading

Machine learning has transformed HFT from simple rule-based algorithms to sophisticated AI-powered trading systems. By leveraging deep learning, reinforcement learning, and NLP, HFT firms can execute trades faster, more accurately, and with greater efficiency than ever before.

However, AI-driven HFT also poses risks of market instability, flash crashes, and regulatory challenges. As AI continues to evolve, the future of HFT will be shaped by quantum computing, decentralized finance, and explainable AI, ensuring a more transparent and efficient financial market.

♦ The race for AI-driven trading dominance is just beginning, and machine learning will continue to revolutionize global financial markets. 🚀

7.3 AI's Role in Portfolio Optimization

In today's fast-paced financial markets, investors seek strategies that maximize returns while minimizing risk. Portfolio optimization, a fundamental concept in investment management, involves balancing assets in a way that achieves the highest possible return for a given level of risk. Traditionally, financial analysts and portfolio managers used historical data, mathematical models, and fundamental analysis to make investment decisions. However, with the rise of Artificial Intelligence (AI), portfolio optimization has become more precise, dynamic, and data-driven.

AI-powered portfolio optimization leverages machine learning (ML), deep learning, and reinforcement learning to analyze vast amounts of market data, identify trends, and rebalance portfolios in real time. These AI-driven systems go beyond human capabilities, automating asset allocation, reducing biases, and improving risk management strategies. This chapter explores how AI is revolutionizing portfolio optimization, the key techniques used, and the benefits and challenges of AI-driven investment strategies.

1. The Fundamentals of Portfolio Optimization

Portfolio optimization is based on the principle of risk-return tradeoff, where investors aim to maximize returns while maintaining an acceptable level of risk. Traditional methods, such as Modern Portfolio Theory (MPT) and Mean-Variance Optimization (MVO), use mathematical formulas to create diversified investment portfolios.

1.1 Traditional Portfolio Optimization Approaches

✓ **Modern Portfolio Theory (MPT):** Introduced by Harry Markowitz, MPT suggests that investors should diversify assets to achieve the best risk-adjusted returns.

✓ **Mean-Variance Optimization (MVO):** Calculates the expected return and risk (volatility) of a portfolio to find the optimal asset allocation.

✓ **Capital Asset Pricing Model (CAPM):** Determines the expected return of an asset based on market risk (beta).

◆ **Limitation**: These models rely on historical data and assumptions, making them less adaptable to rapid market changes.

1.2 Why AI is Transforming Portfolio Optimization

✓ Processes vast amounts of financial data in real time.

✓ Adapts to changing market conditions without relying solely on historical data.

✓ Removes human biases from investment decision-making.

✓ Enhances risk management by detecting hidden market patterns and anomalies.

◆ **Example**: AI-powered hedge funds like Bridgewater Associates and Renaissance Technologies outperform traditional funds using AI-driven strategies.

2. AI Techniques in Portfolio Optimization

AI-powered portfolio optimization uses machine learning, deep learning, and reinforcement learning to analyze financial markets and make data-driven investment decisions.

2.1 Machine Learning for Asset Allocation

✔ **Supervised Learning**: AI models analyze past market data to predict optimal asset allocation.

✔ **Unsupervised Learning**: Clustering algorithms group similar assets to improve diversification strategies.

✔ **Bayesian Networks**: AI models estimate market uncertainty to adjust portfolio weights dynamically.

◆ **Example**: AI models predict how tech stocks react to interest rate hikes and adjust allocations accordingly.

2.2 Deep Learning for Market Trend Prediction

✔ Recurrent Neural Networks (RNNs) & Long Short-Term Memory (LSTMs) analyze time-series financial data.

✔ Convolutional Neural Networks (CNNs) detect trading signals from price charts and technical indicators.

✔ Autoencoders filter out market noise to improve prediction accuracy.

◆ **Example**: AI-driven hedge funds use deep learning to analyze global stock correlations and adjust portfolios dynamically.

2.3 Reinforcement Learning for Dynamic Portfolio Rebalancing

✔ Deep Q-Networks (DQN) help AI agents learn optimal trading decisions through trial and error.

✔ Proximal Policy Optimization (PPO) optimizes risk-adjusted returns.

✔ AI continuously adjusts portfolio weights based on real-time market conditions.

◆ **Example**: AI-powered robo-advisors like Wealthfront and Betterment use reinforcement learning to rebalance portfolios automatically.

3. Benefits of AI-Driven Portfolio Optimization

✓ **Data-Driven Decision Making** – AI removes emotional biases, making investment decisions purely based on data.

✓ **Higher Accuracy in Predictions** – AI detects hidden market trends that traditional models miss.

✓ **Real-Time Portfolio Adjustments** – AI adapts to market volatility faster than human investors.

✓ **Enhanced Risk Management** – AI models identify potential losses before they occur.

◆ **Example**: AI-powered ETFs like BlackRock's iShares use machine learning to optimize portfolio performance.

4. Challenges & Risks of AI in Portfolio Optimization

Despite its advantages, AI-driven portfolio optimization presents several challenges:

4.1 Data Bias & Overfitting

✗ AI models trained on historical data may fail to predict black swan events (e.g., COVID-19 crash).

✗ Overfitting can lead to AI models over-relying on past trends that may not continue.

◆ **Solution**: Use adaptive AI models that incorporate real-time market shifts.

4.2 Lack of Explainability in AI Decisions

✗ Many AI models operate as black boxes, making it difficult for investors to understand why decisions were made.

✗ Explainability is crucial for regulatory compliance and investor trust.

◆ **Solution**: Implement Explainable AI (XAI) to make AI-driven investment decisions more transparent.

4.3 Ethical & Regulatory Concerns

✗ Governments are increasing scrutiny on AI-powered trading algorithms.

✗ AI-driven investment firms must comply with SEC, FINRA, and MiFID II regulations.

♦ **Solution**: Develop ethical AI frameworks to prevent algorithmic market manipulation.

5. The Future of AI in Portfolio Optimization

5.1 Quantum AI for Portfolio Management

✓ Quantum computing will process massive datasets in seconds, revolutionizing asset allocation.

✓ Quantum AI models will outperform classical AI in multi-asset portfolio simulations.

♦ **Example**: Goldman Sachs and IBM are developing quantum-based financial AI models.

5.2 AI-Powered ESG Investing

✓ AI will analyze Environmental, Social, and Governance (ESG) factors to optimize sustainable portfolios.

✓ Investors will use AI to build climate-friendly and socially responsible portfolios.

♦ **Example**: AI-driven ESG funds are gaining popularity among millennial investors and institutional funds.

5.3 Explainable AI (XAI) in Portfolio Management

✓ XAI will make AI-driven investment strategies more transparent and understandable.

✓ Investors will demand AI-generated explanations for trade and portfolio allocation decisions.

♦ **Example**: AI-powered hedge funds are integrating XAI models to comply with investor and regulatory demands.

Conclusion: AI is Reshaping Portfolio Optimization

AI has revolutionized portfolio optimization, making investment strategies smarter, faster, and more data-driven. By leveraging machine learning, deep learning, and reinforcement learning, AI-driven portfolio management systems can optimize asset allocation, predict market trends, and enhance risk management.

However, AI in portfolio optimization comes with challenges such as data bias, lack of explainability, and regulatory scrutiny. As AI technology advances, the future of portfolio optimization will be driven by quantum computing, ESG-focused AI, and explainable AI frameworks.

◆ The investment landscape is evolving, and AI-powered portfolio management is leading the charge toward a more efficient and intelligent financial future. 🚀

7.4 The Risks of AI-Driven Trading

Artificial Intelligence (AI) has transformed financial markets, enabling high-speed algorithmic trading, predictive analytics, and automated portfolio management. AI-driven trading systems can process vast amounts of data, detect market trends, and execute trades faster than human traders. However, despite these advantages, AI-driven trading introduces significant risks that can lead to market instability, financial losses, and regulatory challenges.

This chapter explores the key risks associated with AI-powered trading, including market volatility, model biases, regulatory concerns, cybersecurity threats, and ethical dilemmas. Understanding these risks is crucial for traders, hedge funds, financial institutions, and regulators to ensure a balanced and responsible AI-driven financial ecosystem.

1. Market Volatility & Flash Crashes

One of the most significant risks of AI-driven trading is its potential to cause market volatility and flash crashes. Since AI models react to real-time market conditions in milliseconds, small fluctuations in stock prices can trigger a cascade of automated trades, leading to extreme price swings.

1.1 What is a Flash Crash?

A flash crash occurs when AI and algorithmic trading systems execute large numbers of orders at high speeds, causing a sudden and rapid decline in stock prices, followed by a quick recovery.

◆ **Example: 2010 Flash Crash** – On May 6, 2010, the Dow Jones Industrial Average dropped nearly 1,000 points in minutes due to AI-driven trading algorithms overreacting to market conditions.

◆ **Example: 2021 AMC Stock Volatility** – AI-driven trading contributed to extreme price swings in meme stocks like AMC and GameStop, amplifying retail investor speculation.

1.2 Why AI Contributes to Market Volatility

✓ **Speed of Execution** – AI makes thousands of trades per second, amplifying short-term fluctuations.

✓ **Feedback Loops** – AI models trained on market data can trigger self-reinforcing trading cycles, worsening volatility.

✓ **Lack of Human Oversight** – AI-driven strategies operate without human intervention, making it harder to halt market crashes in real-time.

◆ **Solution**: Regulators have implemented circuit breakers that temporarily halt trading when extreme price movements occur.

2. AI Model Bias & Overfitting

AI models used in trading rely on historical data to make future predictions, but these models can be biased or overfitted to past trends, leading to inaccurate forecasts and financial losses.

2.1 Bias in AI-Driven Trading Models

AI models can develop systematic biases based on the data they are trained on. If a model is trained on data from a bull market, it may fail to predict bear market conditions or financial crashes.

◆ **Example**: An AI model trained on 10 years of bullish stock market data may incorrectly assume that stocks will always rise, leading to overconfident investment strategies.

2.2 Overfitting: When AI Learns the Wrong Patterns

Overfitting occurs when AI models learn patterns that are irrelevant or temporary, leading to poor decision-making in real-world trading.

◆ **Example**: An AI model might find a correlation between Google stock prices and the number of sunny days in New York—a useless and misleading connection.

◆ **Solution**: Use robust validation techniques, ensure AI models are trained on diverse datasets, and incorporate stress-testing methods to account for unexpected market shifts.

3. Regulatory & Compliance Challenges

As AI-driven trading grows, regulators struggle to keep up with automated, high-speed financial decisions that can impact global markets.

3.1 AI and Market Manipulation

AI trading systems can accidentally or deliberately manipulate markets through techniques like:

✓ **Spoofing** – Placing large fake orders to create artificial demand and then canceling them.

✓ **Quote Stuffing** – Flooding the market with orders to slow down competitors.

✓ **Pump and Dump** – AI-driven algorithms detect and exploit rapid price movements.

◆ **Example**: In 2020, the SEC fined an AI-driven hedge fund for using algorithmic strategies that manipulated stock prices.

3.2 The Challenge of Regulating AI-Driven Trading

✓ AI decision-making is opaque, making it difficult for regulators to understand how trading models operate.

✓ AI reacts faster than human regulators, meaning market abuses can occur before authorities intervene.

✓ International regulation conflicts, as different countries have different AI trading rules.

◆ **Solution**: Regulators are developing AI auditing frameworks to ensure transparency in AI-driven trading decisions.

4. Cybersecurity Risks in AI Trading Systems

AI-powered trading systems are vulnerable to cyberattacks, data breaches, and algorithmic hacking, which can lead to financial losses and market instability.

4.1 AI Trading Systems as Cyber Targets

Hackers can exploit AI trading models by injecting fake data, manipulating financial news, or hacking AI algorithms to alter stock prices.

◆ **Example**: In 2013, hackers compromised Twitter and posted false news about an attack on the White House, causing the S&P 500 to drop by $136 billion in minutes. AI trading bots reacted instantly to the fake news, intensifying the market reaction.

4.2 Algorithmic Hacking & Adversarial Attacks

✓ Hackers can use adversarial machine learning to manipulate AI models.

✓ AI models can be fed false data to make bad investment decisions.

✓ Trading algorithms can be sabotaged to favor certain investors over others.

◆ **Solution**: AI trading firms must adopt cybersecurity best practices, including data encryption, anomaly detection, and AI model monitoring.

5. Ethical Concerns in AI-Driven Trading

As AI takes over financial markets, ethical concerns arise regarding job displacement, wealth inequality, and fairness in trading.

5.1 AI and the Displacement of Human Traders

✓ AI-driven trading firms have eliminated many human trading jobs, replacing them with automated systems.

✓ Traditional traders and financial analysts are struggling to compete with AI-powered hedge funds.

◆ **Example**: Goldman Sachs reduced its trading desk staff from 600 to 2 due to AI-driven trading automation.

5.2 AI-Driven Market Inequality

✓ Large firms with advanced AI trading systems dominate financial markets, leaving smaller investors at a disadvantage.

✓ Retail traders have limited access to AI-powered trading tools used by Wall Street giants.

◆ **Solution**: Regulators are considering AI-driven financial fairness laws to prevent large firms from gaining unfair advantages.

6. The Future of AI-Driven Trading Risks

While AI will continue to revolutionize financial markets, it is essential to address its risks through better regulations, cybersecurity measures, and ethical guidelines.

6.1 Explainable AI (XAI) for Transparency

✓ AI-driven trading models must be interpretable so that regulators and investors understand their decision-making processes.

✓ Explainable AI (XAI) will help build trust and reduce black-box trading risks.

6.2 AI-Enhanced Risk Management Systems

✓ AI itself can be used to monitor AI trading risks, providing real-time alerts on suspicious trading activity.

◆ **Example**: AI systems can flag unusual market movements caused by AI-driven trading bots before they escalate.

Conclusion: Managing AI Trading Risks in the Financial World

AI-driven trading offers speed, efficiency, and profitability, but it also comes with risks that can destabilize markets, create ethical concerns, and challenge regulatory frameworks. Market volatility, AI bias, cybersecurity threats, and regulatory gaps must be addressed to ensure responsible AI-driven trading.

As financial markets become increasingly automated, the future will depend on balancing AI's benefits with robust risk management strategies. By adopting explainable AI, improving cybersecurity, and enforcing ethical AI regulations, we can create a safer and fairer financial system powered by AI. 🚀

8. Fraud Detection and Cybersecurity in Finance

As financial transactions become increasingly digital, AI plays a crucial role in detecting fraud and enhancing cybersecurity. Advanced machine learning models analyze transaction patterns, user behavior, and anomalies in real time to identify fraudulent activities such as identity theft, payment fraud, and insider trading. AI-powered cybersecurity systems help financial institutions predict, prevent, and respond to cyber threats, safeguarding sensitive data and ensuring regulatory compliance. This chapter explores how AI-driven fraud detection systems work, their impact on financial security, and the challenges of balancing privacy, accuracy, and ethical concerns in AI-powered risk management.

8.1 AI for Transaction Anomaly Detection

Financial institutions process millions of transactions daily, making it nearly impossible for humans to manually detect fraudulent activities, money laundering, or suspicious transactions. Traditional rule-based fraud detection systems are often slow, prone to false positives, and struggle with evolving fraud tactics. This is where Artificial Intelligence (AI) plays a crucial role.

AI-powered transaction anomaly detection uses machine learning (ML), deep learning, and statistical models to analyze transaction patterns, detect deviations from normal behavior, and flag potential fraudulent activities in real time. This chapter explores how AI detects transaction anomalies, the key techniques used, real-world applications, and the challenges in implementing AI-driven fraud detection systems.

1. What is Transaction Anomaly Detection?

An anomaly in financial transactions refers to any suspicious or unusual activity that deviates from a customer's normal spending behavior. These anomalies can indicate fraud, identity theft, money laundering, or system errors.

◆ **Examples of Anomalous Transactions:**

✓ A sudden large transfer to an offshore account from a customer who usually makes small transactions.

✓ Multiple failed login attempts followed by a high-value transaction.

✓ A customer making purchases from two different locations within minutes (implying stolen credentials).

✓ Small, frequent transactions to the same recipient (often linked to money laundering).

1.1 Traditional vs. AI-Powered Anomaly Detection

Feature	Traditional Rule-Based Systems	AI-Powered Anomaly Detection
Detection Approach	Predefined rules (e.g., flagging transactions above $10,000)	Learns from historical data and detects hidden patterns
Adaptability	Static, requires manual updates	Dynamic, learns from new fraud tactics automatically
False Positives	High (flags many legitimate transactions)	Lower (more accurate detection)
Speed	Slower, batch processing	Real-time transaction monitoring

◆ **Example**: AI detects fraudsters who break large transactions into smaller amounts ("smurfing") to bypass traditional rules.

2. How AI Detects Transaction Anomalies

AI-based fraud detection systems continuously monitor financial transactions to identify unusual activity. They use machine learning models trained on historical transaction data to differentiate between legitimate transactions and fraudulent ones.

2.1 Supervised Machine Learning for Anomaly Detection

✓ Uses labeled datasets (historical fraud data) to train AI models.

✓ **Common algorithms**: Logistic Regression, Random Forest, Support Vector Machines (SVM), and XGBoost.

✓ **Strength**: Effective if a large dataset of past fraud cases is available.

◆ **Example**: If AI has seen thousands of fraud cases where stolen credit cards were used for high-value transactions in foreign countries, it will flag similar transactions in the future.

2.2 Unsupervised Machine Learning for Anomaly Detection

✓ Used when no labeled fraud data is available.

✓ Identifies outliers and unusual transaction behaviors.

✓ **Common algorithms**: K-Means Clustering, Isolation Forest, Autoencoders.

◆ **Example**: If a customer who usually spends $200/month suddenly makes a $10,000 purchase, AI detects it as an anomaly.

2.3 Deep Learning & Neural Networks

✓ Uses Artificial Neural Networks (ANNs) and Long Short-Term Memory (LSTM) networks.

✓ Can analyze sequential transaction behavior over time.

✓ Learns complex fraud patterns, making it more effective for advanced financial crimes.

◆ **Example**: AI can detect sophisticated fraud tactics like synthetic identity fraud, where criminals create fake identities using real and fake data.

3. AI in Real-World Fraud Detection Systems

Many financial institutions and fintech companies use AI-powered fraud detection systems to monitor transactions in real time.

3.1 AI-Powered Credit Card Fraud Detection

✓ AI models analyze spending patterns and detect unusual purchases.

✓ Uses behavioral biometrics (how a user types, swipes, or logs in).

✓ Sends instant alerts or blocks suspicious transactions.

◆ **Example**: Visa and Mastercard use AI to prevent fraudulent purchases before they are completed.

3.2 AI for Money Laundering Detection

✓ Identifies layering techniques (e.g., breaking large transactions into smaller ones).

✓ Detects suspicious account activity, such as frequent international fund transfers.

✓ Helps banks comply with Anti-Money Laundering (AML) regulations.

⬥ **Example**: AI-powered AML solutions flag suspicious banking transactions to comply with global regulations like the Bank Secrecy Act (BSA) and the EU's 6th Anti-Money Laundering Directive (AMLD6).

3.3 AI for Cryptocurrency Fraud Detection

✓ Detects fraudulent crypto transactions on blockchain networks.

✓ Identifies wash trading and pump-and-dump schemes.

✓ Prevents hacks and unauthorized withdrawals.

⬥ **Example**: Chainalysis and CipherTrace use AI to detect illicit crypto transactions linked to dark web marketplaces.

4. Challenges & Limitations of AI in Fraud Detection

Despite its advantages, AI-based fraud detection has challenges that financial institutions must address.

4.1 False Positives & Legitimate Transaction Blocking

✗ AI may flag legitimate transactions as fraudulent, causing customer dissatisfaction.

✗ **Example**: A person traveling abroad may have their credit card blocked due to AI misclassification.

✓ **Solution**: Use hybrid AI-human review systems to verify flagged transactions.

4.2 Evolving Fraud Techniques & AI Adaptation

✗ Criminals use AI to create advanced fraud schemes (e.g., deepfake fraud, AI-generated fake identities).

✗ AI models must continuously learn and adapt to new fraud patterns.

✓ **Solution**: Implement adaptive AI models that update in real-time with new fraud trends.

4.3 Data Privacy & Compliance Issues

✗ AI fraud detection relies on analyzing sensitive financial data, raising privacy concerns.

✗ Financial institutions must comply with GDPR, CCPA, and PCI-DSS regulations.

✓ **Solution**: Use privacy-preserving AI techniques like federated learning and homomorphic encryption.

5. The Future of AI in Transaction Anomaly Detection

As fraud tactics become more sophisticated, AI-powered fraud detection systems will need to evolve.

5.1 Explainable AI (XAI) for Transparent Fraud Detection

✓ AI systems will provide clear explanations for why a transaction is flagged.

✓ Helps regulators and banks understand AI decisions.

◆ **Example**: AI will explain why a $5,000 withdrawal is flagged based on past spending habits.

5.2 AI & Blockchain for Secure Transactions

✓ AI will integrate with blockchain technology to create tamper-proof transaction monitoring.

✓ Helps prevent crypto fraud and identity theft.

◆ **Example**: Decentralized finance (DeFi) platforms will use AI to prevent scams and illegal crypto transactions.

5.3 AI & Behavioral Biometrics for Fraud Prevention

✔ AI will analyze how users interact with devices to detect stolen credentials.

✔ Helps prevent identity fraud, deepfake fraud, and account takeovers.

◆ **Example**: AI will detect if a fraudster is using stolen login credentials based on typing speed and mouse movements.

Conclusion: AI as the Future of Fraud Detection

AI-powered transaction anomaly detection is revolutionizing fraud prevention, enabling financial institutions to detect suspicious transactions in real-time, minimize financial losses, and enhance cybersecurity. By using machine learning, deep learning, and behavioral analytics, AI can identify fraud patterns that traditional systems miss.

However, financial institutions must address challenges like false positives, evolving fraud techniques, and data privacy concerns. As AI continues to advance, integrating explainable AI, blockchain security, and behavioral biometrics will further strengthen fraud detection capabilities.

💡 In the future, AI will not only detect fraud—it will prevent it before it happens! 🚀

8.2 Deep Learning for Identity Verification & Fraud Prevention

As financial transactions move online, fraudsters constantly develop sophisticated techniques to bypass traditional security measures. Identity theft, account takeovers, and synthetic identity fraud have become major threats in banking, fintech, and e-commerce. Traditional rule-based identity verification methods, such as passwords, security questions, and static fraud detection models, are no longer sufficient to combat these advanced fraud tactics.

Deep learning, a subset of artificial intelligence (AI), is revolutionizing identity verification and fraud prevention. By using neural networks, deep learning models can analyze biometric data, behavioral patterns, and transaction anomalies to detect fraud with greater accuracy than ever before.

This chapter explores how deep learning enhances identity verification, prevents fraud, and strengthens financial security, along with real-world applications and challenges.

1. The Growing Threat of Identity Fraud

Identity fraud involves stealing or fabricating identities to gain unauthorized access to financial services, accounts, or personal information. Fraudsters use advanced techniques, including AI-generated deepfake identities, stolen credentials, and synthetic identity fraud, to bypass traditional security systems.

1.1 Common Types of Identity Fraud

✓ **Account Takeover (ATO)** – Hackers steal login credentials and take control of a user's account.

✓ **Synthetic Identity Fraud** – Criminals create fake identities by combining real and fake personal information.

✓ **Biometric Spoofing** – Fraudsters use deepfake videos or voice cloning to bypass biometric authentication.

✓ **Document Forgery** – AI-generated fake IDs, passports, and social security numbers are used for fraudulent transactions.

◆ **Example**: In 2023, financial institutions lost over $50 billion to identity-related fraud, with synthetic identity fraud being the fastest-growing threat.

2. How Deep Learning Enhances Identity Verification

Deep learning models use neural networks to analyze vast amounts of identity-related data, including facial recognition, voice authentication, and behavioral biometrics. These models can detect fraudulent users and unauthorized access attempts with high accuracy.

2.1 Biometric Identity Verification

Deep learning is widely used in biometric security, allowing systems to verify users through:

✓ **Facial Recognition** – Compares a user's face with stored images to verify identity.

✓ **Voice Recognition** – Identifies unique voice patterns for authentication.

✓ **Fingerprint & Iris Scanning** – Uses deep learning models to match biometric features with database records.

◆ **Example**: Apple's Face ID and Microsoft's Windows Hello use deep learning for secure identity verification.

2.2 Behavioral Biometrics for Fraud Detection

Instead of relying on static data like passwords, deep learning models analyze how users interact with devices to detect fraud.

✓ **Typing Patterns** – AI detects if a user's typing speed or rhythm differs from normal behavior.

✓ **Mouse Movements** – Tracks mouse behavior to distinguish between real users and bots.

✓ **Keystroke Dynamics** – Identifies users based on how they type, including speed and pressure.

◆ **Example**: If a fraudster logs into a bank account using stolen credentials but types differently than the real owner, AI can flag it as suspicious.

2.3 AI-Powered Document Verification

Deep learning models can verify identity documents by detecting forgeries, alterations, and fake documents.

✓ **OCR (Optical Character Recognition)** – Extracts text from images to verify authenticity.

✓ **Liveness Detection** – Ensures the user is physically present and not using a photo or deepfake.

✓ **Hologram & Watermark Analysis** – Detects counterfeit documents.

◆ **Example**: Many banks and fintech apps use AI-based document verification during KYC (Know Your Customer) onboarding to prevent fraud.

3. Deep Learning for Fraud Prevention

Deep learning models can detect fraudulent activities by analyzing patterns, anomalies, and behavioral deviations in real time.

3.1 Anomaly Detection in Financial Transactions

✓ AI continuously monitors transactions for irregular spending patterns.

✓ Flags transactions that deviate from a user's normal behavior.

✓ Reduces false positives by learning legitimate spending habits over time.

◆ **Example**: If a customer who usually spends $500 per month suddenly makes a $10,000 purchase in a foreign country, AI will flag it as potential fraud.

3.2 Detecting Deepfake & Synthetic Identity Fraud

✓ AI can detect AI-generated fake faces and videos used for fraudulent identity verification.

✓ **Uses** Generative Adversarial Networks (GANs) to identify synthetic identities.

✓ Prevents deepfake fraud in banking and financial services.

◆ **Example**: Deep learning-based liveness detection ensures that fraudsters cannot use AI-generated deepfake videos to pass facial recognition.

3.3 Fraud Prevention in Online Banking & Fintech

✓ AI-powered risk scoring systems assess the likelihood of fraud before approving transactions.

✓ **Multi-Factor Authentication (MFA) with AI** – Uses biometrics, behavioral analysis, and one-time passwords to enhance security.

✓ Real-time monitoring of login attempts and unusual behaviors.

◆ **Example**: PayPal uses deep learning to detect and block fraudulent transactions before they are completed.

4. Challenges & Limitations of Deep Learning in Fraud Prevention

Despite its effectiveness, deep learning-based identity verification and fraud detection face several challenges.

4.1 Data Privacy & Ethical Concerns

✔ AI fraud detection relies on analyzing sensitive personal data, raising privacy concerns.

✔ Governments enforce strict data protection laws (GDPR, CCPA, PCI-DSS).

◆ **Solution**: Use privacy-preserving AI techniques, such as federated learning and differential privacy, to protect user data.

4.2 Adversarial Attacks on AI Systems

✔ Hackers can trick deep learning models using adversarial machine learning techniques.

✔ **Example**: Manipulating an image slightly can fool a facial recognition AI into misidentifying a user.

◆ **Solution**: Implement robust AI security measures, such as adversarial training and continuous model updates.

4.3 Balancing Security & User Experience

✔ AI fraud detection systems must minimize false positives to avoid blocking legitimate transactions.

✔ Lengthy identity verification processes can frustrate users.

◆ **Solution**: Use adaptive AI models that balance security and convenience by learning from user behavior.

5. Future of Deep Learning in Identity Verification & Fraud Prevention

The future of deep learning in fraud prevention will focus on improving accuracy, reducing fraud, and enhancing user security.

5.1 AI & Blockchain Integration for Secure Identity Management

✓ Blockchain-based decentralized identity verification will reduce identity fraud.

✓ AI-powered smart contracts will prevent unauthorized transactions.

◆ **Example**: Governments and banks are exploring blockchain-based digital IDs for fraud-resistant identity verification.

5.2 Explainable AI (XAI) for Transparent Fraud Detection

✓ AI will provide clear explanations for why a transaction was flagged as fraudulent.

✓ Helps regulators and financial institutions understand AI decision-making.

◆ **Example**: AI models will explain why a login attempt from a new device was flagged as suspicious.

5.3 AI-Driven Biometric Authentication Beyond Face & Fingerprint

✓ Future biometric security may include gait analysis (walking patterns), heartbeat recognition, and brainwave authentication.

✓ AI will analyze multiple biometric factors simultaneously for higher security.

◆ **Example**: AI could authenticate users based on unique heart rhythms detected by wearable devices.

Conclusion: The Future of AI in Identity Security

Deep learning is revolutionizing identity verification and fraud prevention, offering real-time, highly accurate detection of fraudulent activities. From biometric authentication to behavioral analytics, AI-powered security systems are more effective than traditional fraud detection methods.

However, organizations must address privacy concerns, adversarial attacks, and false positives while ensuring a smooth user experience. With advancements in explainable AI, blockchain security, and multi-factor biometric authentication, deep learning will continue to be a game-changer in preventing identity fraud and securing financial transactions. 🚀

8.3 AI in Financial Cybersecurity & Threat Intelligence

In an era where financial transactions are increasingly digital, the threat landscape for cyberattacks, data breaches, and financial fraud continues to expand. Cybercriminals leverage sophisticated tactics such as ransomware, phishing, AI-generated deepfake scams, and bot-driven attacks to compromise financial institutions. Traditional cybersecurity measures, such as rule-based threat detection and manual monitoring, struggle to keep up with rapidly evolving threats.

This is where artificial intelligence (AI) and machine learning (ML) step in, revolutionizing financial cybersecurity and threat intelligence. AI-driven systems analyze massive amounts of security data in real time, identifying vulnerabilities, predicting cyberattacks, and automating threat response mechanisms. This chapter explores how AI strengthens cybersecurity in finance, covering real-world applications, challenges, and future trends.

1. The Rising Threat Landscape in Financial Cybersecurity

1.1 The Cost of Cybercrime in Finance

Financial institutions are prime targets for cybercriminals due to their sensitive customer data, vast financial assets, and complex digital infrastructures. According to industry reports:

✓ **$4.45 million** – The average cost of a financial data breach (IBM, 2023).

✓ 300% increase in AI-driven phishing attacks since 2021.

✓ 90% of cyberattacks target financial institutions.

1.2 Common Cyber Threats in Finance

✓ **Phishing & Social Engineering** – Attackers trick employees or customers into revealing credentials.

✓ **Ransomware** – Hackers encrypt financial data and demand payment for decryption.

✔ **DDoS Attacks** – Cybercriminals overload banking servers, causing outages.

✔ **Deepfake & AI-Generated Scams** – AI-powered fraudsters create fake voices and videos to impersonate financial executives.

✔ **Insider Threats** – Employees with malicious intent steal or misuse financial data.

◆ **Example**: In 2020, hackers used AI-powered deepfake audio to impersonate a bank CEO, successfully tricking employees into transferring $35 million.

2. How AI Strengthens Financial Cybersecurity

AI-driven cybersecurity solutions use machine learning algorithms, natural language processing (NLP), and real-time anomaly detection to predict, prevent, and respond to cyber threats in financial institutions.

2.1 AI for Threat Detection & Prevention

AI models analyze historical cyberattack patterns, network traffic, and user behavior to detect threats before they cause damage.

✔ **Anomaly Detection** – AI identifies suspicious transactions, unauthorized access attempts, and unusual login locations.

✔ **Predictive Threat Intelligence** – Machine learning models analyze global cyberattack trends to forecast potential risks.

✔ **Automated Threat Response** – AI-powered security systems neutralize threats in real time by blocking malicious IPs or isolating infected devices.

◆ **Example**: JPMorgan Chase uses AI-driven security analytics to monitor billions of transactions per second, preventing fraud and cyberattacks.

2.2 AI for Identity and Access Management (IAM)

AI improves user authentication and access control by continuously monitoring login behaviors and detecting potential identity compromises.

✔ **Behavioral Biometrics** – AI detects changes in typing speed, mouse movements, and login habits to identify potential fraud.

✓ **Adaptive Authentication** – AI dynamically adjusts security levels based on risk assessment, requiring multi-factor authentication (MFA) for suspicious logins.

✓ **Zero Trust Security Models** – AI ensures that no user or device is trusted by default, verifying credentials continuously.

◆ **Example**: Many financial institutions now use AI-powered risk-based authentication, where additional verification steps are triggered only when login behavior deviates from the norm.

2.3 AI-Powered Phishing & Social Engineering Detection

Phishing attacks have become increasingly sophisticated, using AI-generated emails and deepfake videos to trick employees and customers. AI-driven cybersecurity tools help:

✓ Detect AI-generated phishing emails using NLP and sentiment analysis.

✓ Analyze email sender reputation to block suspicious messages.

✓ Monitor voice and video communications for deepfake impersonations.

◆ **Example**: Banks like Citibank and Wells Fargo use AI-based anti-phishing tools to analyze email patterns and block phishing attempts before they reach users.

2.4 AI in Fraud & Insider Threat Detection

AI-powered fraud detection tools identify suspicious transactions, detect insider threats, and monitor employee activities to prevent security breaches.

✓ **Real-Time Transaction Monitoring** – AI scans transactions for fraud indicators (e.g., unusual spending behavior).

✓ **Insider Threat Detection** – AI analyzes employee activities to detect unauthorized data access.

✓ **AI-Based Behavioral Risk Scoring** – Assigns risk scores to employees based on security behavior.

◆ **Example**: Goldman Sachs uses AI-driven security analytics to monitor employee activity and prevent insider trading.

3. Challenges of AI in Financial Cybersecurity

3.1 Adversarial AI & Evasion Techniques

✔ Cybercriminals train AI models to bypass AI-powered cybersecurity defenses.

✔ Hackers create adversarial machine learning attacks by subtly manipulating data to fool AI security systems.

✔ AI-powered malware evolves continuously, making it harder to detect.

◆ **Solution**: Financial institutions must develop AI adversarial training models to counter evolving threats.

3.2 Balancing Security with User Privacy

✔ AI cybersecurity tools require large amounts of user data for accurate threat detection.

✔ Strict regulations like GDPR, CCPA, and PCI-DSS limit data collection practices.

✔ Overly aggressive security measures may lead to false positives, blocking legitimate users.

◆ **Solution**: Use privacy-preserving AI (e.g., federated learning, homomorphic encryption) to enhance security while protecting user data.

3.3 AI Model Bias & Ethical Concerns

✔ AI models may incorrectly flag legitimate users as security threats due to biased training data.

✔ Over-reliance on AI security can reduce human oversight, leading to unexpected security loopholes.

◆ **Solution**: Financial institutions should adopt explainable AI (XAI) to ensure transparent decision-making.

4. The Future of AI in Financial Cybersecurity

4.1 AI & Blockchain for Secure Transactions

✓ AI-powered fraud detection combined with blockchain-based transaction verification will enhance security.

✓ Smart contracts will automatically detect and prevent fraudulent financial activities.

◆ **Example**: Blockchain-based decentralized finance (DeFi) platforms are integrating AI-powered security mechanisms to prevent cyberattacks.

4.2 Quantum AI for Cybersecurity

✓ Quantum computing will break traditional encryption, forcing banks to adopt quantum-safe AI encryption.

✓ AI-powered quantum cryptography will secure financial transactions against future cyber threats.

◆ **Example**: IBM and Google are researching quantum AI for next-generation financial cybersecurity solutions.

4.3 Autonomous AI Security Agents

✓ AI-driven autonomous cybersecurity agents will proactively detect and neutralize cyber threats.

✓ These AI models will self-learn from evolving attack techniques, making security systems more adaptive.

◆ **Example**: AI-based Cyber Defense Neural Networks (CDNNs) are being tested for real-time cyber threat mitigation.

Conclusion: The AI-Powered Cybersecurity Revolution

AI is rapidly transforming financial cybersecurity and threat intelligence, providing real-time threat detection, predictive analytics, and automated response mechanisms.

Financial institutions must leverage AI-powered fraud detection, identity verification, and cybersecurity automation to stay ahead of evolving cyber threats.

However, AI-driven cybersecurity must overcome challenges like adversarial AI attacks, ethical concerns, and data privacy regulations. The future of financial cybersecurity will involve quantum AI encryption, blockchain integration, and autonomous AI threat detection systems, ensuring a safer digital financial ecosystem. 🚀

8.4 Ethical and Legal Considerations in AI-Based Fraud Detection

AI-driven fraud detection is revolutionizing financial security, allowing institutions to identify fraudulent activities with greater speed and accuracy. Machine learning models can analyze vast amounts of transaction data, detect anomalies, and predict fraud patterns in real time. However, while AI enhances fraud prevention, it also introduces ethical and legal challenges, including privacy concerns, algorithmic bias, regulatory compliance, and the potential for false positives that impact legitimate users.

This chapter explores the ethical dilemmas and legal complexities associated with AI-based fraud detection, discussing how financial institutions can balance security with fairness, transparency, and compliance.

1. Ethical Challenges in AI Fraud Detection

1.1 Bias in AI Models

AI fraud detection systems are trained on historical financial data, but this data may contain inherent biases that lead to unfair outcomes.

✓ **Racial & Socioeconomic Bias** – If past fraud cases disproportionately involve certain demographics, the AI may unfairly flag individuals from those groups as high-risk.

✓ **Geographical Bias** – Fraud models may mistakenly classify transactions from specific regions as fraudulent, leading to unnecessary account freezes.

✓ **Creditworthiness Discrimination** – Some AI models might unintentionally penalize customers based on socioeconomic status rather than actual fraud risks.

◆ **Example**: In 2019, a major financial institution faced backlash when its AI-powered fraud detection system disproportionately flagged low-income users for suspicious transactions, resulting in unfair banking restrictions.

◆ **Solution**: Financial institutions must regularly audit AI models for bias, ensuring fairness in fraud detection.

1.2 False Positives & Customer Impact

✓ AI-driven fraud detection sometimes misidentifies legitimate transactions as fraudulent, leading to:

- Blocked accounts and declined transactions.
- Inconvenience for customers, especially in urgent situations.
- Loss of trust in financial institutions.

✓ False positives occur when AI models rely on overly strict patterns that fail to account for unique but legitimate behaviors.

◆ **Example**: A business traveler making transactions across multiple countries might trigger fraud alerts, resulting in account suspension, even though the transactions are genuine.

◆ **Solution**: Financial institutions should implement adaptive AI models that learn individual spending behaviors to reduce false positives.

1.3 Privacy & Data Security Concerns

AI fraud detection relies on massive amounts of customer data, including:

✓ Banking transactions

✓ Credit history

✓ Online behavior

✓ Biometric data (for identity verification)

While this data helps AI detect fraud, it also raises concerns about:

✔ **Customer consent** – Are customers fully aware of how their data is used?

✔ **Data breaches** – Storing sensitive financial data makes institutions vulnerable to cyberattacks.

✔ **AI surveillance** – Over-monitoring can feel intrusive, leading to a loss of personal privacy.

◆ **Example**: In 2023, a major bank faced legal action for failing to disclose how its AI system tracked and stored customer transaction data, violating privacy laws.

◆ **Solution**: Companies must ensure data transparency, encryption, and compliance with data protection regulations to maintain customer trust.

2. Legal Considerations in AI-Based Fraud Detection

Financial institutions must comply with strict regulations when deploying AI-powered fraud detection systems. Regulatory frameworks vary globally, but key legal considerations include data protection laws, AI accountability, and explainability requirements.

2.1 Compliance with Data Protection Laws

Several global regulations impact how AI fraud detection systems handle customer data:

✔ **General Data Protection Regulation (GDPR - Europe)** – Requires AI models to provide explainable fraud detection decisions and obtain customer consent for data processing.

✔ **California Consumer Privacy Act (CCPA - USA)** – Gives consumers the right to know how AI systems use their financial data.

✔ **Payment Card Industry Data Security Standard (PCI DSS)** – Mandates strict security protocols for handling credit card transaction data.

◆ **Example**: Under GDPR Article 22, if an AI system declines a loan or flags a transaction as fraud, the affected customer has the right to request an explanation and human review.

◆ **Solution**: Banks and fintech companies must ensure AI-driven fraud detection systems adhere to transparency laws and offer appeal mechanisms.

2.2 Explainability & AI Accountability

✓ Regulators demand transparency in AI decision-making.

✓ AI fraud detection models must provide clear, explainable reasons when flagging transactions.

✓ Customers should have the option to contest AI-based fraud decisions and request human intervention.

⬧ **Example**: The European Banking Authority (EBA) requires AI fraud models to offer "human-in-the-loop" oversight, ensuring that important financial decisions are not solely automated.

⬧ **Solution**: Institutions must use explainable AI (XAI) techniques that allow regulators and customers to understand how fraud detection decisions are made.

2.3 AI Ethics & Legal Responsibility

✓ If an AI fraud detection system wrongfully penalizes a customer, who is responsible— the bank, the AI provider, or the data scientists?

✓ Legal frameworks are evolving to assign responsibility for AI errors, ensuring customers have legal recourse in case of unjust fraud accusations.

⬧ **Example**: A UK-based fintech company was sued after its AI fraud detection system erroneously flagged thousands of legitimate transactions, leading to massive financial losses for small businesses.

⬧ **Solution**: Financial institutions should establish AI governance policies to ensure ethical accountability and compliance.

3. Best Practices for Ethical & Legal AI Fraud Detection

To balance security, fairness, and compliance, financial institutions should adopt the following best practices:

3.1 Fair & Bias-Free AI Models

✓ Regularly audit AI fraud detection models for unintended biases.

✓ Train models on diverse, unbiased datasets.

✓ Implement fairness metrics to ensure AI does not disproportionately impact specific groups.

3.2 Transparency & Customer Rights

✓ Provide explainable AI decisions to customers affected by fraud detection systems.

✓ Allow customers to challenge AI decisions and request human review.

✓ Ensure fraud detection models comply with global regulatory transparency requirements.

3.3 Strong Data Privacy & Security Measures

✓ Encrypt customer transaction data to prevent breaches and misuse.

✓ Use privacy-preserving AI (e.g., federated learning) to analyze fraud without exposing raw data.

✓ Ensure AI systems comply with GDPR, CCPA, and PCI DSS standards.

3.4 Human Oversight in AI-Based Decisions

✓ Implement human-in-the-loop systems where AI decisions require human review for high-impact cases.

✓ Avoid fully automated fraud decisions that could unjustly block legitimate transactions.

Conclusion: Building Trust in AI Fraud Detection

AI-based fraud detection is essential for securing financial transactions, preventing cybercrime, and enhancing fraud prevention. However, its effectiveness must be balanced with ethical considerations and legal compliance. Institutions must:

✓ Minimize bias in AI models to ensure fairness.

✓ Reduce false positives to prevent blocking legitimate transactions.

✓ Ensure transparency & explainability in fraud detection decisions.

✓ Follow global data privacy laws to protect customer information.

✓ Implement human oversight to maintain accountability in AI fraud detection.

By addressing these ethical and legal challenges, financial institutions can build AI fraud detection systems that are secure, fair, and legally compliant, ensuring customer trust and regulatory approval in the AI-driven financial landscape. 🚀

9. Personalized AI in Banking & Fintech

AI is redefining banking and fintech by delivering hyper-personalized financial services, improving customer experience, and optimizing operations. From AI-powered chatbots and virtual financial advisors to personalized loan offerings and robo-advisors for investment management, AI enables banks and fintech firms to provide tailored solutions based on customer behavior, spending patterns, and financial goals. Machine learning algorithms enhance credit risk assessment, fraud detection, and transaction security, making banking smarter and more efficient. This chapter explores the role of AI in modern banking, fintech innovations, and the challenges of data privacy, transparency, and regulatory compliance in AI-driven financial services.

9.1 AI-Powered Credit Scoring & Risk Assessment

Traditional credit scoring systems, such as FICO scores and manual risk assessments, have long been the backbone of financial decision-making. However, they often suffer from limited data scope, bias, and outdated evaluation techniques. AI-powered credit scoring and risk assessment systems are revolutionizing the financial industry by incorporating machine learning (ML), big data analytics, and alternative data sources to provide more accurate, fair, and real-time assessments of creditworthiness.

In this chapter, we will explore how AI-driven credit scoring enhances financial inclusivity, improves risk assessment accuracy, and mitigates bias, while also addressing ethical concerns, regulatory challenges, and real-world applications.

1. The Evolution of Credit Scoring

1.1 Traditional Credit Scoring: Limitations & Challenges

Traditional credit scoring models rely on a fixed set of financial indicators, such as:

✓ Credit history (loan repayments, credit card usage).

✓ Income level & employment history.

✓ Debt-to-income ratio.

✓ Credit utilization rate.

However, these methods present several challenges:

✓ **Limited Data Scope** – Many people (especially those without prior credit history) are excluded from the system.

✓ **Static & Inflexible Models** – Traditional credit scores are updated infrequently, leading to delayed risk assessments.

✓ **Bias & Inequity** – Credit scores can be biased against certain demographics, disproportionately affecting low-income individuals and minorities.

◈ **Example**: Millions of people globally remain "credit invisible", meaning they cannot access loans or credit due to a lack of sufficient financial history.

2. How AI is Transforming Credit Scoring & Risk Assessment

AI-powered credit scoring uses machine learning algorithms and big data analytics to create dynamic, personalized risk profiles that adapt in real-time. These systems incorporate:

✓ **Alternative Data Sources** – AI considers rental payments, utility bills, online spending habits, and even social media behavior.

✓ **Real-Time Analysis** – AI evaluates financial behavior dynamically, offering more accurate and updated risk assessments.

✓ **Predictive Modeling** – Machine learning algorithms identify patterns and trends to predict credit risk before defaults occur.

◈ **Example**: Fintech companies like Upstart and ZestFinance use AI to evaluate non-traditional borrowers, increasing approval rates while reducing loan defaults.

3. AI Techniques in Credit Scoring

3.1 Machine Learning for Risk Prediction

AI models analyze large datasets to detect patterns that indicate creditworthiness. Popular machine learning techniques include:

✓ **Supervised Learning** – AI trains on past loan repayment data to predict future defaults.

✓ **Neural Networks** – Advanced models analyze complex credit behaviors beyond traditional risk factors.

✓ **Decision Trees & Random Forests** – AI identifies key risk indicators by analyzing multiple variables simultaneously.

◆ **Example**: A bank can use AI to detect that a borrower with frequent short-term loans but no defaults is a lower risk than one with a high credit score but irregular payments.

3.2 Alternative Data for More Inclusive Credit Scoring

Traditional credit models ignore people with little or no credit history. AI-based systems can assess alternative financial behaviors, such as:

✓ **Rent & Utility Payments** – Consistent payments show financial reliability.

✓ **E-commerce Spending Patterns** – AI can analyze online purchase behavior as an indicator of financial responsibility.

✓ **Employment & Education Data** – Stable jobs and higher education levels may correlate with lower credit risk.

✓ **Social Media & Digital Footprint** – AI can evaluate social behavior, professional networks, and transaction history to assess risk.

◆ **Example**: WeBank, a Chinese fintech company, uses AI-powered credit scoring based on digital transaction data, approving millions of first-time borrowers.

3.3 Real-Time Risk Monitoring & Adaptive Credit Scoring

Unlike static credit scores, AI-powered credit risk models continuously monitor and update borrower profiles based on real-time financial behavior.

✓ **Dynamic Score Adjustments** – AI can instantly adjust credit limits based on spending patterns.

✓ **Early Default Warnings** – AI can detect early signs of financial distress, allowing lenders to take proactive measures.

✓ **Personalized Loan Offers** – AI helps financial institutions tailor interest rates and credit limits based on individual risk profiles.

◆ **Example**: AI-driven systems can reduce loan defaults by up to 30% by identifying at-risk borrowers early.

4. Ethical & Legal Concerns in AI-Based Credit Scoring

4.1 Algorithmic Bias & Fairness

✓ AI models can inherit biases from historical credit data, unfairly penalizing certain demographics.

✓ Lack of transparency in AI decision-making makes it difficult to detect discrimination.

✓ Unethical use of personal data (e.g., social media activity) raises privacy concerns.

◆ **Solution**: Regulators and companies must ensure "fair AI" practices, including bias audits and transparent AI models.

4.2 Compliance with Financial Regulations

AI-based credit scoring must comply with global regulations, including:

✓ **Fair Credit Reporting Act (FCRA - USA)** – Requires AI-driven decisions to be explainable and allows consumers to dispute inaccuracies.

✓ **General Data Protection Regulation (GDPR - Europe)** – Mandates data protection, transparency, and the right to opt out of AI-based decisions.

✓ **Equal Credit Opportunity Act (ECOA - USA)** – Prohibits credit discrimination based on race, gender, or age.

◆ **Solution**: Financial institutions must use explainable AI (XAI) to justify credit decisions and comply with regulatory requirements.

4.3 Privacy & Data Security Risks

✓ AI credit scoring models rely on sensitive personal and financial data.

✓ Cyberattacks on AI systems could expose confidential customer data.

✓ Unauthorized use of alternative data raises ethical concerns about surveillance.

◆ **Solution**: Institutions should implement data encryption, access controls, and ethical AI guidelines to protect customer privacy.

5. The Future of AI in Credit Scoring & Risk Assessment

5.1 AI & Blockchain Integration for Secure Credit Scoring

✓ Blockchain can provide tamper-proof, decentralized credit histories, reducing fraud.

✓ Smart contracts can automate loan approvals based on AI-driven credit scores.

◆ **Example**: Decentralized finance (DeFi) platforms are using AI and blockchain to offer global microloans without traditional credit checks.

5.2 Quantum AI for Ultra-Accurate Credit Risk Models

✓ Quantum computing will enable hyper-accurate credit risk predictions by processing massive datasets.

✓ AI-powered quantum simulations will model complex borrower behaviors in real-time.

◆ **Example**: Financial firms are investing in Quantum AI labs to develop next-generation credit risk assessment tools.

5.3 The Rise of Explainable AI (XAI) in Credit Scoring

✓ Regulators and consumers demand greater transparency in AI-driven financial decisions.

✓ XAI ensures that AI-generated credit scores can be explained in human terms.

✓ Future credit models will use interpretable AI algorithms to enhance trust.

◆ **Example**: Banks like HSBC and Citibank are deploying Explainable AI systems to provide detailed justifications for AI-generated credit scores.

Conclusion: The AI-Powered Future of Credit Scoring

AI-driven credit scoring and risk assessment are transforming the financial landscape, making credit decisions faster, more inclusive, and more accurate. By incorporating alternative data, real-time monitoring, and machine learning, AI enhances credit evaluation while minimizing fraud.

However, to ensure fairness, transparency, and compliance, financial institutions must address ethical concerns, regulatory challenges, and data security risks. The future of AI-powered credit assessment will involve blockchain integration, quantum computing, and explainable AI models, paving the way for a more secure and inclusive financial ecosystem. 🚀

9.2 AI-Driven Chatbots & Virtual Banking Assistants

The banking industry is undergoing a digital transformation, with AI-powered chatbots and virtual banking assistants redefining customer service, financial management, and operational efficiency. By leveraging natural language processing (NLP), machine learning (ML), and conversational AI, these AI-driven assistants can handle customer inquiries, provide financial advice, automate transactions, and detect fraud—all in real-time.

In this chapter, we will explore how AI-powered chatbots enhance banking experiences, their benefits, challenges, ethical considerations, and the future of virtual banking assistants in the financial sector.

1. The Rise of AI Chatbots in Banking

1.1 Traditional Banking vs. AI-Powered Digital Banking

Historically, banking services were conducted in-person or over the phone, requiring customers to wait in long queues or deal with inefficient support systems. With AI-driven chatbots and virtual assistants, banks can now provide:

✓ 24/7 customer support without human intervention.

✓ Instant responses to customer queries.

✓ Personalized financial advice based on customer data.

✓ Seamless transaction automation (bill payments, fund transfers, loan applications).

◆ **Example**: Bank of America's Erica, an AI-driven banking assistant, has handled over 1 billion interactions, assisting customers with account management, credit monitoring, and financial planning.

1.2 How AI Chatbots Work in Banking

AI-driven chatbots use machine learning, natural language understanding (NLU), and predictive analytics to interpret customer queries and respond intelligently. Key components include:

✓ **Natural Language Processing (NLP)** – Enables chatbots to understand and process human speech and text.

✓ **Machine Learning (ML)** – Allows AI assistants to learn from customer interactions and improve over time.

✓ **Sentiment Analysis** – Helps chatbots detect customer emotions and provide appropriate responses.

✓ **Data Analytics** – AI analyzes user behavior to offer personalized financial insights.

◆ **Example**: Apple's Siri and Google Assistant can now execute voice-based banking commands, such as checking balances or making payments.

2. Key Benefits of AI-Powered Banking Assistants

2.1 Enhanced Customer Service & Engagement

✓ AI chatbots provide instant, accurate responses to banking-related queries.

✓ Reduces customer wait times and enhances satisfaction.

✓ Supports multiple languages, making banking more inclusive.

◆ **Example**: HSBC's AI chatbot Amy handles over 100,000 customer inquiries per month, reducing workload for human agents.

2.2 Personalized Financial Advice

✓ AI assistants analyze spending habits and income patterns to provide:

- Budgeting recommendations
- Savings strategies
- Investment advice

✓ Helps customers track expenses, manage loans, and optimize financial goals.

◆ **Example**: Capital One's chatbot Eno proactively alerts users about unusual transactions and spending trends.

2.3 Fraud Prevention & Security Alerts

✓ AI chatbots monitor transactions in real-time to detect fraud.

✓ Alerts customers about suspicious activities, unauthorized transactions, and account breaches.

✓ Uses multi-factor authentication (MFA) and biometric verification for added security.

◆ **Example**: Wells Fargo's AI assistant monitors transactions and alerts customers about potential fraud risks via mobile notifications.

2.4 Cost Savings & Operational Efficiency

✓ AI-driven chatbots reduce the need for large customer service teams, saving banks millions in operational costs.

✓ Automates routine banking tasks, such as:

- Password resets
- Loan application processing
- Account balance inquiries

◆ **Example**: JPMorgan Chase's AI-powered system COiN analyzes legal contracts in seconds—tasks that previously took human employees 360,000 hours per year.

3. Use Cases of AI Chatbots in Banking

3.1 Conversational Banking & Voice Assistants

✓ Customers can use voice commands to:

- Check account balances
- Transfer funds
- Pay bills

✓ Integrated with Amazon Alexa, Google Assistant, and Apple Siri.

◆ **Example**: U.S. Bank's AI assistant allows customers to perform transactions hands-free via smart speakers.

3.2 AI for Loan & Mortgage Processing

✓ AI chatbots guide customers through loan applications, offering instant approvals.

✓ Analyzes credit history and financial behavior to suggest customized loan options.

◆ **Example**: HDFC Bank's AI chatbot Eva answers loan eligibility queries and automates approvals, reducing paperwork.

3.3 AI-Driven Investment & Wealth Management Assistants

✓ Robo-advisors provide AI-powered investment recommendations.

✓ Monitors stock market trends to help users diversify portfolios.

✓ Offers risk assessment and savings strategies.

◆ **Example**: Charles Schwab's Intelligent Portfolios use AI to manage customer investments without human intervention.

3.4 AI for Customer Onboarding & KYC Compliance

✓ AI chatbots streamline Know Your Customer (KYC) verification.

✓ Uses facial recognition, biometrics, and ID scanning for instant account opening.

◈ **Example**: Revolut's AI assistant automates KYC verification, reducing account setup time from days to minutes.

4. Challenges & Ethical Considerations in AI Banking Assistants

4.1 Data Privacy & Security Concerns

✓ AI chatbots collect sensitive financial data, raising privacy risks.

✓ Cybercriminals can exploit chatbots to phish customer credentials.

◈ **Solution**: Banks must implement end-to-end encryption, biometric authentication, and AI-driven fraud detection to enhance security.

4.2 Bias in AI Decision-Making

✓ AI chatbots may inherit biases from training data, leading to unfair lending or investment advice.

◈ **Solution**: Banks should regularly audit AI algorithms to ensure fairness and transparency.

4.3 Trust & Transparency Issues

✓ Customers may hesitate to trust AI with high-value transactions or complex banking queries.

◈ **Solution**: Implement human-AI collaboration, where complex inquiries are transferred to human agents.

5. The Future of AI-Driven Banking Assistants

5.1 Hyper-Personalized AI Banking

✓ Future AI chatbots will use predictive analytics to offer highly personalized financial insights.

✓ AI will anticipate customer needs before they arise.

5.2 AI-Powered Emotional Intelligence

✓ Next-gen chatbots will detect customer emotions and adjust responses accordingly.

✓ AI will provide empathetic support during financial distress.

5.3 Blockchain Integration for AI Chatbots

✓ Blockchain will enhance data security and transparency in AI-powered banking.

✓ AI chatbots will facilitate decentralized finance (DeFi) transactions.

Conclusion: The AI Revolution in Banking

AI-driven chatbots and virtual banking assistants are transforming customer experiences, optimizing financial operations, and enhancing security. By providing 24/7 support, personalized financial insights, and fraud detection, AI is making banking faster, smarter, and more accessible.

However, to ensure trust, fairness, and security, banks must:

✓ Address data privacy concerns and implement strong encryption.

✓ Continuously audit AI systems to eliminate bias.

✓ Ensure human oversight for complex banking interactions.

As AI technology advances, the future of banking will be more intuitive, customer-centric, and secure than ever before. 🚀

9.3 Personalized Financial Advice via AI

In today's fast-paced financial landscape, customers demand tailored financial guidance that adapts to their unique needs. Traditional financial advisory services, often expensive and limited to high-net-worth individuals, are being transformed by AI-driven financial advisory systems. Using machine learning (ML), natural language processing (NLP), predictive analytics, and big data, AI-powered platforms can provide customized investment strategies, budgeting recommendations, debt management plans, and retirement planning—all in real-time.

This chapter explores how AI is redefining personalized financial advice, its benefits, challenges, ethical considerations, and future advancements.

1. The Shift from Traditional to AI-Powered Financial Advice

1.1 Traditional Financial Advisors: Challenges & Limitations

✓ **High Costs** – Hiring human financial advisors can be expensive, often limiting access to wealthy individuals.

✓ **Limited Availability** – Traditional advisors can only handle a limited number of clients at a time.

✓ **Subjectivity & Human Bias** – Advisors may have conflicts of interest or provide biased recommendations.

◆ **Example**: A human financial planner might favor investment options with higher commission incentives, leading to potential conflicts of interest.

1.2 The AI Revolution in Personalized Financial Advice

AI-powered advisory platforms overcome traditional limitations by:

✓ Providing 24/7 financial guidance.

✓ Analyzing massive datasets to detect investment opportunities.

✓ Offering unbiased recommendations based on data-driven insights.

✓ Adapting strategies in real-time as market conditions change.

◆ **Example**: Robo-advisors like Betterment and Wealthfront provide AI-driven investment strategies based on a user's financial goals, risk tolerance, and market trends.

2. How AI Provides Personalized Financial Advice

2.1 AI-Powered Budgeting & Expense Tracking

✓ AI-powered apps analyze income, spending habits, and financial goals to suggest personalized budgeting strategies.

✓ Identifies overspending trends and recommends cost-cutting measures.

✓ Automates savings by allocating funds to emergency savings or investments.

◆ **Example**: Mint and YNAB (You Need a Budget) use AI to categorize expenses, predict future spending, and offer budgeting tips.

2.2 AI for Investment & Portfolio Management

✓ Uses machine learning algorithms to analyze market trends, risk levels, and investment behaviors.

✓ Provides real-time stock recommendations based on an individual's risk tolerance.

✓ Continuously rebalances portfolios for optimal returns.

◆ **Example**: AI-driven robo-advisors like Wealthsimple use automated rebalancing to maintain optimal asset allocation.

2.3 AI in Debt Management & Loan Optimization

✓ AI assesses loan history, income stability, and creditworthiness to recommend:

- Optimal debt repayment strategies (e.g., avalanche vs. snowball method).
- Refinancing opportunities for lower interest rates.

✓ Helps users improve credit scores by analyzing financial behaviors.

◆ **Example**: Tally uses AI to automate credit card debt repayment, optimizing payments to reduce interest costs.

2.4 AI for Retirement & Long-Term Financial Planning

✓ Uses predictive analytics to estimate future expenses, inflation rates, and retirement needs.

✓ Provides tax-efficient withdrawal strategies for retirees.

✓ Recommends diversified investment plans for long-term growth.

◆ **Example**: Personal Capital offers AI-powered retirement forecasting tools, helping users plan for future financial security.

3. Benefits of AI-Driven Personalized Financial Advice

3.1 Accessibility & Affordability

✓ AI democratizes financial advice, making it available to all income groups.

✓ Reduces reliance on high-cost human financial advisors.

3.2 Data-Driven Decision-Making

✓ AI removes human bias and makes recommendations purely based on historical and real-time financial data.

3.3 Real-Time Adjustments & Market Adaptability

✓ AI can adapt investment strategies instantly in response to market fluctuations.

✓ Provides dynamic risk assessment based on changing financial situations.

◆ **Example**: AI-driven platforms can automatically shift funds to safer assets during a market downturn.

4. Challenges & Ethical Concerns in AI-Driven Financial Advice

4.1 Data Privacy & Security Risks

✓ AI-driven financial platforms require access to sensitive personal data.

✓ Risk of data breaches and cyberattacks.

◆ **Solution**: Financial institutions must implement end-to-end encryption, secure authentication, and compliance with data privacy laws (e.g., GDPR, CCPA).

4.2 Algorithmic Bias & Fairness

✔ AI models may develop biases based on historical financial data, leading to unfair lending or investment advice.

◆ **Solution**: Regular bias audits and transparent AI models are essential to ensure fairness.

4.3 Lack of Human Intuition & Emotional Understanding

✔ AI lacks the emotional intelligence that human financial advisors offer.

✔ May not fully understand personal financial crises or unique life circumstances.

◆ **Solution**: Hybrid models where AI handles routine tasks while human advisors provide emotional guidance.

5. The Future of AI in Personalized Financial Advice

5.1 AI-Powered Voice Assistants for Finance

✔ AI-driven voice assistants will allow users to:

- Check financial health.
- Make investments.
- Get real-time financial coaching via Alexa, Siri, or Google Assistant.

◆ **Example**: JP Morgan Chase's AI assistant can execute trades and provide market insights using voice commands.

5.2 AI & Blockchain for Transparent Financial Advisory

✔ Blockchain will enhance security and transparency in AI-driven financial advice.

✔ AI-driven smart contracts will automate investment and wealth management.

◆ **Example**: DeFi (Decentralized Finance) platforms are integrating AI and blockchain for trustless investment automation.

5.3 AI for Hyper-Personalized Financial Strategies

✓ AI will continuously analyze life events (job changes, home purchases, economic shifts) to update financial plans in real-time.

✓ Future AI assistants will predict financial needs before customers even realize them.

◆ **Example**: A future AI assistant could automatically adjust investment allocations when a user's salary increases.

Conclusion: The AI-Powered Future of Financial Advisory

AI-driven personalized financial advice is revolutionizing the way individuals manage money, invest, and plan for the future. By leveraging machine learning, predictive analytics, and real-time data processing, AI provides affordable, data-driven, and accessible financial guidance to a broader audience.

However, to ensure fairness, security, and trust, financial institutions must:

✓ Implement strong data privacy measures.

✓ Address algorithmic biases.

✓ Develop human-AI hybrid advisory models to combine emotional intelligence with AI's analytical power.

As AI continues to evolve, the future of financial advisory will be more automated, personalized, and predictive, enabling individuals to make smarter financial decisions with ease. 🚀

9.4 Regulatory Challenges in AI-Powered Finance

As artificial intelligence (AI) transforms the financial sector, regulatory bodies worldwide face the challenge of ensuring fairness, security, and compliance while allowing innovation to thrive. AI is now embedded in credit scoring, fraud detection, algorithmic trading, robo-advisors, and risk assessment, making financial services faster and more efficient. However, this technological shift introduces ethical dilemmas, bias risks, cybersecurity threats, and legal complexities that demand stringent oversight.

This chapter explores the regulatory landscape, key challenges, and future directions for AI governance in finance.

1. The Growing Need for AI Regulations in Finance

1.1 Why Regulating AI in Finance is Essential

✓ **Consumer Protection** – Prevents AI from making biased lending or investment decisions.

✓ **Financial Stability** – Reduces risks from AI-driven trading volatility.

✓ **Data Privacy & Security** – Protects sensitive financial data from misuse or breaches.

✓ **Transparency & Explainability** – Ensures fair and interpretable AI decision-making.

◆ **Example**: The 2010 Flash Crash demonstrated how AI-driven high-frequency trading algorithms can cause extreme market instability within minutes.

1.2 Key Global Regulatory Bodies Governing AI in Finance

✓ **United States** – The SEC (Securities and Exchange Commission), Federal Reserve, and CFPB (Consumer Financial Protection Bureau) oversee AI applications in banking and trading.

✓ **European Union** – The AI Act and GDPR (General Data Protection Regulation) regulate financial AI usage.

✓ **United Kingdom** – The Financial Conduct Authority (FCA) enforces AI risk and compliance.

✓ **China** – The Cyberspace Administration of China (CAC) enforces strict AI security laws in financial services.

◆ **Example**: The EU AI Act (2024) classifies AI-driven financial systems as high-risk, requiring transparency and human oversight.

2. Key Regulatory Challenges in AI-Powered Finance

2.1 Bias and Discrimination in AI Decision-Making

✓ AI models used in credit scoring and lending can inherit biases from historical data.

✓ Discriminatory outcomes may unfairly reject loan applications from minorities or low-income groups.

◈ **Case Study**: In 2019, Apple's AI-driven credit card was found to offer lower credit limits to women, raising concerns over algorithmic bias.

◈ **Solution**: Regulators are demanding fair AI auditing, explainability, and bias mitigation techniques to ensure ethical AI lending practices.

2.2 Data Privacy & Security Risks in AI-Driven Finance

✓ AI systems process massive amounts of financial data, increasing the risk of hacking and misuse.

✓ Compliance with GDPR, CCPA, and other privacy regulations is critical.

◈ **Example**: In 2022, a large AI-powered fintech company suffered a data breach, exposing millions of customer transactions.

◈ **Solution**: Regulators require banks and fintech firms to implement:

✓ End-to-end encryption.

✓ AI-driven fraud detection.

✓ Multi-factor authentication (MFA).

2.3 Lack of Explainability in AI Models

✓ AI-driven trading algorithms, robo-advisors, and loan approval systems often operate as black boxes.

✓ Regulators demand explainability so financial decisions can be audited and justified.

◆ **Example**: The EU AI Act mandates that AI systems in financial services must be interpretable and explainable to ensure accountability.

◆ **Solution**: AI-driven finance firms are developing Explainable AI (XAI) to enhance transparency.

2.4 Algorithmic Trading & Market Manipulation Risks

✓ AI-driven high-frequency trading (HFT) algorithms can cause market instability and flash crashes.

✓ Regulators worry about AI market manipulation and insider trading risks.

◆ **Example**: The SEC has fined multiple hedge funds for using AI-driven trading algorithms to engage in manipulative trading practices.

◆ **Solution:**

✓ Implement AI-driven trade monitoring systems.

✓ Enforce AI trading regulations that require human oversight.

3. Compliance Strategies for AI-Driven Financial Services

3.1 Ethical AI Audits & Bias Testing

✓ Regular AI audits ensure fair, unbiased, and compliant AI decision-making.

✓ Regulators require firms to test AI models for discrimination and bias.

◆ **Example**: Financial institutions now use Fairness-Aware AI models to prevent biased lending practices.

3.2 Implementing Explainable AI (XAI) for Compliance

✓ Banks and fintech firms must develop transparent AI models that regulators can audit.

✓ Explainability techniques include:

- **SHAP** (Shapley Additive Explanations) for AI decision tracking.
- **LIME** (Local Interpretable Model-Agnostic Explanations) for understanding predictions.

◆ **Example**: The FCA requires AI-powered financial services to provide clear explanations for credit approvals and investment recommendations.

3.3 Strengthening AI Cybersecurity & Data Protection

✓ AI-driven financial institutions must adopt zero-trust security frameworks.

✓ Implement blockchain-based AI security to enhance data integrity and privacy.

◆ **Example**: The U.S. Treasury Department mandates financial AI models to comply with strict cybersecurity standards.

4. The Future of AI Regulations in Finance

4.1 Stricter AI Compliance Laws

✓ Governments will introduce stricter AI financial regulations to protect consumers.

✓ More oversight on AI-powered lending, trading, and risk assessment.

◆ **Example**: The EU's Digital Finance Strategy aims to regulate AI-based fintech platforms.

4.2 Global AI Financial Regulation Standards

✓ Regulators may develop global AI governance frameworks to ensure consistency across markets.

◆ **Example**: The Financial Stability Board (FSB) is working on global AI regulatory policies for finance.

4.3 AI-Blockchain Integration for Regulatory Compliance

✓ Blockchain will enhance AI decision traceability and compliance.

✓ Smart contracts will be used for automated AI regulatory reporting.

◆ **Example**: AI-powered RegTech (Regulatory Technology) solutions use blockchain to automate compliance monitoring.

Conclusion: Balancing AI Innovation & Financial Regulations

AI-powered finance is revolutionizing banking, trading, lending, and fraud detection, but it also introduces bias risks, security threats, market instability, and transparency concerns. Regulators worldwide are tightening AI governance to ensure ethical, fair, and compliant financial services.

For AI-driven financial firms to thrive in a heavily regulated landscape, they must:

✓ Implement transparent AI models with explainability features.

✓ Strengthen cybersecurity and data privacy protections.

✓ Conduct regular AI audits to eliminate bias.

✓ Follow global regulatory frameworks to ensure compliance.

The future of AI in finance will depend on responsible innovation—where advanced AI technologies and regulatory oversight work together to create a fair, secure, and efficient financial ecosystem. 🚀

10. AI in Manufacturing: Smart Factories & Predictive Maintenance

AI is revolutionizing manufacturing by enabling smart factories, automation, and predictive maintenance, leading to increased efficiency, reduced downtime, and cost savings. AI-powered robotics, IoT sensors, and machine learning models allow factories to optimize production lines, detect equipment failures before they occur, and enhance supply chain management. Predictive maintenance helps manufacturers anticipate machinery breakdowns, minimize disruptions, and extend equipment lifespan. This chapter explores how AI-driven automation is transforming industrial processes, the role of digital twins in manufacturing, and the challenges of AI adoption, workforce integration, and cybersecurity in smart factories.

10.1 AI & IoT for Industrial Automation

The combination of Artificial Intelligence (AI) and the Internet of Things (IoT) is revolutionizing industrial automation, enabling smarter, more efficient, and highly adaptive manufacturing processes. AI-powered IoT (AIoT) enhances automation by integrating real-time data collection, predictive analytics, and machine learning (ML) to optimize production lines, reduce downtime, and improve safety. Industries such as manufacturing, logistics, energy, and construction are leveraging AIoT to create smart factories, autonomous systems, and self-optimizing supply chains.

In this chapter, we explore how AI and IoT are reshaping industrial automation, their benefits, challenges, and real-world applications.

1. Understanding AIoT: The Intersection of AI and IoT

1.1 What is AIoT?

✓ **IoT (Internet of Things):** A network of connected sensors, machines, and devices that collect and transmit data in real-time.

✓ **AI (Artificial Intelligence):** Machine learning and data analytics techniques that process and interpret IoT-generated data for decision-making.

✔ **AIoT (AI + IoT):** A smart system where AI enhances IoT capabilities by providing predictive analytics, real-time automation, and autonomous decision-making.

◆ **Example:** In smart factories, IoT sensors monitor machine performance, while AI predicts equipment failures before they happen.

1.2 How AI Enhances IoT for Industrial Automation

✔ **Predictive Maintenance** – AI detects potential machine failures using IoT sensor data.

✔ **Autonomous Operations** – AI-driven robotic arms and self-learning machines optimize production efficiency.

✔ **Real-Time Analytics** – AI processes IoT data instantly to make faster operational decisions.

✔ **Supply Chain Optimization** – AI analyzes IoT-generated logistics data to reduce delays and costs.

◆ **Example:** Siemens' AI-powered factories use IoT-connected robots and smart sensors to improve manufacturing efficiency and reduce energy waste.

2. Applications of AI & IoT in Industrial Automation

2.1 Smart Factories: The Rise of Industry 4.0

✔ AIoT-powered factories use robotic automation, digital twins, and machine learning to self-optimize production lines.

✔ AI analyzes sensor data from machines to adjust workflow and prevent breakdowns.

◆ **Example:** General Electric (GE) Digital's Brilliant Manufacturing Suite integrates AIoT to enhance factory automation and predictive maintenance.

2.2 AIoT for Predictive Maintenance

✔ IoT sensors collect vibration, temperature, and pressure data from machines.

✔ AI algorithms detect early signs of wear and tear to prevent unplanned downtime.

◆ **Case Study**: Rolls-Royce's AI-driven aircraft engines use IoT sensors to predict failures and schedule maintenance, saving millions in operational costs.

2.3 AI-Driven Robotics for Automated Manufacturing

✓ AI-powered collaborative robots (cobots) work alongside human employees to enhance efficiency.

✓ Machine learning enables robots to self-learn and improve performance over time.

◆ **Example**: Tesla's Gigafactories use AI-driven robotics for precision assembly and automated quality control.

2.4 AIoT in Supply Chain & Logistics

✓ AI-powered IoT devices track inventory, shipments, and warehouse conditions in real-time.

✓ AI predicts delivery delays, optimizes routing, and improves fleet management.

◆ **Example**: Amazon's AI-driven logistics system automates warehouse management using IoT-connected robots.

2.5 AI for Quality Control & Defect Detection

✓ AI-powered computer vision analyzes product defects faster than human inspectors.

✓ IoT sensors detect temperature, pressure, and humidity variations affecting product quality.

◆ **Example**: Foxconn, a major electronics manufacturer, uses AIoT-based defect detection to reduce waste and improve product reliability.

3. Benefits of AI & IoT in Industrial Automation

3.1 Increased Efficiency & Productivity

✔ AI-powered automation speeds up manufacturing, logistics, and inventory management.

✔ Smart factories self-optimize workflows, reducing human errors.

3.2 Reduced Downtime & Maintenance Costs

✔ Predictive maintenance prevents unexpected machine breakdowns, saving companies millions.

✔ AI-driven monitoring systems ensure continuous production flow.

3.3 Improved Workplace Safety

✔ AI-powered IoT wearables detect hazards and ensure worker safety in industrial environments.

✔ AI-driven robotics handle dangerous tasks, reducing workplace injuries.

◆ **Example**: Boeing's AI-driven robotic assembly lines improve worker safety by automating repetitive tasks.

3.4 Lower Operational Costs

✔ AIoT automation reduces waste, optimizes energy consumption, and streamlines supply chains.

✔ Self-learning AI models improve decision-making, minimizing costly errors.

4. Challenges & Risks of AIoT in Industrial Automation

4.1 Cybersecurity Risks

✔ AIoT systems are vulnerable to hacking, data breaches, and cyberattacks.

✔ AI-driven intrusion detection systems (IDS) must be implemented for security.

◈ **Example**: In 2020, a cyberattack on a major European factory disrupted AI-driven production lines.

4.2 High Implementation Costs

✓ AIoT adoption requires significant upfront investment in sensors, AI models, and infrastructure.

✓ Companies need skilled professionals for AIoT system management.

◈ **Solution**: Cloud-based AIoT platforms help reduce cost barriers for small & medium enterprises (SMEs).

4.3 Data Privacy & Compliance Issues

✓ AIoT collects massive amounts of sensitive industrial and employee data.

✓ Companies must comply with GDPR, CCPA, and industry-specific data regulations.

◈ **Solution**: Implement strong data encryption, access controls, and AI-powered compliance monitoring.

5. The Future of AI & IoT in Industrial Automation

5.1 AIoT-Powered Edge Computing

✓ AI models will run directly on IoT devices (Edge AI), reducing latency and improving real-time decision-making.

◈ **Example**: NVIDIA's AI Edge devices enable real-time AIoT automation in factories.

5.2 Digital Twins for Smart Manufacturing

✓ AI-driven digital twins will simulate and optimize industrial operations.

✓ Virtual models will help predict failures and improve efficiency.

◆ **Example**: Siemens' AI-powered digital twin technology enhances factory performance monitoring.

5.3 AIoT & 5G Integration

✓ High-speed 5G networks will enhance AIoT performance by enabling real-time data transfer and automation.

◆ **Example**: Ford's AI-driven smart factories use 5G-powered IoT for faster production line automation.

Conclusion: AI & IoT – The Future of Industrial Automation

The integration of AI and IoT is reshaping industrial automation, leading to smarter, safer, and more efficient operations. AI-powered predictive maintenance, robotics, smart factories, and supply chain automation are unlocking new levels of productivity while reducing costs. However, challenges like cybersecurity risks, high implementation costs, and data privacy concerns must be addressed.

As AIoT continues to evolve, innovations in Edge AI, digital twins, and 5G will drive the next wave of industrial automation, making factories more intelligent, connected, and autonomous than ever before. 🚀

10.2 Predictive Maintenance with AI-Powered Sensors

Predictive maintenance, powered by AI-driven sensors and IoT (Internet of Things) technology, is transforming industrial operations by minimizing downtime, optimizing equipment efficiency, and reducing maintenance costs. Traditional reactive and preventive maintenance methods often lead to unnecessary repairs or unexpected failures, causing financial losses. However, AI-powered predictive maintenance (PdM) leverages machine learning (ML), big data analytics, and real-time sensor monitoring to detect early signs of equipment failure before they occur.

In this chapter, we explore how AI-powered sensors revolutionize predictive maintenance, the key benefits, challenges, and real-world applications.

1. Understanding Predictive Maintenance with AI

1.1 What is Predictive Maintenance (PdM)?

✓ Traditional Maintenance Approaches:

- **Reactive Maintenance**: Fixing equipment after failure occurs (high risk, high cost).
- **Preventive Maintenance**: Regular scheduled servicing, even if no issue exists (often inefficient).

✓ **Predictive Maintenance (PdM):** Uses AI and IoT sensors to analyze real-time equipment data and predict failures before they happen.

♦ **Example**: Instead of manually checking a factory machine every month, AI sensors monitor temperature, vibrations, and pressure in real-time to detect early warning signs of failure.

1.2 How AI-Powered Sensors Enable PdM

✓ **IoT Sensors Collect Data**: Installed on machines to measure temperature, vibration, pressure, humidity, and performance levels.

✓ **AI & ML Algorithms Analyze Patterns**: AI detects anomalies, unusual trends, and failure indicators in sensor data.

✓ **Real-Time Alerts**: AI predicts failures and notifies maintenance teams before breakdowns occur.

♦ **Example**: In aircraft maintenance, AI-powered sensors monitor jet engine performance to prevent mid-flight failures, reducing operational risks.

2. Key Components of AI-Powered Predictive Maintenance

2.1 IoT-Enabled Smart Sensors

✓ Collect real-time machine data and detect minor fluctuations that could indicate future failures.

✓ Installed on motors, pumps, turbines, conveyor belts, and industrial robots.

◆ **Example**: Siemens' AI-powered factory sensors detect micro-vibrations in machines, predicting failures weeks in advance.

2.2 AI & Machine Learning Models for Failure Prediction

✓ AI learns historical failure patterns and identifies abnormal behavior.

✓ Uses techniques like:

- **Time Series Analysis**: Predicts when a failure is likely to happen.
- **Anomaly Detection**: Identifies unexpected sensor readings.
- **Deep Learning Models**: Recognizes complex failure patterns over time

.

◆ **Example**: GE Aviation's AI models predict engine failures, saving millions in maintenance costs.

2.3 Cloud & Edge Computing for Data Processing

✓ **Cloud AI Models**: Analyze sensor data from multiple machines and optimize maintenance schedules.

✓ **Edge AI**: Processes data locally on IoT devices, allowing faster failure predictions.

◆ **Example**: Rolls-Royce's AI-powered aircraft engines use Edge AI to make real-time maintenance decisions mid-flight.

3. Applications of AI-Powered Predictive Maintenance

3.1 Manufacturing & Industrial Automation

✓ AI-powered sensors monitor production lines, preventing sudden machine breakdowns.

✓ Ensures continuous factory operations and minimal downtime.

◆ **Case Study**: General Motors (GM) uses AI-driven PdM to reduce assembly line failures by 30%, improving overall efficiency.

3.2 Energy Sector (Power Plants & Wind Turbines)

✓ AI analyzes oil pipelines, turbines, and power grids for early failure detection.

✓ Reduces maintenance costs and prevents hazardous failures.

◆ **Example**: Siemens Gamesa Wind Turbines use AI-powered sensors to predict gearbox failures, reducing maintenance expenses.

3.3 Transportation & Automotive Industry

✓ AI sensors in trucks, trains, and aircraft detect engine wear and fuel efficiency issues.

✓ Reduces unexpected breakdowns and improves safety.

◆ **Example**: Boeing's AI-driven predictive maintenance system identifies potential aircraft part failures before takeoff, enhancing flight safety.

3.4 Oil & Gas Industry

✓ AI-powered pipeline sensors detect leaks, pressure drops, and corrosion early.

✓ Prevents environmental disasters and costly repairs.

◆ **Example**: Shell's AI-driven PdM system reduces offshore drilling maintenance costs by over 20%.

4. Benefits of AI-Powered Predictive Maintenance

4.1 Reduced Downtime & Increased Productivity

✓ AI predicts failures before they occur, avoiding unplanned shutdowns.

✓ Companies experience higher efficiency and smoother operations.

◆ **Example**: AI-driven maintenance at Tesla's Gigafactories keeps production running 24/7.

4.2 Cost Savings on Repairs & Labor

✓ Proactive maintenance prevents costly emergency repairs.

✓ Reduces the need for manual inspections and unnecessary servicing.

◆ **Example**: AI-powered predictive maintenance in oil rigs saves millions in repair costs annually.

4.3 Improved Equipment Lifespan

✓ AI-driven insights optimize machine performance, reducing wear and tear.

✓ Extends the life of expensive industrial machinery.

◆ **Example**: AI-powered sensors in nuclear plants extend reactor lifespan by detecting early signs of material degradation.

4.4 Enhanced Safety & Risk Prevention

✓ AI detects hazardous conditions before accidents occur.

✓ Ensures compliance with safety regulations and industry standards.

◆ **Example**: AI-powered PdM in mining equipment prevents mechanical failures, reducing worker injuries.

5. Challenges of AI-Driven Predictive Maintenance

5.1 High Initial Investment

✓ AI-powered sensors and ML models require high upfront costs.

✓ Companies need data scientists and skilled technicians for AI system management.

◆ **Solution**: Cloud-based PdM solutions offer subscription-based pricing, reducing capital expenses.

5.2 Data Quality & Integration Issues

✓ AI models require high-quality historical failure data for accurate predictions.

✔ Many industries still rely on legacy equipment without IoT sensors.

◆ **Solution**: Use retrofitted AI sensors for older machines and apply data fusion techniques for better AI insights.

5.3 Cybersecurity Risks

✔ AI-driven PdM systems depend on cloud and IoT networks, making them vulnerable to cyberattacks.

✔ Industrial cyber threats can manipulate sensor data and cause system failures.

◆ **Solution**: Implement AI-powered cybersecurity systems, blockchain-based data protection, and secure cloud architectures.

6. The Future of AI-Powered Predictive Maintenance

6.1 AI & 5G for Real-Time Predictive Maintenance

✔ 5G-powered AI sensors enable instant failure detection and faster decision-making.

◆ **Example**: BMW uses 5G-enabled AI sensors for predictive maintenance in autonomous vehicles.

6.2 Digital Twins for Predictive Maintenance

✔ AI-driven digital twins simulate machine operations to predict failures more accurately.

◆ **Example**: NASA uses AI-powered digital twins to predict failures in spacecraft components.

6.3 Self-Healing AI-Driven Machines

✔ AI will enable autonomous machines that repair themselves without human intervention.

◆ **Example**: Future AI-driven industrial robots will detect minor defects and self-correct without stopping production.

Conclusion: The Future of AI-Driven Predictive Maintenance

AI-powered predictive maintenance is revolutionizing industrial automation, reducing downtime, cutting costs, and improving operational efficiency. While challenges like high implementation costs and cybersecurity risks remain, the benefits far outweigh the drawbacks. As AI, 5G, digital twins, and self-healing machines evolve, predictive maintenance will become even more accurate, autonomous, and essential for future industries. 🚀

10.3 AI in Supply Chain Optimization

Supply chains are the backbone of global commerce, ensuring products move efficiently from manufacturers to consumers. However, traditional supply chain management faces challenges like demand fluctuations, logistics delays, inventory mismanagement, and unforeseen disruptions (e.g., pandemics, natural disasters). AI-powered supply chain optimization is revolutionizing logistics by improving efficiency, reducing costs, and enhancing decision-making.

This chapter explores how AI-driven technologies such as machine learning (ML), predictive analytics, robotic process automation (RPA), and real-time data monitoring are transforming supply chain operations.

1. Understanding AI in Supply Chain Optimization

1.1 The Role of AI in Supply Chain Management

✓ AI enhances supply chain operations by automating processes, analyzing vast data sets, and improving accuracy in demand forecasting.

✓ It replaces outdated manual systems with self-learning algorithms that adapt to market changes in real time.

◆ **Example**: Amazon's AI-powered supply chain predicts customer demand and automatically adjusts inventory and delivery routes.

1.2 Key AI Technologies Used in Supply Chains

✔ **Machine Learning (ML):** Identifies patterns in supply chain data for better decision-making.

✔ **Predictive Analytics**: Forecasts demand, supplier performance, and potential disruptions.

✔ **Natural Language Processing (NLP):** Automates communication in logistics operations.

✔ **Computer Vision**: Scans barcodes, detects product defects, and manages warehouse automation.

✔ **Robotic Process Automation (RPA):** Reduces human intervention in repetitive tasks (e.g., invoicing, order processing).

◈ **Example**: Walmart uses AI-powered computer vision and predictive analytics to track inventory shortages in real time.

2. AI in Demand Forecasting & Inventory Management

2.1 AI-Powered Demand Forecasting

✔ AI analyzes historical sales data, market trends, and consumer behavior to predict future demand.

✔ Helps businesses avoid stockouts and overstocking, optimizing inventory levels.

◈ **Example**: Nike uses AI-driven demand forecasting to align production with consumer trends, reducing waste and maximizing sales.

2.2 AI for Smart Inventory Management

✔ AI-driven systems track inventory in real-time and send automatic alerts when stock is low.

✔ Uses automated warehouse robots to manage and move goods efficiently.

◆ **Example**: Alibaba's AI warehouse robots increase order fulfillment speed by 70%, reducing errors and operational costs.

3. AI in Logistics & Transportation Optimization

3.1 AI for Route Optimization

✓ AI analyzes traffic patterns, weather conditions, and delivery schedules to create optimal transportation routes.

✓ Reduces fuel costs, delivery times, and transportation inefficiencies.

◆ **Example**: UPS uses AI-powered route optimization, saving 10 million gallons of fuel annually and reducing emissions.

3.2 Autonomous Vehicles & Drones in Supply Chains

✓ AI enables self-driving trucks and delivery drones, reducing reliance on human drivers.

✓ Improves last-mile delivery speed and efficiency.

◆ **Example**: Amazon's AI-powered drones are being tested for autonomous package delivery.

3.3 AI-Powered Warehouse Automation

✓ AI-driven robotic arms, automated sorting systems, and smart conveyor belts streamline warehouse operations.

✓ Reduces errors and speeds up order fulfillment processes.

◆ **Example**: Amazon's AI-driven fulfillment centers use robotic arms to automate 75% of warehouse operations.

4. AI for Supplier & Risk Management

4.1 AI-Powered Supplier Performance Analysis

✔ AI assesses supplier reliability, delivery speed, and compliance based on historical data.

✔ Helps businesses choose the best suppliers and mitigate risks.

◆ **Example**: Coca-Cola's AI-driven supplier management system reduces procurement risks by analyzing vendor reliability.

4.2 AI for Risk Detection & Disruption Management

✔ AI predicts supply chain disruptions caused by natural disasters, pandemics, or geopolitical tensions.

✔ Uses real-time data from weather reports, economic trends, and global news to recommend solutions.

◆ **Example**: AI-driven supply chain models helped companies predict and manage COVID-19-related disruptions by adjusting inventory and logistics.

5. Benefits of AI in Supply Chain Optimization

5.1 Cost Reduction & Increased Efficiency

✔ AI eliminates inefficiencies, reduces waste, and optimizes transportation and inventory management.

✔ Automation reduces the need for manual intervention, lowering labor costs.

◆ **Example**: AI-driven supply chain analytics at Siemens reduced operational costs by 15%.

5.2 Faster & More Accurate Decision-Making

✔ AI processes vast amounts of data in seconds, providing real-time insights for decision-making.

✔ Helps businesses react quickly to market changes and consumer demands.

◆ **Example**: Tesla uses AI-powered demand forecasting to optimize vehicle production based on customer preferences.

5.3 Sustainability & Environmental Impact

✓ AI helps reduce carbon footprints by optimizing transportation routes and energy-efficient warehouses.

✓ Predicts waste levels and suggests ways to minimize excess inventory.

◆ **Example**: AI-driven logistics at DHL reduced CO_2 emissions by 30% using smarter route planning.

6. Challenges of AI-Powered Supply Chain Management

6.1 High Implementation Costs

✓ AI adoption requires significant investment in technology, skilled workforce, and system integration.

✓ Small and mid-sized businesses may struggle with upfront costs.

◆ **Solution**: Cloud-based AI supply chain solutions offer subscription models, making AI adoption more affordable.

6.2 Data Privacy & Cybersecurity Risks

✓ AI-powered supply chains rely on cloud networks, making them vulnerable to cyber threats.

✓ Sensitive supplier and inventory data must be secured against breaches.

◆ **Solution**: Companies are implementing blockchain technology and AI-driven cybersecurity to enhance protection.

6.3 Resistance to AI Adoption

✓ Some industries face resistance to AI-driven automation due to job displacement concerns.

✓ Employees may need reskilling to work with AI-powered supply chain tools.

◆ **Solution**: Companies should focus on AI-human collaboration, ensuring that AI assists workers rather than replaces them.

7. Future of AI in Supply Chain Optimization

7.1 AI & Blockchain for Transparent Supply Chains

✓ AI and blockchain improve supply chain visibility and traceability.

✓ Ensures authenticity and ethical sourcing of products.

◆ **Example**: IBM's AI-powered blockchain tracks food supply chains to prevent contamination.

7.2 Quantum AI for Complex Supply Chain Problems

✓ Quantum computing will allow AI to solve highly complex supply chain issues instantly.

✓ Helps in real-time global logistics optimization.

◆ **Example**: DHL & Google are developing Quantum AI to optimize international shipping routes.

7.3 AI-Enabled Circular Supply Chains

✓ AI will help companies reduce waste and recycle materials efficiently.

✓ Supports the shift toward sustainable and eco-friendly supply chains.

◆ **Example**: Unilever's AI-driven circular supply chain model improves plastic recycling efficiency.

Conclusion: The Future of AI in Supply Chains

AI-powered supply chain optimization is reshaping global logistics, making them more efficient, cost-effective, and resilient. Companies leveraging AI for demand forecasting, warehouse automation, transportation management, and risk mitigation will have a competitive advantage in the future. Despite challenges like high costs and cybersecurity risks, the benefits of AI-driven supply chains far outweigh the challenges. As AI continues to evolve with quantum computing, blockchain, and autonomous logistics, supply chains will become smarter, faster, and more sustainable in the coming years. 🚀

10.4 Real-World Applications: AI in Smart Factories

Artificial intelligence (AI) is revolutionizing manufacturing through smart factories, where automation, real-time data analytics, and machine learning drive productivity and efficiency. Traditional manufacturing processes, once dependent on manual labor and static production lines, are now becoming highly adaptive, self-learning, and data-driven. AI-powered smart factories integrate robotics, IoT sensors, predictive analytics, and computer vision to optimize operations, reduce waste, and enhance product quality.

This chapter explores real-world applications of AI in smart factories, showcasing how leading industries are leveraging AI-driven automation, predictive maintenance, and intelligent supply chain management to stay competitive in the digital age.

1. What Are Smart Factories?

A smart factory is a digitally connected and AI-powered manufacturing facility where machines, sensors, and systems communicate in real time. Unlike traditional factories, which rely on human intervention for decision-making, smart factories leverage AI to automate processes, predict failures, and optimize workflows dynamically.

✔ Key Features of Smart Factories:

- ◆ AI-driven robotics & automation
- ◆ IoT-enabled real-time monitoring
- ◆ Predictive maintenance using machine learning
- ◆ Computer vision for quality control
- ◆ Autonomous decision-making via AI-powered analytics

✦ **Example**: Siemens' smart factories use AI-driven automation to reduce production errors by 30% and increase output efficiency.

2. AI Applications in Smart Factories

2.1 AI for Predictive Maintenance

✓ AI-driven predictive maintenance helps manufacturers detect equipment failures before they occur, reducing downtime and maintenance costs.

✓ Machine learning algorithms analyze sensor data from equipment, predicting failures based on vibration, temperature, and performance metrics.

✦ **Example**: General Electric (GE) uses AI-powered predictive maintenance to reduce unexpected machine failures by 40% in its aircraft engine production.

2.2 AI-Enabled Robotics & Automation

✓ AI-powered collaborative robots (cobots) work alongside human operators to handle repetitive tasks, improving efficiency and safety.

✓ AI-driven robotic arms and automated assembly lines adjust to production demands in real-time.

✦ **Example**: Tesla's Gigafactories use AI-powered robots to assemble electric vehicles with precision, reducing defects and boosting efficiency.

2.3 Computer Vision for Quality Control

✓ AI-driven computer vision systems detect defects, anomalies, and inconsistencies in real-time, ensuring higher product quality and less waste.

✓ Machine learning models continuously improve defect detection over time.

✦ **Example**: BMW's AI-powered quality control system inspects car components with 99% accuracy, reducing production errors.

2.4 AI for Smart Supply Chain & Inventory Management

✓ AI-powered real-time demand forecasting ensures optimal raw material inventory.

✓ AI systems predict supply chain disruptions and recommend alternative solutions.

◆ **Example**: Foxconn, Apple's largest supplier, uses AI to optimize supply chain logistics, reducing delays and excess inventory costs.

2.5 Digital Twins for Factory Simulation

✓ AI-powered digital twins create virtual replicas of production lines, allowing manufacturers to simulate and optimize operations before implementation.

✓ Helps identify bottlenecks and inefficiencies in factory workflows.

◆ **Example**: Siemens uses digital twin technology to simulate factory layouts, improving production planning and efficiency.

3. Benefits of AI in Smart Factories

3.1 Increased Production Efficiency

✓ AI reduces bottlenecks, automates repetitive tasks, and optimizes machine performance, leading to faster production cycles.

◆ **Example**: AI-powered automation at Boeing's aircraft manufacturing reduced assembly time by 25%, boosting output.

3.2 Cost Savings & Reduced Waste

✓ AI-powered predictive maintenance lowers repair costs by preventing unexpected breakdowns.

✓ Automated quality control reduces material waste and ensures higher product quality.

◆ **Example**: AI-driven automation at Toyota cut manufacturing costs by 20% while improving efficiency.

3.3 Enhanced Workplace Safety

✔ AI-powered robotic systems handle hazardous tasks, reducing workplace accidents.

✔ AI-driven computer vision monitors factory environments for safety violations.

◈ **Example**: AI-driven safety monitoring at Daimler factories reduced workplace incidents by 40%.

4. Challenges in AI-Driven Smart Factories

4.1 High Implementation Costs

✔ Smart factories require significant upfront investment in AI infrastructure, robotics, and cloud computing.

✔ Small manufacturers may struggle with budget constraints for AI adoption.

◈ **Solution**: Cloud-based AI platforms offer scalable AI solutions for cost-effective implementation.

4.2 Data Security & Cyber Threats

✔ AI-driven smart factories rely on cloud computing, making them vulnerable to cyberattacks.

✔ Protecting sensitive factory data from hacking and breaches is a growing challenge.

◈ **Solution**: AI-driven cybersecurity measures (e.g., anomaly detection, blockchain-based authentication) enhance security.

4.3 Workforce Adaptation & AI Integration

✔ AI automation can replace some traditional jobs, leading to concerns about workforce displacement.

✓ Employees need upskilling in AI, robotics, and data analytics to work alongside smart factory technology.

♦ **Solution**: Companies should invest in reskilling programs to ensure AI-human collaboration in factories.

5. Future Trends in AI-Powered Smart Factories

5.1 Edge AI for Real-Time Processing

✓ AI models will move from cloud-based computing to edge AI, enabling real-time analytics and faster decision-making on factory floors.

♦ **Example**: Bosch is developing edge AI-based factory systems to enable real-time machine learning on industrial devices.

5.2 AI & 5G-Powered Smart Manufacturing

✓ 5G networks will enhance AI-driven factory automation by enabling ultra-fast data transmission between machines and sensors.

♦ **Example**: Ericsson and ABB are testing 5G-enabled AI automation to improve smart factory communication.

5.3 AI-Enabled Circular Manufacturing

✓ AI will optimize recycling, waste management, and energy efficiency in smart factories.
✓ AI-powered circular supply chains will promote sustainable manufacturing.

♦ **Example**: Unilever uses AI-powered circular economy models to reduce plastic waste in its supply chain.

6. Conclusion: AI is Shaping the Future of Smart Factories

AI-powered smart factories are revolutionizing global manufacturing, making them faster, smarter, and more efficient. By integrating AI-driven automation, predictive analytics, robotics, and computer vision, industries are achieving higher productivity, reduced costs, and improved quality control. Despite challenges such as high costs and cybersecurity risks, the benefits of AI-driven manufacturing far outweigh the drawbacks.

As AI technologies continue to advance with edge computing, 5G, and digital twins, smart factories will become fully autonomous, enabling manufacturers to meet global demand with greater efficiency and sustainability. 🚀

11. Retail AI: Personalized Shopping & Demand Forecasting

AI is transforming the retail industry by delivering personalized shopping experiences and highly accurate demand forecasting. Machine learning algorithms analyze customer preferences, browsing behavior, and purchase history to provide tailored product recommendations, dynamic pricing, and targeted marketing. AI-powered demand forecasting helps retailers predict inventory needs, optimize supply chains, and reduce waste, ensuring products are available when and where customers need them. This chapter explores how AI enhances customer engagement, streamlines retail operations, and addresses challenges like data privacy, AI-driven pricing strategies, and the future of AI in e-commerce and brick-and-mortar stores.

11.1 AI-Powered Recommendation Systems & Personalization

In today's digital world, personalization is key to enhancing customer experience, and AI-powered recommendation systems play a crucial role in delivering tailored content, products, and services. From e-commerce platforms and streaming services to financial planning and healthcare, businesses leverage AI to analyze user behavior, predict preferences, and provide personalized recommendations in real time.

This chapter explores how AI-driven recommendation engines work, their applications in various industries, and the benefits and challenges of implementing AI-based personalization.

1. Understanding AI-Powered Recommendation Systems

AI recommendation systems use machine learning, deep learning, and data analytics to analyze customer behavior and provide tailored product or content suggestions. These systems process massive amounts of data from customer interactions, browsing history, purchases, and preferences to predict what users are most likely to engage with.

1.1 Types of AI Recommendation Models

✓ **Collaborative Filtering**: Analyzes past user interactions and recommends items based on similar user preferences.

✓ **Content-Based Filtering**: Recommends items similar to those a user has previously engaged with.

✓ **Hybrid Recommendation Systems**: Combines both collaborative and content-based filtering for higher accuracy.

◆ **Example**: Netflix's AI-powered recommendation engine analyzes viewing history and user preferences to suggest personalized shows and movies.

2. Applications of AI Recommendation Systems

2.1 AI in E-Commerce: Personalized Shopping

✓ AI-driven recommendation engines in e-commerce suggest products based on user behavior, preferences, and purchase history.

✓ Enhances customer experience and boosts conversion rates.

◆ **Example**: Amazon's AI recommendation system drives 35% of its total sales by suggesting relevant products to customers.

2.2 AI in Streaming Services: Personalized Content Recommendations

✓ AI analyzes watch history, search patterns, and viewing time to suggest personalized content.

✓ Enhances engagement by ensuring users find content that aligns with their interests.

◆ **Example**: Spotify's AI-based recommendation engine creates personalized playlists like "Discover Weekly" based on user listening habits.

2.3 AI in Financial Services: Personalized Investment & Credit Offers

✓ AI analyzes customer spending habits, income levels, and risk profiles to recommend financial products (e.g., credit cards, loans, and investment plans).

✓ Enhances financial planning by suggesting customized savings and investment strategies.

◆ **Example**: Robo-advisors like Betterment and Wealthfront use AI to create personalized investment portfolios based on user goals and risk tolerance.

2.4 AI in Healthcare: Personalized Treatment Plans

✓ AI-driven recommendation systems in healthcare suggest personalized treatment plans, medications, and lifestyle changes based on patient data.

✓ Enhances preventive care and chronic disease management.

◆ **Example**: IBM Watson uses AI to recommend personalized cancer treatment plans based on a patient's medical history and genetic profile.

2.5 AI in Retail: Hyper-Personalized Customer Experience

✓ AI recommendation engines in retail suggest personalized discounts, loyalty rewards, and in-store experiences based on purchase history and preferences.

✓ Enhances customer retention and engagement.

◆ **Example**: Sephora uses AI-driven beauty advisors to suggest personalized skincare and makeup products based on skin type and previous purchases.

3. Benefits of AI-Powered Recommendation Systems

3.1 Improved Customer Engagement & Satisfaction

✓ AI-powered personalization enhances user experience by showing content or products relevant to individual preferences.

✓ Leads to higher engagement, increased customer retention, and brand loyalty.

◆ **Example**: Netflix's AI recommendations reduce content search time by 80%, improving user experience.

3.2 Increased Sales & Revenue Growth

✓ AI-driven product recommendations increase average order value and conversion rates in e-commerce.

✓ Businesses generate higher revenue by targeting customers with personalized promotions and offers.

◈ **Example**: AI-powered recommendations contribute to Amazon's $280 billion annual revenue growth.

3.3 Enhanced User Experience & Time Efficiency

✓ AI helps users find relevant content/products faster, reducing frustration and decision fatigue.

✓ Creates seamless and intuitive digital experiences.

◈ **Example**: Google News' AI recommendation engine personalizes news articles based on user interests, improving content discovery.

3.4 Data-Driven Insights for Businesses

✓ AI provides businesses with valuable insights into consumer behavior, preferences, and trends.

✓ Helps companies refine marketing strategies, product offerings, and inventory management.

◈ **Example**: AI-powered analytics help fashion retailers predict seasonal trends and optimize inventory based on demand forecasts.

4. Challenges in AI-Powered Personalization

4.1 Data Privacy & Security Concerns

✓ AI personalization relies on large-scale data collection, raising concerns about user privacy and data security.

✓ Compliance with GDPR, CCPA, and other data protection regulations is critical.

♦ **Solution**: Businesses should implement transparent data policies, encryption, and opt-in consent mechanisms for AI-driven personalization.

4.2 Bias & Fairness in AI Recommendations

✓ AI algorithms can develop biases based on skewed training data, leading to unfair or discriminatory recommendations.

✓ AI must be regularly audited for biases to ensure fairness.

♦ **Solution**: Companies should use diverse and inclusive datasets to train AI models and implement bias-detection tools.

4.3 Over-Personalization Risks

✓ Excessive personalization can make users feel overly monitored or restricted, reducing trust in AI systems.

✓ Users should have the option to adjust recommendation settings.

♦ **Solution**: Provide user control features, such as feedback mechanisms and personalization settings, to balance recommendations.

4.4 High Computational & Maintenance Costs

✓ AI-driven recommendation systems require massive computing power and continuous updates to stay relevant.

✓ Small businesses may struggle with the cost of implementing AI-based personalization.

♦ **Solution**: Cloud-based AI solutions and AI-as-a-Service (AIaaS) platforms offer affordable personalization tools for businesses.

5. Future Trends in AI-Powered Personalization

5.1 AI-Powered Voice Assistants for Personalized Recommendations

✓ AI-driven voice assistants like Amazon Alexa and Google Assistant will enhance personalized shopping and content recommendations.

◆ **Example**: AI voice assistants will suggest customized meal plans, music playlists, and shopping deals based on voice interactions.

5.2 AI-Powered Hyper-Personalization in Real-Time

✓ Future AI recommendation engines will analyze emotions, real-time interactions, and biometric data to offer even more personalized experiences.

◆ **Example**: AI-powered emotion recognition technology will recommend content based on user mood and facial expressions.

5.3 AI & Augmented Reality (AR) for Personalized Shopping

✓ AI will integrate with AR technology to provide virtual try-ons and personalized product recommendations in real time.

◆ **Example**: AI-driven AR fitting rooms in fashion retail will recommend outfits based on body shape and style preferences.

6. Conclusion: AI-Driven Personalization is the Future

AI-powered recommendation systems are reshaping industries by delivering personalized shopping, entertainment, financial planning, and healthcare solutions. Businesses that embrace AI-driven personalization will see higher customer engagement, increased sales, and long-term brand loyalty.

While challenges such as data privacy, algorithmic bias, and computational costs exist, AI innovations continue to enhance recommendation systems. As AI evolves with real-time personalization, emotion recognition, and AR integration, the future of hyper-personalized user experiences looks more promising than ever. 🚀

11.2 Demand Forecasting with AI in Retail

In the fast-paced world of retail, accurate demand forecasting is crucial for inventory management, cost reduction, and meeting consumer demand efficiently. Traditionally, retailers relied on historical sales data and human judgment to predict future demand. However, these methods often led to overstocking, understocking, or missed revenue opportunities. With the rise of artificial intelligence (AI), businesses can now leverage machine learning, predictive analytics, and real-time data to make highly accurate demand forecasts.

This chapter explores how AI-driven demand forecasting works, its benefits, challenges, and real-world applications in the retail industry.

1. What is Demand Forecasting in Retail?

Demand forecasting is the process of predicting future consumer demand for products or services based on historical data, market trends, and external factors. AI enhances this process by using real-time data, machine learning models, and deep learning algorithms to make more precise predictions.

✓ Traditional Demand Forecasting

- Based on historical sales data and seasonal trends
- Limited accuracy due to changing customer behavior
- Prone to errors caused by unexpected events

✓ AI-Powered Demand Forecasting

- Uses real-time sales data, weather patterns, social media trends, and economic indicators
- Continuously learns and adapts to changing market conditions
- Improves forecast accuracy and inventory management

- **Example**: Walmart's AI-driven demand forecasting system analyzes millions of data points daily, helping the company optimize inventory and reduce waste.

2. How AI-Driven Demand Forecasting Works

AI-based demand forecasting leverages advanced analytics, machine learning, and big data to improve accuracy. The key components include:

2.1 Machine Learning Models for Forecasting

✓ AI uses supervised and unsupervised machine learning models to predict demand based on historical sales, customer behavior, and market trends.

✓ Algorithms such as Random Forest, Gradient Boosting, and Neural Networks identify complex patterns and correlations.

◈ **Example**: Amazon's AI-driven demand forecasting system uses deep learning models to analyze past purchases, competitor prices, and user searches to predict future demand.

2.2 Real-Time Data Analysis & Predictive Analytics

✓ AI integrates real-time data from multiple sources, including:

- POS (Point-of-Sale) data
- Online shopping trends & social media sentiment analysis
- Weather patterns & economic conditions

✓ Predicts demand fluctuations based on current market conditions.

◈ **Example**: H&M uses AI-powered predictive analytics to forecast seasonal demand and optimize store inventory.

2.3 AI & Natural Language Processing (NLP) for Consumer Insights

✓ AI-powered NLP analyzes customer reviews, online feedback, and social media discussions to detect emerging trends and shifts in consumer preferences.

✓ Helps retailers adjust product offerings and marketing campaigns accordingly.

◆ **Example**: Nike's AI-driven demand forecasting system analyzes social media conversations to anticipate trends and adjust production.

2.4 AI & IoT for Supply Chain Optimization

✓ AI integrates with IoT (Internet of Things) sensors in warehouses and stores to track real-time inventory levels.

✓ Automatically adjusts stock levels based on real-time demand forecasts.

◆ **Example**: Zara uses AI-powered demand forecasting and IoT-based inventory tracking to respond to changing fashion trends faster than competitors.

3. Benefits of AI in Demand Forecasting

3.1 Improved Forecast Accuracy & Reduced Stockouts

✓ AI eliminates human errors and increases forecast accuracy by up to 50%.

✓ Helps retailers prevent stock shortages, ensuring products are available when customers need them.

◆ **Example**: Target's AI-driven demand forecasting reduced stockouts by 30%, improving customer satisfaction.

3.2 Reduced Overstocking & Lower Inventory Costs

✓ AI optimizes inventory by predicting demand more accurately, reducing over-purchasing and storage costs.

✓ Prevents product waste, especially in perishable goods like groceries.

◆ **Example**: Kroger uses AI-powered forecasting to reduce perishable food waste, saving millions annually.

3.3 Faster & More Agile Decision-Making

✓ AI provides real-time demand insights, allowing retailers to respond quickly to market changes.

✓ Helps businesses adjust pricing, promotions, and inventory in real-time.

◆ **Example**: Adidas uses AI-powered forecasting to adapt pricing strategies dynamically, maximizing revenue.

3.4 Enhanced Customer Experience

✓ Ensures that high-demand products are always in stock, improving customer satisfaction.

✓ Helps retailers create personalized promotions based on predicted customer needs.

◆ **Example**: Sephora's AI-based demand forecasting ensures popular beauty products remain stocked while preventing overstock of low-demand items.

4. Challenges in AI-Driven Demand Forecasting

4.1 Data Quality & Integration Issues

✓ AI models require high-quality, real-time data from multiple sources to be effective.

✓ Many retailers struggle with integrating AI with legacy systems.

◆ **Solution**: Invest in cloud-based AI platforms that aggregate and clean data automatically.

4.2 Sudden Market Disruptions & Unpredictability

✓ AI models may struggle to predict unforeseen events like pandemics, natural disasters, or sudden economic downturns.

✓ Retailers must combine AI forecasting with human expertise for best results.

◆ **Solution**: Implement hybrid AI-human decision-making models for demand planning.

4.3 High Implementation & Maintenance Costs

✓ AI demand forecasting requires significant investment in infrastructure, cloud computing, and data science expertise.

✓ Small retailers may struggle with the cost of AI adoption.

◆ **Solution**: Use AI-as-a-Service (AIaaS) solutions like Google Cloud AI or Amazon Forecast to reduce costs.

4.4 Ethical Concerns & Bias in AI Forecasting

✓ AI models can reinforce biases if trained on skewed historical data.

✓ Biased demand predictions may negatively impact product availability in certain regions or demographics.

◆ **Solution**: Regularly audit AI models for bias and use diverse datasets for training.

5. Future Trends in AI-Driven Demand Forecasting

5.1 AI & Blockchain for Transparent Supply Chains

✓ AI combined with blockchain technology will enhance demand forecasting by providing transparent and tamper-proof supply chain data.

◆ **Example**: Walmart is exploring AI-blockchain integration to improve inventory transparency.

5.2 AI-Powered Hyper-Personalization in Retail Forecasting

✓ AI will predict individual customer demand for personalized shopping experiences.

◆ **Example**: Amazon's AI predicts which products customers will need soon, even before they search for them.

5.3 Edge AI for Faster Forecasting Decisions

✔ AI will move from cloud-based models to edge computing, enabling real-time demand forecasting at retail locations.

◆ **Example**: AI-powered smart shelves will automatically adjust inventory based on real-time demand.

6. Conclusion: AI is Revolutionizing Retail Demand Forecasting

AI-powered demand forecasting is transforming retail by enhancing accuracy, reducing inventory costs, preventing stockouts, and improving customer experiences. As AI continues to evolve with real-time data processing, IoT integration, and hyper-personalization, retailers that embrace AI forecasting will gain a competitive advantage in the global market.

While challenges such as data quality, market disruptions, and implementation costs remain, AI-driven demand forecasting is the future of retail decision-making. Businesses that leverage AI for demand prediction will be able to adapt quickly to changing consumer needs, optimize inventory, and maximize profits in the years ahead. 🚀

11.3 AI-Driven Inventory Management & Dynamic Pricing

In the fast-evolving retail landscape, inventory management and pricing strategies are crucial for maximizing profitability and ensuring customer satisfaction. Traditionally, businesses relied on static inventory control methods and fixed pricing models based on historical sales data. However, these outdated approaches often led to overstocking, stockouts, and missed revenue opportunities.

With the rise of artificial intelligence (AI), machine learning (ML), and real-time analytics, businesses can now adopt AI-driven inventory management and dynamic pricing to optimize supply chains, reduce waste, and enhance revenue. This chapter explores how AI is transforming inventory management and pricing strategies, the benefits, challenges, and real-world applications in the retail industry.

1. AI-Driven Inventory Management: How It Works

Inventory management is one of the most complex aspects of retail, requiring accurate demand forecasting, real-time tracking, and optimized supply chains. AI enhances inventory management by leveraging real-time data, predictive analytics, and automation to streamline operations.

1.1 Key Components of AI-Powered Inventory Management

✓ Predictive Analytics for Demand Forecasting

AI algorithms analyze historical sales data, seasonality, and external factors to predict future demand trends. This helps businesses avoid stock shortages and excess inventory.

◆ **Example**: Walmart uses AI-powered predictive analytics to anticipate demand shifts and optimize inventory across its stores.

✓ Real-Time Inventory Tracking

AI integrates with IoT (Internet of Things) sensors and RFID tags to track inventory levels in real time. This ensures faster restocking, reduced losses, and better inventory accuracy.

◆ **Example**: Amazon's fulfillment centers use AI-powered robots and IoT-based inventory tracking to manage warehouse stock efficiently.

✓ Automated Replenishment Systems

AI-driven inventory management systems can automatically place orders when stock reaches a certain threshold, reducing manual intervention and stockouts.

◆ **Example**: Zara's AI-based inventory system automatically adjusts stock levels based on sales trends, ensuring optimal availability.

✓ Supply Chain Optimization with AI

AI enhances supply chain efficiency by analyzing supplier performance, transportation logistics, and storage conditions to minimize delays and disruptions.

◆ **Example**: Nike uses AI-driven supply chain analytics to improve logistics and reduce shipping delays.

2. Dynamic Pricing: AI-Driven Price Optimization

Dynamic pricing is a real-time pricing strategy where product prices fluctuate based on demand, competitor pricing, market conditions, and consumer behavior. AI enables businesses to automate and optimize pricing decisions using advanced data analytics.

2.1 How AI-Powered Dynamic Pricing Works

✓ Competitive Price Monitoring

AI continuously monitors competitor prices and adjusts pricing strategies to remain competitive.

◆ **Example**: Amazon's AI-driven pricing system updates prices every 10 minutes based on competitor activity.

✓ Real-Time Demand Analysis

AI dynamically adjusts prices based on supply and demand trends, customer purchasing patterns, and market conditions.

◆ **Example**: Uber's surge pricing uses AI to increase fares when demand is high and supply is low.

✓ Customer Segmentation & Personalized Pricing

AI can analyze customer behavior and segment users based on past purchases, browsing history, and willingness to pay. This allows for personalized discounts and promotions.

◆ **Example**: E-commerce platforms like eBay and Alibaba use AI-driven personalized pricing to offer customized discounts to specific customer segments.

✓ AI for Markdown & Clearance Sales

Retailers can use AI to predict when to reduce prices for slow-moving inventory, minimizing losses while optimizing sales.

⬧ **Example**: Walmart's AI-powered markdown optimization helps reduce unsold stock and prevent over-discounting.

3. Benefits of AI-Driven Inventory Management & Dynamic Pricing

3.1 Reduced Inventory Costs & Increased Efficiency

✓ AI optimizes stock levels, reducing storage costs and preventing dead stock.

✓ Helps businesses allocate inventory more efficiently across multiple locations.

⬧ **Example**: H&M reduced inventory costs by 20% using AI-driven demand forecasting and automated stock management.

3.2 Maximized Revenue & Profit Margins

✓ AI-powered dynamic pricing helps businesses increase profit margins by adjusting prices dynamically based on demand.

✓ AI pricing algorithms ensure optimal pricing strategies without over-discounting.

⬧ **Example**: Airlines use AI-driven dynamic pricing to maximize ticket revenue based on booking patterns.

3.3 Enhanced Customer Experience & Loyalty

✓ AI ensures popular products are always available, improving customer satisfaction.

✓ Personalized pricing offers help retain customers and increase conversions.

⬧ **Example**: Starbucks uses AI-based pricing models to offer personalized discounts based on customer preferences.

3.4 Faster Decision-Making with Real-Time Analytics

✓ AI provides retailers with real-time insights into sales, stock levels, and market trends, enabling faster decisions.

✓ AI-driven automation reduces human errors and delays in inventory restocking.

◆ **Example**: Home Depot's AI-driven inventory system helped reduce stockouts by 30%, improving operational efficiency.

4. Challenges of AI in Inventory & Pricing Optimization

4.1 Data Quality & Integration Issues

✓ AI models require high-quality, real-time data from multiple sources. Many businesses struggle to integrate AI with legacy systems.

✓ Poor data quality can lead to inaccurate forecasts and pricing decisions.

◆ **Solution**: Retailers should invest in AI-driven data integration platforms to unify data sources.

4.2 Customer Perception & Ethical Concerns

✓ Dynamic pricing can sometimes cause customer frustration if they notice price fluctuations.

✓ Over-aggressive pricing strategies may be perceived as unfair or exploitative.

◆ **Solution**: Retailers should maintain pricing transparency and communicate value-based pricing strategies to customers.

4.3 High Implementation Costs

✓ AI-driven inventory and pricing systems require significant investment in technology, cloud computing, and data science expertise.

✓ Smaller retailers may face budget constraints in adopting AI solutions.

♦ **Solution**: Businesses can use AI-as-a-Service (AIaaS) solutions like Google Cloud AI, AWS AI, or IBM Watson for cost-effective AI adoption.

4.4 AI Algorithm Bias & Accuracy Issues

✓ AI models may be biased if trained on skewed historical data, leading to pricing discrimination or inaccurate demand forecasts.

✓ AI systems need continuous monitoring and retraining to remain effective.

♦ **Solution**: Retailers must regularly audit AI models for fairness and accuracy.

5. Future of AI in Inventory Management & Pricing

5.1 AI & Blockchain for Supply Chain Transparency

✓ Combining AI with blockchain will create tamper-proof, transparent inventory tracking systems.

♦ **Example**: Walmart is piloting AI-blockchain technology for tracking food supply chains.

5.2 Hyper-Personalized Pricing with AI & NLP

✓ AI-powered natural language processing (NLP) will help retailers analyze customer conversations and tailor pricing strategies accordingly.

♦ **Example**: E-commerce giants like Amazon & Alibaba are investing in AI-driven hyper-personalization for pricing.

5.3 Edge AI for Faster Inventory Decisions

✓ AI will shift from cloud-based models to edge computing, allowing real-time inventory adjustments at store locations.

♦ **Example**: AI-powered smart shelves will adjust pricing and stock levels instantly based on demand.

6. Conclusion: AI is the Future of Retail Optimization

AI-driven inventory management and dynamic pricing are revolutionizing the retail industry by enhancing efficiency, reducing costs, and maximizing revenue. Businesses that leverage AI gain a competitive edge through real-time inventory tracking, automated restocking, predictive demand forecasting, and adaptive pricing strategies.

Despite challenges such as data integration, customer perception, and high costs, AI-powered solutions are becoming more accessible and essential for modern retail success. By adopting AI-driven inventory and pricing strategies, retailers can ensure optimized stock levels, fair pricing, and enhanced customer experiences, shaping the future of the retail industry. 🚀

11.4 Case Studies: AI in E-commerce & Brick-and-Mortar Stores

Artificial intelligence (AI) is reshaping both e-commerce and brick-and-mortar retail, optimizing everything from personalized recommendations to supply chain logistics and checkout automation. Businesses that harness AI effectively can enhance customer experiences, increase sales, and streamline operations. This chapter explores real-world case studies of AI adoption in leading e-commerce platforms and physical retail stores, showcasing the impact of AI-driven strategies on the retail landscape.

1. AI in E-Commerce: Transforming Online Retail

E-commerce platforms have been early adopters of AI, leveraging machine learning, natural language processing (NLP), and predictive analytics to create seamless, personalized shopping experiences. The following case studies illustrate how AI has revolutionized online retail.

1.1 Amazon: AI-Powered Personalized Shopping & Logistics

Amazon has built its business on AI-driven automation, using AI across its entire ecosystem—from product recommendations to warehouse robotics.

✔ AI-Powered Recommendation Engine

- Amazon's personalized recommendation system generates 35% of its total sales.
- AI analyzes customer browsing history, past purchases, and real-time behavior to suggest relevant products.

✓ AI in Supply Chain & Warehouse Automation

- Amazon uses Kiva robots in its fulfillment centers to automate order picking, sorting, and packing, reducing operational costs and speeding up deliveries.
- AI-powered demand forecasting helps Amazon stock inventory efficiently, reducing overstock and stockouts.

✓ AI Chatbots & Voice Assistants

- Alexa, Amazon's AI-powered virtual assistant, allows customers to shop hands-free.
- AI-driven customer service chatbots handle routine inquiries, improving response times.

☞ **Impact**: AI-driven recommendations, automation, and logistics optimization have helped Amazon maintain its dominance in global e-commerce while reducing operational costs and enhancing customer engagement.

1.2 Alibaba: AI for Dynamic Pricing & Fraud Detection

Alibaba, China's largest e-commerce platform, has integrated AI into every aspect of its business, from pricing optimization to AI-powered fraud detection.

✓ Smart Pricing & Dynamic Discounts

- Alibaba uses AI to analyze market trends, competitor pricing, and customer demand to optimize product prices in real time.
- AI ensures that discounts are personalized, maximizing conversion rates while protecting profit margins.

✓ AI in Fraud Detection & Payment Security

- AI analyzes billions of transactions daily to detect anomalies and prevent fraud.

- Alibaba's City Brain AI system detects fraudulent transactions with 99% accuracy using machine learning.

✔ AI in Customer Engagement & Marketing

- AI-powered virtual shopping assistants offer personalized product recommendations and real-time customer support.
- AI analyzes consumer behavior to optimize ad targeting and marketing campaigns, increasing ROI.

☞ **Impact**: AI has helped Alibaba improve conversion rates, reduce fraud, and enhance customer loyalty, making it a leader in AI-driven e-commerce innovation.

1.3 Shopify: AI-Powered E-Commerce for Small Businesses

Shopify, a leading e-commerce platform, integrates AI to help small and medium-sized businesses (SMBs) compete with larger retailers.

✔ AI-Powered Chatbots & Customer Support

- Shopify's "Kit" AI assistant helps merchants automate marketing campaigns, send personalized emails, and manage social media ads.

✔ AI for Smart Inventory Management

- AI predicts demand and automatically suggests stock replenishment for Shopify merchants.
- Machine learning analyzes seasonality and shopping trends to optimize inventory decisions.

✔ AI for Image Search & Visual Recommendations

- Shopify enables shoppers to search for products using AI-powered image recognition, improving product discovery.

☞ **Impact**: AI allows Shopify merchants to scale their businesses efficiently, enhancing customer engagement, marketing automation, and inventory control.

2. AI in Brick-and-Mortar Retail: Enhancing Physical Store Experiences

AI is also transforming brick-and-mortar stores by enabling smart inventory tracking, cashierless checkouts, and AI-powered customer analytics. These case studies highlight how major retailers are integrating AI into physical store operations.

2.1 Walmart: AI-Powered Inventory Management & Customer Analytics

Walmart has heavily invested in AI to improve supply chain efficiency, in-store experiences, and operational automation.

✓ **AI-Powered Inventory Robots**

- Walmart's AI-driven robots scan shelves in real time to detect out-of-stock products, misplaced items, and pricing discrepancies.
- These robots reduce manual labor costs and improve stock accuracy.

✓ **AI for Demand Forecasting & Logistics Optimization**

- Walmart uses AI to predict consumer demand, ensuring that fast-moving products are restocked quickly.
- AI-powered supply chain analytics help Walmart optimize delivery routes and reduce transportation costs.

✓ **Facial Recognition for Customer Experience**

- AI-powered facial recognition analyzes customer moods and foot traffic patterns to enhance in-store engagement.

☞ **Impact**: AI has improved Walmart's supply chain efficiency, reduced stockouts, and enhanced customer satisfaction through better product availability.

2.2 Amazon Go: AI-Driven Cashierless Shopping

Amazon Go has revolutionized physical retail with its "Just Walk Out" AI-powered checkout technology, eliminating traditional cashiers and long checkout lines.

✓ **Computer Vision & Sensor Fusion for Checkout-Free Shopping**

AI-powered cameras track customer movements and automatically charge their accounts when they leave the store.

✓ AI for Real-Time Product Recognition

AI ensures accurate inventory tracking and fraud prevention, making shopping more convenient.

☞ **Impact**: Amazon Go showcases how AI can eliminate checkout friction, reduce labor costs, and enhance customer convenience.

2.3 Sephora: AI-Powered Virtual Try-On & Beauty Assistants

Sephora integrates AI to enhance beauty shopping experiences both online and in-store.

✓ AI Virtual Try-On with Augmented Reality (AR)

Sephora's "Virtual Artist" uses AI-powered AR to let customers try on makeup virtually before purchasing.

✓ AI-Powered Beauty Chatbots

AI-driven chatbots provide personalized skincare recommendations based on user preferences and skin type.

✓ Smart Mirror Technology for Personalized Beauty Advice

In-store smart mirrors use AI and facial recognition to suggest makeup products that best match skin tone and facial features.

☞ **Impact**: AI has helped Sephora create a hyper-personalized beauty shopping experience, increasing customer engagement and satisfaction.

3. Key Takeaways: How AI is Reshaping Retail

3.1 AI Benefits for E-Commerce & Brick-and-Mortar Stores

✓ **Personalized Shopping Experiences** → AI-powered recommendations boost sales & customer loyalty.

✓ **Inventory Optimization** → AI-driven demand forecasting & supply chain automation reduce stock issues.

✓ **Fraud Prevention & Security** → AI enhances transaction security & fraud detection.

✓ **Checkout Automation** → AI-powered cashierless stores eliminate long queues & improve convenience.

✓ **AI-Powered Marketing** → AI-driven insights optimize pricing, advertising, and customer engagement.

3.2 Future of AI in Retail

✓ **AI + IoT for Smart Stores** → More retailers will adopt AI-driven smart shelves & automated inventory systems.

✓ **Hyper-Personalization with AI** → AI will enhance real-time price adjustments & tailored product recommendations.

✓ **Voice Commerce & AI Assistants** → AI-powered voice search & chatbots will further streamline shopping.

4. Conclusion: AI is the Future of Retail Innovation

AI is revolutionizing both e-commerce and physical retail, enabling businesses to offer personalized shopping experiences, optimize supply chains, and enhance customer engagement. Companies that invest in AI-powered recommendation engines, demand forecasting, cashierless checkouts, and fraud prevention will gain a competitive edge in the retail industry.

As AI technology continues to evolve, the future of retail will be driven by automation, personalization, and data-driven decision-making, ensuring a seamless, intelligent shopping experience for customers worldwide. 🚀

12. AI in Transportation & Supply Chain Optimization

AI is revolutionizing transportation and supply chain management by enhancing efficiency, reducing costs, and improving decision-making. From AI-powered route optimization and autonomous vehicles to predictive analytics for demand forecasting and warehouse automation, businesses are leveraging AI to streamline logistics operations. Machine learning models help companies anticipate disruptions, optimize inventory levels, and reduce delivery times, making global supply chains more resilient. This chapter explores how AI is transforming transportation, logistics, and supply chain management, highlighting key innovations, real-world applications, and challenges such as cybersecurity risks and ethical AI deployment.

12.1 AI-Driven Route Optimization & Logistics Management

Efficient logistics and transportation are the backbone of global commerce, and AI-driven route optimization is revolutionizing the way businesses manage supply chains. With rising consumer expectations, fluctuating fuel costs, and complex delivery networks, companies are turning to artificial intelligence (AI) and machine learning (ML) algorithms to optimize transportation, reduce costs, and enhance delivery efficiency.

In this chapter, we will explore how AI is transforming route optimization and logistics management, covering real-world applications, benefits, challenges, and future trends in the industry.

1. The Role of AI in Modern Logistics

Traditional logistics management relied on static route planning, human decision-making, and rule-based systems. However, these approaches often resulted in inefficiencies, delays, and increased costs due to unforeseen circumstances such as traffic congestion, weather conditions, and last-minute order changes.

AI-powered route optimization and logistics management leverage:

✓ **Big Data & Real-Time Analytics** → AI processes vast amounts of traffic, weather, and delivery data to create optimized routes.

✓ **Machine Learning Algorithms** → AI learns from historical data to predict bottlenecks and optimize fleet efficiency.

✓ **Computer Vision & IoT Sensors** → AI-driven smart cameras and sensors track vehicle performance and detect potential delays.

✓ **Predictive Analytics** → AI forecasts demand and adjusts logistics strategies dynamically.

By integrating AI into logistics, companies can achieve faster deliveries, lower operational costs, reduced fuel consumption, and improved customer satisfaction.

2. AI-Powered Route Optimization: How It Works

2.1 Real-Time Traffic Analysis & Dynamic Routing

AI analyzes real-time traffic patterns, road closures, weather conditions, and historical data to suggest the most efficient delivery routes.

✓ AI-powered GPS tracking systems continuously monitor road conditions and recalculate routes dynamically.

✓ Companies like UPS and FedEx use AI-driven tools to minimize left turns, reducing fuel costs and improving delivery speeds.

☞ **Case Study:**

UPS's ORION System uses AI to process over 250 million data points daily, optimizing routes for 110,000+ delivery vehicles, saving 10 million gallons of fuel annually.

2.2 AI & IoT for Smart Fleet Management

AI-powered fleet management systems optimize vehicle usage, monitor fuel efficiency, and predict maintenance needs.

✓ IoT sensors in vehicles track speed, fuel consumption, and braking patterns to reduce wear and tear.

✓ AI automatically schedules vehicle maintenance before failures occur, preventing costly breakdowns.

✓ Self-driving trucks, powered by AI, are being tested for long-haul freight to reduce human dependency and increase efficiency.

☞ **Case Study:**

DHL's AI-driven SmartFleet System reduced delivery time by 15% and fuel costs by 10% by optimizing fleet routes dynamically.

2.3 AI for Last-Mile Delivery Optimization

The last-mile delivery—the final step in a product's journey to the customer—is often the most expensive and time-consuming part of logistics. AI optimizes last-mile delivery by:

✓ Predicting demand fluctuations to adjust delivery schedules.

✓ Using AI-powered drones & autonomous delivery robots for contactless deliveries.

✓ Analyzing customer preferences to determine the best delivery windows.

☞ **Case Study:**

Amazon's AI-driven delivery robots and autonomous Prime Air drones are reducing last-mile delivery times significantly.

3. The Business Impact of AI in Logistics

3.1 Benefits of AI-Driven Route Optimization

✅ **Cost Savings** → AI reduces fuel consumption, labor costs, and vehicle wear-and-tear.

✅ **Faster Deliveries** → AI-powered predictive traffic analysis and real-time routing optimize delivery times.

✅ **Lower Carbon Footprint** → AI helps logistics companies adopt eco-friendly route planning, cutting emissions.

✅ **Better Resource Utilization** → AI improves fleet efficiency, reducing idle time and maximizing productivity.

3.2 Challenges in AI-Powered Logistics

⚠ **Data Privacy & Security Risks** → AI logistics platforms handle vast amounts of sensitive data.

⚠ **High Implementation Costs** → AI-driven logistics requires significant investment in software, hardware, and infrastructure.

⚠ **Regulatory & Compliance Issues** → Autonomous vehicles and AI-driven drones face strict government regulations.

⚠ **Human Workforce Adaptation** → AI-powered automation may disrupt traditional logistics jobs, requiring workforce reskilling.

4. Future Trends: The Next Evolution of AI in Logistics

🚀 **AI-Powered Self-Driving Trucks** → Autonomous freight transport will eliminate human driver limitations and reduce long-haul shipping costs.

🚀 **Hyper-Personalized Delivery Windows** → AI will analyze consumer habits to schedule deliveries when customers are home, reducing failed delivery attempts.

🚀 **5G & AI for Ultra-Fast Logistics** → 5G networks will enable AI-powered logistics systems to process data in real time, enhancing route optimization and delivery accuracy.

🚀 **Blockchain + AI for Supply Chain Transparency** → AI-driven blockchain solutions will track shipments securely, preventing fraud and improving supply chain visibility.

5. Conclusion: AI is Reshaping the Future of Logistics

AI-driven route optimization and logistics management are revolutionizing the transportation industry by making deliveries faster, more cost-efficient, and environmentally friendly. From predictive traffic analytics to smart fleet management and last-mile delivery automation, AI is at the heart of logistics innovation.

Companies that embrace AI-powered logistics solutions will gain a competitive edge by enhancing operational efficiency, reducing costs, and improving customer satisfaction. As AI technology evolves, we can expect even smarter, fully autonomous logistics systems that redefine global supply chains. 🚀

12.2 Self-Driving Vehicles & AI-Powered Fleet Management

The transportation and logistics industry is undergoing a significant transformation with the integration of self-driving vehicles and AI-powered fleet management systems. As global supply chains become more complex and customer expectations for faster deliveries increase, businesses are turning to autonomous vehicles, machine learning algorithms, and IoT-based fleet monitoring to enhance efficiency, reduce costs, and improve safety.

In this chapter, we explore how self-driving vehicles and AI-driven fleet management are revolutionizing logistics, covering key technologies, benefits, challenges, and real-world case studies.

1. The Role of AI in Autonomous Vehicles & Fleet Management

AI plays a critical role in both self-driving vehicle technology and fleet management systems by enabling:

✓ **Computer Vision & Sensor Fusion** → AI-powered cameras, LiDAR, and radar help autonomous vehicles navigate complex environments.

✓ **Machine Learning for Decision-Making** → AI predicts road conditions, traffic patterns, and driver behaviors to optimize vehicle performance.

✓ **Predictive Maintenance & Fuel Optimization** → AI-powered fleet management software detects wear-and-tear issues and improves fuel efficiency.

✓ **Smart Routing & Traffic Optimization** → AI dynamically adjusts routes based on real-time road conditions, reducing delivery delays.

By integrating AI into transportation, companies can increase safety, enhance operational efficiency, and lower costs while moving towards a more sustainable, automated future.

2. Self-Driving Vehicles: How AI Enables Autonomous Transportation

2.1 Core Technologies Behind Self-Driving Vehicles

Self-driving vehicles rely on multiple AI-driven technologies to operate safely and efficiently:

✓ Computer Vision & Deep Learning

- AI processes real-time video feeds from onboard cameras to recognize pedestrians, vehicles, traffic signs, and obstacles.
- Deep learning models enable vehicles to "learn" from driving data and improve navigation over time.

✓ LiDAR & Radar for 3D Mapping

- Self-driving vehicles use LiDAR (Light Detection and Ranging) to create high-resolution 3D maps of their surroundings.
- AI analyzes LiDAR and radar signals to detect distance, speed, and movement patterns of nearby objects.

✓ AI for Path Planning & Decision Making

- AI-powered self-driving systems predict lane changes, braking patterns, and acceleration based on real-time road conditions.
- Reinforcement learning models allow vehicles to adapt to new driving scenarios autonomously.

☞ Case Study: Waymo (Google's Self-Driving Car Division)

- Waymo's AI-powered autonomous taxi fleet has driven over 20 million miles on public roads with a safety record surpassing human drivers.
- AI models process 20 terabytes of sensor data per day, optimizing vehicle movements in real time.

2.2 Autonomous Trucks: AI in Long-Haul Freight

The trucking industry is one of the biggest beneficiaries of self-driving technology, as autonomous trucks can:

✓ Operate 24/7 without driver fatigue, reducing delivery times.

✓ Optimize fuel efficiency through AI-driven acceleration and braking.

✓ Minimize human errors, reducing accidents caused by distracted or drowsy drivers.

☞ Case Study: Tesla's AI-Powered Semi Trucks

- Tesla's Autopilot & Full Self-Driving (FSD) system enables semi-autonomous freight transportation.
- AI-powered convoy technology allows multiple autonomous trucks to follow each other efficiently, reducing aerodynamic drag and cutting fuel consumption by up to 10%.

2.3 AI-Driven Last-Mile Autonomous Delivery

Last-mile delivery—the final step in the logistics chain—is being revolutionized by AI-powered self-driving robots and drones.

✓ **Autonomous Delivery Robots** → Companies like Starship Technologies and Nuro deploy AI-driven delivery robots for contactless, on-demand deliveries.

✓ **AI-Powered Drones** → Amazon's Prime Air drones use AI to navigate urban environments and deliver packages in under 30 minutes.

☞ Case Study: Nuro's AI-Powered Autonomous Delivery Vehicles

- Nuro's electric self-driving vehicles transport groceries, pharmacy items, and restaurant orders without human drivers.
- AI-driven path planning and obstacle detection ensure safe and efficient last-mile delivery.

3. AI-Powered Fleet Management: Optimizing Vehicle Operations

3.1 How AI is Transforming Fleet Management

Fleet management involves tracking, optimizing, and maintaining commercial vehicle operations. AI-powered fleet management software helps companies:

✔ **Predict Maintenance Needs** → AI detects engine performance issues before breakdowns occur, reducing repair costs.

✔ **Optimize Fuel Efficiency** → AI analyzes driver behavior and suggests fuel-saving driving techniques.

✔ **Improve Safety with Driver Monitoring** → AI-powered in-cabin cameras detect distracted driving, fatigue, and risky behaviors.

✔ **Enhance Route Planning & Dispatching** → AI-powered logistics platforms optimize vehicle dispatching and real-time rerouting.

☞ **Case Study: UPS's AI-Powered Fleet Optimization**

- UPS's AI-driven On-Road Integrated Optimization and Navigation (ORION) system saves 10 million gallons of fuel per year.
- AI-powered telematics monitor vehicle performance, reducing downtime and improving fleet longevity.

3.2 AI & IoT for Smart Fleet Monitoring

The integration of AI and IoT (Internet of Things) sensors enables fleet managers to:

✔ Track vehicles in real time via GPS and AI-powered dashboards.

✔ Monitor tire pressure, fuel levels, and engine health remotely.

✔ Reduce emissions by optimizing fuel consumption and vehicle maintenance schedules.

☞ **Case Study: Daimler's AI-Powered Fleet Management System**

Daimler uses AI-driven predictive analytics to monitor vehicle components and prevent mechanical failures before they happen.

4. Challenges & Ethical Considerations in AI-Powered Transportation

While AI-powered autonomous vehicles and fleet management bring numerous benefits, there are challenges to consider:

⚠ **Safety & Liability Issues** → Who is responsible in case of an AI-driven vehicle accident?

⚠ **Regulatory Uncertainty** → Governments are still developing legal frameworks for self-driving cars.

⚠ **Cybersecurity Threats** → AI-powered fleets are vulnerable to hacking and cyberattacks.

⚠ **Job Displacement** → Autonomous vehicles may replace millions of truck drivers and delivery personnel, requiring workforce reskilling.

5. The Future of AI in Transportation & Fleet Management

🚀 **Full Autonomy in Logistics** → Self-driving trucks will dominate long-haul freight transport by 2035.

🚀 **AI-Powered Green Logistics** → AI will help logistics companies achieve carbon neutrality through electric and hydrogen-powered fleets.

🚀 **5G & AI for Instant Decision-Making** → AI-powered vehicle-to-vehicle (V2V) communication will enhance road safety and traffic flow.

🚀 **AI + Blockchain for Secure Logistics** → AI-driven blockchain systems will track shipments with tamper-proof transparency.

6. Conclusion: AI is the Future of Logistics & Fleet Management

AI-powered self-driving vehicles and fleet management systems are revolutionizing the transportation industry, offering greater efficiency, lower costs, and enhanced safety. From autonomous long-haul trucking to AI-optimized last-mile delivery, the future of logistics is increasingly automated.

Companies that embrace AI-driven fleet management and self-driving technology will lead the industry by delivering faster, safer, and more cost-effective transportation solutions. As AI continues to evolve, fully autonomous logistics ecosystems will soon become a reality. 🚀

12.3 Predictive AI for Demand Planning & Warehousing

In today's fast-paced global economy, efficient demand planning and warehousing are critical for businesses looking to optimize inventory, reduce waste, and improve customer satisfaction. Artificial Intelligence (AI) and predictive analytics have emerged as game-changers in this domain, helping companies anticipate market demand, streamline supply chain operations, and enhance warehouse management.

This chapter explores how AI-powered predictive analytics is transforming demand forecasting and warehouse optimization, the key technologies involved, real-world applications, and challenges that businesses must overcome.

1. The Role of AI in Demand Planning & Warehousing

Traditional demand planning relied on historical sales data, human intuition, and basic statistical models, often leading to inaccurate forecasts, stockouts, and excess inventory. AI-driven predictive analytics overcomes these limitations by:

✓ Analyzing vast datasets from multiple sources, including sales trends, weather conditions, economic indicators, and social media sentiment.

✓ Detecting hidden patterns and seasonality to generate accurate demand forecasts.

✓ Adjusting forecasts dynamically in response to market fluctuations, supply chain disruptions, and consumer behavior changes.

✓ Optimizing warehouse storage and replenishment using AI-driven inventory management systems.

With AI, businesses can move from reactive decision-making to proactive planning, leading to greater efficiency and cost savings.

2. AI-Powered Demand Forecasting: How It Works

2.1 Key Technologies Behind Predictive AI in Demand Planning

✓ **Machine Learning (ML) & Deep Learning** → AI algorithms analyze historical sales data, identify demand patterns, and adjust forecasts dynamically.

✓ **Natural Language Processing (NLP)** → AI processes external data sources such as news articles, market reports, and customer reviews to predict demand shifts.

✓ **Time-Series Forecasting Models** → AI-driven models like ARIMA, LSTMs, and Prophet enhance accuracy in long-term demand predictions.

✓ **AI-Enabled Prescriptive Analytics** → AI not only predicts demand but also recommends optimal inventory levels and distribution strategies.

☞ **Case Study: Walmart's AI-Powered Demand Forecasting**

- Walmart uses AI-driven predictive analytics to forecast seasonal and promotional demand fluctuations across its 10,000+ stores.
- AI integrates real-time weather data and regional economic indicators to predict shifts in customer purchasing behavior.
- This system reduces stockouts by 30% and minimizes excess inventory costs.

2.2 AI for Dynamic Inventory Optimization

AI-powered demand forecasting ensures that businesses:

✓ Maintain optimal stock levels, preventing overstocking or understocking.

✓ Reduce waste and carrying costs by aligning inventory levels with demand.

✓ Adjust order quantities dynamically based on real-time data.

☞ **Case Study: Amazon's AI-Driven Inventory Management**

- Amazon's AI-based demand forecasting predicts customer demand at a granular level, enabling just-in-time inventory replenishment.
- The system automatically reorders stock based on real-time data, reducing warehouse storage costs and improving efficiency.

3. AI in Warehousing: Smart Storage & Automation

3.1 AI-Powered Warehouse Management Systems (WMS)

AI is revolutionizing warehouse operations by enabling:

✓ **Real-Time Stock Monitoring** → AI tracks inventory levels using RFID tags, IoT sensors, and computer vision.

✓ **Automated Warehouse Layout Optimization** → AI analyzes item popularity and movement to suggest the most efficient storage configurations.

✓ **AI-Driven Picking & Packing Optimization** → AI optimizes pick paths and order fulfillment, reducing labor costs and increasing efficiency.

☞ **Case Study: Ocado's AI-Powered Automated Warehouses**

- Ocado, a UK-based online grocery retailer, uses AI-powered robots to manage its high-speed fulfillment centers.
- The AI system coordinates 1,000+ robots, improving efficiency and enabling 30-minute grocery deliveries.

3.2 Robotics & AI in Warehouse Automation

✓ **Autonomous Mobile Robots (AMRs)** → AI-powered robots assist in picking, packing, and transporting goods.

✓ **AI-Enabled Drones for Inventory Scanning** → AI-driven drones scan warehouse shelves to track stock levels.

✓ **Computer Vision for Quality Control** → AI inspects damaged products and packaging errors automatically.

☞ **Case Study: Alibaba's AI-Driven Warehouse Automation**

Alibaba's smart warehouses use AI-powered robots that handle 70% of total order fulfillment, reducing manual labor costs by 50%.

4. Business Benefits of AI in Demand Planning & Warehousing

✓ **Increased Forecast Accuracy** → AI enhances demand forecasting, reducing errors by 20-50%.

✓ **Lower Inventory Holding Costs** → AI minimizes excess stock and storage expenses.

✓ **Faster Order Fulfillment** → AI-driven automation speeds up picking, packing, and shipping.

✓ **Enhanced Supply Chain Resilience** → AI identifies disruptions early, allowing for proactive risk management.

5. Challenges in AI-Powered Demand Planning & Warehousing

⚠ **Data Quality Issues** → AI relies on accurate, high-quality data for effective predictions.

⚠ **High Implementation Costs** → AI-powered warehouse automation requires significant investment in hardware and software.

⚠ **Workforce Adaptation & Reskilling** → Employees must be trained to work alongside AI-powered systems.

⚠ **Integration with Legacy Systems** → Many companies struggle to integrate AI with existing supply chain software.

6. The Future of AI in Demand Planning & Warehousing

🔋 **AI + IoT for Fully Automated Warehouses** → Smart sensors and AI-driven robots will eliminate manual warehouse tasks.

🔋 **Hyper-Personalized Demand Forecasting** → AI will predict customer preferences at an individual level, enabling micro-inventory planning.

🔋 **AI-Powered Autonomous Delivery** → Self-driving trucks and drones will streamline supply chain logistics.

🔋 **AI & Blockchain for Transparent Supply Chains** → AI-driven blockchain solutions will ensure secure, real-time inventory tracking.

7. Conclusion: AI is Reshaping Demand Planning & Warehousing

AI-driven predictive analytics is revolutionizing demand planning and warehouse management, offering businesses greater efficiency, cost savings, and improved customer satisfaction. By leveraging machine learning, robotics, and real-time data analysis, companies can optimize inventory levels, automate warehouse operations, and enhance supply chain resilience.

As AI technology continues to evolve, the future of logistics will be defined by fully automated, AI-driven smart warehouses and predictive demand forecasting systems that deliver unprecedented accuracy and efficiency. Companies that invest in AI now will lead the industry into the next era of intelligent supply chain management. 🚀

12.4 AI in Reducing Carbon Footprint in Logistics

As climate change concerns continue to rise, industries worldwide are under increasing pressure to reduce their environmental impact. The logistics and transportation sector is a major contributor to global carbon emissions, accounting for nearly 14% of total greenhouse gas emissions. With the rapid advancements in Artificial Intelligence (AI), businesses are leveraging AI-powered solutions to make supply chains more sustainable, optimize transportation routes, reduce energy consumption, and minimize waste.

This chapter explores how AI is transforming logistics to lower carbon emissions, the key technologies enabling this shift, real-world applications, and the challenges businesses must address.

1. The Environmental Impact of Logistics

The logistics industry is one of the largest contributors to carbon emissions, driven by:

✔ **Fossil Fuel Dependency** → Most transportation relies on diesel and gasoline-powered vehicles, producing CO_2 and nitrogen oxide emissions.

✔ **Inefficient Routing** → Poor route planning leads to longer trips, excessive fuel consumption, and unnecessary emissions.

✓ **Empty Miles & Underutilized Vehicles** → Many trucks travel partially loaded or empty, leading to wasted energy and higher emissions.

✓ **Warehouse Energy Consumption** → Large warehouses consume significant electricity for lighting, heating, and cooling.

✓ **Excess Packaging & Waste** → Logistics generates huge amounts of plastic waste, contributing to environmental degradation.

AI is now being adopted to address these challenges and create a greener, more sustainable logistics ecosystem.

2. AI-Powered Solutions for Reducing Carbon Emissions

2.1 AI for Smart Route Optimization

One of the most effective ways AI reduces carbon emissions is through smart route planning. AI-powered route optimization software:

✓ Uses real-time traffic data to identify the fastest and most fuel-efficient routes.

✓ Analyzes weather conditions, road closures, and traffic congestion to minimize delays and fuel consumption.

✓ Optimizes delivery sequences to reduce unnecessary mileage and emissions.

☞ **Case Study: UPS's AI-Powered ORION System**

- UPS's On-Road Integrated Optimization and Navigation (ORION) uses AI to optimize delivery routes.
- ORION has eliminated 100 million miles of unnecessary travel per year, saving 10 million gallons of fuel and reducing CO_2 emissions by 100,000 metric tons annually.

2.2 AI-Driven Fleet Electrification & Fuel Efficiency

AI plays a critical role in transitioning logistics fleets to electric and hybrid vehicles by:

✓ Identifying optimal fleet electrification strategies based on route length, charging station availability, and energy costs.

✓ Monitoring driver behavior and suggesting fuel-efficient driving techniques (e.g., eco-driving).

✓ Using AI-powered predictive maintenance to ensure fuel efficiency and reduce carbon emissions.

☞ Case Study: DHL's AI-Based Green Fleet Strategy

- DHL uses AI-powered fleet management systems to track fuel consumption and suggest optimal driving patterns.
- AI has helped DHL reduce fuel use by 15% and cut CO_2 emissions by over 50,000 metric tons annually.

2.3 AI in Smart Warehousing & Energy Efficiency

Warehouses consume large amounts of energy for lighting, cooling, and automated machinery. AI-driven energy management systems help reduce carbon footprints by:

✓ Optimizing warehouse layout to minimize energy-intensive transportation within facilities.

✓ Using AI-powered climate control systems to adjust heating, cooling, and ventilation based on real-time conditions.

✓ Deploying autonomous robots to improve efficiency and reduce manual energy-intensive processes.

☞ Case Study: Amazon's AI-Optimized Warehouses

- Amazon's warehouses use AI-powered energy optimization, reducing electricity use by 25%.
- AI-powered predictive maintenance detects faulty HVAC systems, preventing unnecessary energy waste.

2.4 AI for Reducing Empty Miles & Load Optimization

One of the biggest inefficiencies in logistics is empty miles, where trucks return without cargo after a delivery. AI-powered logistics platforms:

✓ Use machine learning algorithms to match return shipments with trucks that would otherwise be empty.

✓ Optimize load distribution and truck capacity, reducing the number of vehicles on the road.

✓ Enable shared logistics and freight pooling, cutting emissions significantly.

☞ **Case Study: Convoy's AI-Powered Load Matching**

- Convoy, an AI-driven freight logistics company, uses AI to optimize truckloads and reduce empty miles.
- Its AI system has reduced carbon emissions by 35% for partner fleets by ensuring trucks operate at full capacity.

3. AI for Sustainable Packaging & Waste Reduction

3.1 AI in Smart Packaging Optimization

AI-driven solutions are transforming packaging sustainability by:

✓ Analyzing package dimensions and weight to reduce material waste.

✓ Using AI-powered robotics to customize packaging based on product size, minimizing excessive use of plastic and cardboard.

✓ Implementing AI-based predictive analytics to prevent overproduction of packaging materials.

☞ **Case Study: FedEx's AI-Optimized Packaging**

FedEx uses AI-driven packaging solutions to reduce cardboard waste by 20%, cutting thousands of tons of CO_2 emissions.

3.2 AI for Reducing Reverse Logistics Waste

Returns and reverse logistics create additional emissions and packaging waste. AI-powered returns management systems:

✓ Predict return trends and optimize reverse logistics routes.

✓ Identify resellable and recyclable returned products to minimize landfill waste.

✓ Optimize warehouse space allocation for handling returned goods efficiently.

☞ **Case Study: Zara's AI-Powered Returns Management**

AI-driven reverse logistics optimization has helped Zara reduce return-related carbon emissions by 25%.

4. Challenges in AI-Driven Sustainable Logistics

⚠ **High Implementation Costs** → AI-powered green logistics solutions require significant upfront investment.

⚠ **Data Integration Issues** → Businesses struggle to integrate AI with existing logistics and fleet management systems.

⚠ **Limited Green Infrastructure** → The transition to electric vehicles and AI-powered charging stations is still in progress.

⚠ **Regulatory Uncertainty** → Sustainability policies and carbon taxes are constantly evolving, requiring flexible AI strategies.

5. The Future of AI in Green Logistics

🖋 **AI-Powered Carbon Footprint Tracking** → AI will provide real-time emissions monitoring for supply chains.

🖋 **Autonomous Electric Vehicles & Drones** → AI-driven EVs and delivery drones will replace fossil-fuel-based logistics.

🖋 **AI + Blockchain for Sustainable Logistics** → AI-powered blockchain solutions will ensure transparent and eco-friendly supply chains.

🚀 **AI-Driven Circular Supply Chains** → AI will optimize recycling, reuse, and material recovery in logistics.

6. Conclusion: AI is Driving the Future of Green Logistics

AI is playing a transformative role in reducing the carbon footprint of logistics, making supply chains more sustainable, efficient, and cost-effective. From route optimization and fleet electrification to smart warehousing and packaging waste reduction, AI is enabling businesses to cut emissions, lower energy consumption, and improve sustainability efforts.

As AI technology continues to evolve, net-zero logistics will become a reality, paving the way for a greener, smarter, and more environmentally responsible future. 🌍💡

13. AI in Education: Personalized Learning & Automated Grading

AI is reshaping education by enabling personalized learning experiences, intelligent tutoring systems, and automated grading solutions. Machine learning algorithms analyze student performance data to adapt lesson plans, recommend customized study materials, and provide real-time feedback, ensuring a more tailored and effective learning journey. AI-driven grading systems streamline assessments by automating essay evaluations, detecting plagiarism, and offering data-driven insights to educators. This chapter explores how AI is transforming education, the benefits and challenges of AI-driven learning, and the future of AI-powered classrooms, online learning platforms, and academic institutions.

13.1 NLP & AI-Driven Chatbots in E-Learning

The integration of Artificial Intelligence (AI) and Natural Language Processing (NLP) in e-learning is revolutionizing education by enhancing personalized learning experiences, student engagement, and administrative efficiency. Among AI-powered tools, chatbots stand out as game-changers in virtual classrooms, learning management systems (LMS), and online education platforms. These AI-driven assistants can answer queries, provide tutoring, assess student progress, and deliver real-time feedback, making learning more interactive and efficient.

This chapter explores the role of NLP-powered chatbots in e-learning, the key technologies driving them, their benefits, real-world applications, and the challenges in implementing AI-driven educational tools.

1. The Role of AI Chatbots in E-Learning

AI-driven chatbots serve as virtual teaching assistants in e-learning environments, handling a wide range of tasks such as:

✓ Providing instant answers to students' academic queries.

✓ Offering personalized tutoring based on a student's learning style and progress.

✓ Assisting educators by automating administrative tasks like grading and attendance tracking.

✓ Enhancing engagement through interactive quizzes, gamification, and real-time feedback.

✓ Supporting multilingual learning by breaking language barriers using NLP.

With AI chatbots, students receive 24/7 academic support, reducing dependency on human instructors and fostering a self-paced learning environment.

2. Key Technologies Powering AI Chatbots in E-Learning

2.1 Natural Language Processing (NLP)

✓ Enables chatbots to understand, interpret, and respond to human language.

✓ Helps chatbots analyze student queries, detect sentiment, and personalize responses.

2.2 Machine Learning & Deep Learning

✓ AI chatbots learn from student interactions, improving accuracy over time.

✓ Deep learning algorithms allow chatbots to adapt to individual learning patterns.

2.3 Speech Recognition & Text-to-Speech (TTS) Technologies

✓ Allows voice-based interaction for students who prefer audio learning.

✓ Enhances accessibility for visually impaired learners.

2.4 Integration with Learning Management Systems (LMS)

✓ Chatbots can be integrated into platforms like Moodle, Blackboard, and Google Classroom.

✓ Helps automate assignment submissions, reminders, and exam notifications.

3. AI Chatbots in Personalized Learning

3.1 Adaptive Learning with AI

AI chatbots use student performance data to create personalized learning paths by:

✓ Identifying knowledge gaps and recommending relevant resources.

✓ Adjusting difficulty levels based on student progress.

✓ Providing real-time feedback to improve learning outcomes.

☞ Case Study: Duolingo's AI-Powered Chatbots

- Duolingo uses NLP-powered chatbots to provide conversational language practice.
- The AI adjusts questions based on user proficiency, making language learning more interactive and personalized.

3.2 AI Chatbots as Virtual Tutors

✓ AI chatbots act as 24/7 virtual tutors, assisting students with complex concepts.

✓ Provides step-by-step explanations and instant solutions to doubts.

✓ Uses gamification techniques like quizzes and rewards to maintain engagement.

☞ Case Study: Carnegie Learning's MATHia AI Tutor

- MATHia's AI-driven chatbot tutor provides real-time math tutoring, tracking student progress and adjusting lessons accordingly.
- Helps students grasp complex mathematical concepts through interactive explanations.

4. AI Chatbots for Administrative & Instructor Support

✓ Automates grading of assignments and quizzes, saving educators time.

✓ Sends course reminders, deadlines, and personalized study plans.

✓ Reduces the teacher workload, allowing them to focus on interactive teaching.

☞ Case Study: IBM Watson in Education

- IBM Watson's AI chatbot assists teachers in grading assignments, answering student queries, and tracking performance.
- Reduces administrative burden and improves teacher efficiency.

5. AI Chatbots for Student Engagement & Gamification

5.1 AI-Powered Interactive Learning

✓ AI chatbots can create gamified quizzes, challenges, and interactive simulations.

✓ Boosts student motivation and participation.

☞ **Example: QuizBot by Stanford University**

- QuizBot uses NLP-powered AI to engage students in chat-based quiz sessions.
- Improves knowledge retention through interactive revision sessions.

5.2 Multilingual AI Chatbots for Global Learning

✓ NLP-powered chatbots translate lessons into multiple languages.

✓ Helps international students overcome language barriers.

☞ **Example: Microsoft's AI-Powered Translator Chatbot**

- Assists students in understanding course material in their native language.
- Supports inclusive education across different linguistic backgrounds.

6. Challenges in AI-Driven Chatbots for E-Learning

⚠ **Contextual Understanding Issues** → NLP chatbots may misinterpret complex student queries.

⚠ **Lack of Human Emotion** → AI chatbots lack the empathy and creativity of human teachers.

⚠ **Privacy & Data Security Concerns** → AI chatbots store student interactions, raising privacy issues.

⚠ **Integration with Legacy Systems** → Some educational institutions struggle to adopt AI due to outdated infrastructure.

7. Future of AI Chatbots in Education

🚀 **Emotionally Intelligent AI Tutors** → Future chatbots will use sentiment analysis to detect student frustration and adjust teaching styles.

🚀 **Voice-Based Learning Assistants** → AI will enable fully voice-driven e-learning experiences.

🚀 **AI-Powered Peer Learning Networks** → Chatbots will connect students with similar learning needs for collaborative learning.

🚀 **AI-Driven AR & VR Chatbots** → AI will integrate with Augmented & Virtual Reality (AR/VR) for immersive learning experiences.

8. Conclusion: AI Chatbots are Transforming E-Learning

AI-driven chatbots, powered by Natural Language Processing (NLP), are revolutionizing e-learning by offering instant support, personalized tutoring, and enhanced engagement. By automating administrative tasks, optimizing learning experiences, and enabling 24/7 student assistance, chatbots are shaping the future of digital education.

As AI technology continues to evolve, chatbots will become even more sophisticated, bridging the gap between human instructors and digital learning, ultimately making education more accessible, interactive, and efficient. 🚀🎓

13.2 AI-Powered Adaptive Learning Platforms

The traditional "one-size-fits-all" education model is rapidly evolving, thanks to Artificial Intelligence (AI)-powered adaptive learning platforms. These platforms leverage machine learning, data analytics, and natural language processing (NLP) to create personalized learning experiences tailored to each student's strengths, weaknesses, and learning pace. By continuously analyzing student performance and behavior, AI-driven systems dynamically adjust content, recommend resources, and provide real-time feedback, ensuring more effective and engaging education.

This chapter explores how AI-powered adaptive learning platforms are transforming education, their key components, benefits, challenges, and real-world applications.

1. What is Adaptive Learning?

Adaptive learning is an educational approach that uses AI and data-driven algorithms to modify learning materials in real time based on individual student needs. Unlike traditional education methods that follow a fixed curriculum, AI-driven adaptive platforms continuously assess students and adjust content dynamically.

1.1 How AI Enables Adaptive Learning

✓ **Personalized Learning Paths** → AI tailors content to match each student's progress.

✓ **Real-Time Assessments** → AI evaluates student responses and adjusts difficulty levels accordingly.

✓ **Automated Feedback** → AI provides instant explanations and recommendations for improvement.

✓ **Predictive Analytics** → AI predicts future learning outcomes and identifies struggling students early.

☞ **Example: Khan Academy's AI-Based Learning Model**

Khan Academy uses AI-driven adaptive learning to customize math and science lessons based on a student's performance, offering personalized hints and guidance.

2. Key Technologies Behind AI-Powered Adaptive Learning

2.1 Machine Learning & Data Analytics

✓ AI analyzes student behavior, quiz results, and engagement metrics to modify lesson plans.

✓ Predicts learning patterns and suggests personalized study plans.

2.2 Natural Language Processing (NLP)

✓ Enables AI to understand student questions, responses, and feedback.

✓ Powers interactive AI tutors and chatbots for real-time student support.

2.3 Deep Learning for Personalized Content Recommendation

✓ AI recommends relevant articles, videos, and exercises tailored to student progress.

✓ Adjusts content based on learning speed, retention rate, and knowledge gaps.

☞ Example: Coursera's AI-Powered Recommendation Engine

Coursera suggests personalized courses and video lectures based on learner preferences and past performance.

3. Benefits of AI-Powered Adaptive Learning

3.1 Personalized Learning Experience

✓ AI customizes lesson plans to fit individual learning speeds and styles.

✓ Provides extra practice for weaker areas and accelerates learning for advanced students.

3.2 Increased Student Engagement

✓ AI-powered gamification techniques, quizzes, and interactive exercises keep students engaged.

✓ Real-time performance tracking helps maintain motivation and reduce frustration.

3.3 24/7 AI Tutoring & Support

✓ AI-driven virtual tutors and chatbots provide instant explanations.

✓ Enables self-paced learning without requiring human intervention.

☞ **Example: Duolingo's AI Adaptive Language Learning**

Duolingo adjusts difficulty levels based on user accuracy, providing personalized language learning experiences.

4. AI-Driven Adaptive Learning in Different Education Sectors

4.1 AI in K-12 Education

✓ Helps teachers identify struggling students early and adjust lesson plans accordingly.

✓ Provides customized exercises for students with different learning abilities.

☞ **Example: DreamBox Learning (AI Math Tutor for K-12)**

Uses AI to analyze student performance and adjust math problems in real time.

4.2 AI in Higher Education

✓ AI-powered platforms recommend study materials based on university coursework.

✓ Automates grading and provides personalized course assistance.

☞ **Example: Carnegie Mellon University's AI-Powered Learning**

Uses AI to personalize computer science courses, helping students progress at their own pace.

4.3 AI in Corporate Training & Professional Development

✓ AI tailors training programs based on employee skill levels.

✓ Provides personalized career growth recommendations.

☞ **Example: LinkedIn Learning's AI-Powered Skill Development**

Recommends courses based on career goals and skill proficiency.

5. Challenges in AI-Powered Adaptive Learning

⚠ **Bias in AI Algorithms** → AI models may favor certain learning patterns and unintentionally disadvantage others.

⚠ **Data Privacy Concerns** → AI platforms collect student learning data, raising ethical issues.

⚠ **High Implementation Costs** → Developing AI-powered educational tools requires significant investment.

⚠ **Teacher Adaptation** → Educators must adapt to AI-driven teaching methodologies.

☞ **Solution:**

✓ **Ethical AI Guidelines** → Ensure bias-free and transparent AI models.

✓ **Data Security Measures** → Implement strong encryption and data protection.

✓ **AI Training for Educators** → Help teachers integrate AI tools effectively.

6. The Future of AI in Adaptive Learning

🖋 **Emotionally Intelligent AI Tutors** → AI will detect student frustration, boredom, and motivation levels.

🖋 **AI-Powered AR/VR Learning Environments** → Adaptive virtual reality-based learning experiences will enhance engagement.

🖋 **AI + Blockchain for Secure Learning Records** → Blockchain will store verified learning achievements securely.

🖋 **AI-Driven Peer-to-Peer Learning** → AI will match students with similar learning goals for collaborative education.

☞ **Example: Google's AI-Driven Learning Tools**

Google is investing in AI-powered virtual tutors and interactive learning experiences to make education more accessible and engaging.

7. Conclusion: AI is Shaping the Future of Learning

AI-powered adaptive learning platforms are revolutionizing education by personalizing learning experiences, improving student engagement, and enhancing knowledge retention. By leveraging machine learning, NLP, and real-time analytics, AI enables educators to create dynamic and responsive learning environments that cater to individual student needs.

As AI technology continues to advance, adaptive learning platforms will become even more intuitive, accessible, and effective, paving the way for a future where education is truly personalized for every learner. 🚀🎓

13.3 Automated Essay Scoring & Student Performance Prediction

The integration of Artificial Intelligence (AI) and Natural Language Processing (NLP) in education has revolutionized the way essays are graded and student performance is predicted. Automated essay scoring (AES) systems use AI to evaluate written responses, providing fast, objective, and consistent assessments. Additionally, AI-driven predictive analytics can forecast student success, identify struggling learners, and recommend personalized interventions to improve learning outcomes.

In this chapter, we explore how AI-powered essay grading systems work, their benefits and limitations, and how predictive analytics is transforming academic performance monitoring.

1. What is Automated Essay Scoring (AES)?

Automated essay scoring (AES) is an AI-based grading system that evaluates written assignments by analyzing language, structure, coherence, and argument quality. These systems use machine learning, NLP, and deep learning to mimic human grading patterns while ensuring speed and consistency.

1.1 How AES Works

✓ **Text Preprocessing** → AI tokenizes the text, removing irrelevant elements (e.g., stop words, punctuation).

✓ **Feature Extraction** → AI analyzes grammar, vocabulary richness, coherence, and argument structure.

✓ **Scoring Algorithm** → Uses a pre-trained model that compares the essay to graded examples.

✓ **Feedback Generation** → AI provides detailed feedback on writing quality, readability, and areas for improvement.

☞ **Example**: E-Rater by ETS (Used in TOEFL & GRE Exams)

ETS's E-Rater system evaluates essays based on grammar, structure, coherence, and content relevance, offering quick and fair assessments.

2. Key Technologies Behind Automated Essay Scoring

2.1 Natural Language Processing (NLP)

✓ Helps AI understand and evaluate text based on linguistic patterns.

✓ Assesses sentence structure, readability, and semantic meaning.

2.2 Machine Learning & Deep Learning

✓ AI learns from large datasets of human-graded essays to mimic human evaluation.

✓ Uses neural networks to recognize complex writing patterns.

2.3 Sentiment & Semantic Analysis

✓ AI detects tone, argument quality, and clarity in essays.

✓ Identifies logical reasoning and coherence in student responses.

☞ **Example**: Grammarly's AI-Powered Writing Assistant

Uses NLP and deep learning to provide automated grammar, structure, and readability improvements.

3. Benefits of Automated Essay Scoring

3.1 Speed & Efficiency

✓ AES systems can evaluate thousands of essays in seconds, reducing grading workload for teachers.

✓ Ideal for large-scale exams and online learning platforms.

3.2 Consistency & Objectivity

✓ Unlike human graders, AI does not suffer from fatigue or subjective bias.

✓ Ensures uniform grading criteria across all students.

3.3 Instant & Detailed Feedback

✓ Provides students with immediate scoring and suggestions for improvement.

✓ Helps learners refine their writing skills through AI-driven analysis.

☞ **Example**: Pearson's Intelligent Essay Assessor (IEA)

Uses AI-based scoring to provide detailed feedback on writing clarity, coherence, and grammar.

4. Limitations & Challenges of AES

⚠ **Lack of Deep Comprehension** → AI struggles to understand creativity, humor, or abstract arguments.

⚠ **Bias in AI Models** → AI may favor certain writing styles over others, leading to grading inconsistencies.

⚠ **Vulnerability to Tricks** → Some AES systems reward longer essays with more complex vocabulary, even if content quality is poor.

⚠ **Limited Handling of Subjective Essays** → AI struggles to assess personal reflections, opinions, or highly creative responses.

☞ **Solution:**

✓ Combine AI scoring with human oversight for more accurate grading.

✓ Train AI models on diverse datasets to reduce bias.

5. AI in Student Performance Prediction

5.1 What is AI-Powered Student Performance Prediction?

AI uses predictive analytics to assess student learning patterns, past performance, and engagement levels to forecast academic success.

5.2 How AI Predicts Student Performance

✓ **Analyzing Assignment & Exam Scores** → AI tracks trends in student performance over time.

✓ **Monitoring Engagement Levels** → AI evaluates class participation, attendance, and LMS activity.

✓ **Behavioral Analytics** → AI detects patterns in study habits, assignment submissions, and learning interactions.

☞ **Example**: IBM Watson's AI for Student Success

IBM Watson helps universities analyze student learning data to predict dropout risks and recommend interventions.

6. Benefits of AI-Driven Student Performance Prediction

6.1 Early Intervention for Struggling Students

✓ AI identifies at-risk students and recommends personalized support.

✓ Helps educators design targeted learning strategies.

6.2 Personalized Learning Plans

✓ AI suggests customized study plans based on a student's strengths and weaknesses.

✓ Improves learning efficiency through adaptive learning models.

6.3 Reducing Dropout Rates

✓ AI flags low-engagement students and suggests remedial actions.

✓ Helps universities implement personalized mentoring programs.

☞ **Example**: Georgia State University's AI-Based Dropout Prediction Model

Uses AI to predict student dropout risks and offers proactive academic support.

7. Challenges in AI-Driven Performance Prediction

⚠ **Privacy Concerns** → AI collects student learning data, raising ethical issues.

⚠ **Bias in AI Models** → AI may unintentionally favor certain demographics.

⚠ **Over-Reliance on AI** → Human mentorship is still crucial for student success.

⚠ **Data Quality Issues** → Inaccurate or incomplete data can affect AI predictions.

☞ **Solution:**

✓ **Transparent AI Models** → Ensure fairness in AI decision-making.

✓ **Strict Data Protection Policies** → Protect student privacy and security.

8. The Future of AI in Automated Essay Scoring & Performance Prediction

🔋 **AI-Powered Emotion Detection** → AI will analyze student sentiment in essays to assess deeper understanding.

🔋 **Advanced AI Feedback Systems** → AI will provide interactive writing feedback in real time.

✒ AI + Blockchain for Secure Student Records → Blockchain will protect AI-generated student performance reports.

✒ AI-Driven Adaptive Exams → AI will create customized test questions based on student strengths & weaknesses.

☞ **Example: Turnitin's AI-Based Writing Insights**

Uses AI to detect plagiarism, analyze writing styles, and provide real-time feedback.

9. Conclusion: AI is Revolutionizing Assessment & Performance Tracking

AI-driven automated essay scoring and student performance prediction are transforming the education system by making assessments faster, fairer, and more personalized. By leveraging machine learning, NLP, and predictive analytics, AI provides instant feedback, customized learning plans, and early intervention for struggling students.

While challenges remain, continuous AI advancements will make assessments more accurate, insightful, and student-friendly. The future of education lies in intelligent, adaptive, and data-driven learning experiences that empower students to reach their full potential. ✒🎓

13.4 Ethical Considerations in AI-Based Learning

As Artificial Intelligence (AI) continues to revolutionize education, ethical concerns surrounding AI-based learning have become increasingly significant. While AI-driven educational tools offer personalized learning, automated assessments, and predictive analytics, they also raise critical issues related to privacy, bias, transparency, and the role of human educators. Ensuring that AI in education is fair, ethical, and beneficial to all learners requires careful consideration and responsible implementation.

This chapter explores the key ethical concerns in AI-powered education, the potential risks of AI-driven learning systems, and strategies for developing ethical AI models that enhance education without compromising student rights and educational integrity.

1. The Ethical Dilemmas in AI-Based Learning

AI-powered education tools are designed to improve learning outcomes, but they also introduce several ethical dilemmas. These include concerns about data privacy, algorithmic bias, student autonomy, and the over-reliance on AI for learning.

1.1 AI and Student Data Privacy

✓ AI systems collect, analyze, and store vast amounts of student data.

✓ This data includes learning patterns, behavioral analytics, and personal information.

✓ If improperly managed, student data can be misused, leaked, or exploited by third parties.

☞ **Example**: AI Learning Platforms & Data Collection

Platforms like Google Classroom, Coursera, and Khan Academy track student interactions, raising concerns about who controls the data and how it is used.

⚠ **Potential Risk:**

- Student data might be sold to advertisers or used for unauthorized purposes.

✓ **Solution:**

- Implement strict data encryption, transparent privacy policies, and opt-in data collection systems.
- Adopt federal regulations (e.g., FERPA, GDPR) to protect student information.

2. Bias & Fairness in AI-Driven Learning

AI models are trained on historical data, which can sometimes contain biases that disadvantage certain student groups. Algorithmic bias in AI learning systems can lead to inequitable learning opportunities.

2.1 How Bias Appears in AI Education Systems

✓ **Language Bias** → AI chatbots or grading systems may struggle with non-native English speakers.

✓ **Cultural Bias** → AI training data might favor certain cultural norms, leaving out diverse perspectives.

✓ **Demographic Bias** → AI-powered adaptive learning may unintentionally disadvantage students from lower-income backgrounds.

☞ **Example**: Bias in Automated Essay Scoring (AES)

Studies have shown that some AI essay graders favor longer essays with complex vocabulary, disadvantaging students with simpler writing styles or different linguistic backgrounds.

⚠ **Potential Risk:**

- AI may unintentionally discriminate against students based on race, gender, or socioeconomic status.

✓ **Solution:**

- Train AI models on diverse datasets to ensure fair assessment.
- Implement human oversight in AI grading to counteract algorithmic biases.

3. Transparency & Explainability in AI-Based Learning

Many AI-driven educational systems function as "black boxes," where their decision-making process is not fully transparent. This lack of explainability raises concerns about fairness, accountability, and trust in AI-driven education.

3.1 Why AI Transparency Matters

✓ Students and educators need to understand how AI makes decisions (e.g., grading, recommendations, performance tracking).

✓ AI-powered grading and feedback should be explainable, auditable, and interpretable.

☞ **Example**: AI-Based College Admissions Screening

Some universities use AI algorithms to filter student applications, but the lack of transparency in the selection process has led to ethical concerns.

⚠ Potential Risk:

Opaque AI models can result in unfair evaluations and lack of accountability.

✓ Solution:

- Develop explainable AI (XAI) models that clearly outline how decisions are made.
- Ensure that students and educators can challenge AI-driven assessments.

4. The Role of Human Educators in AI-Based Learning

While AI enhances learning, it cannot replace human educators. The over-reliance on AI-powered teaching and assessment tools may lead to a loss of human interaction and mentorship in education.

4.1 The Limits of AI in Teaching

✓ AI can personalize learning, but it cannot understand student emotions, social factors, or personal challenges.

✓ AI-driven chatbots lack empathy and emotional intelligence, which are crucial in education.

☞ **Example**: AI Chatbots vs. Human Teachers

AI tutors can provide instant feedback, but they lack the ability to inspire, motivate, or mentor students the way human teachers can.

⚠ Potential Risk:

Over-dependence on AI may reduce human interaction in classrooms, leading to weaker social skills in students.

✓ Solution:

- Use AI as a support tool, not a replacement for human teachers.
- Develop hybrid AI-human learning models that integrate AI assistance with teacher guidance.

5. Ethical AI Development for Education

Ensuring ethical AI in education requires clear guidelines, accountability, and responsible AI development.

5.1 Ethical AI Development Principles

✓ **Fairness & Bias Reduction** → Train AI with inclusive datasets.

✓ **Transparency & Explainability** → Provide clear insights into how AI makes decisions.

✓ **Privacy & Security** → Protect student data with encryption and strict access controls.

✓ **Human-AI Collaboration** → Use AI to enhance, not replace, human educators.

☞ **Example**: UNESCO's AI in Education Policy

UNESCO has outlined global AI ethics guidelines, ensuring AI benefits all students without discrimination or harm.

6. The Future of Ethical AI in Education

✦ **Bias-Free AI Models** → More efforts will be made to reduce AI biases in grading and learning recommendations.

✦ **Transparent AI Systems** → AI-powered grading and assessment tools will provide detailed explanations.

✦ **Privacy-First AI Learning** → Schools and universities will adopt stronger AI data protection policies.

✦ **AI & Human Collaboration** → Future classrooms will integrate AI with human-driven mentoring and teaching strategies.

☞ **Example**: Microsoft's AI Ethics Initiative

Microsoft is working on ethical AI policies to ensure fair, transparent, and inclusive AI applications in education.

7. Conclusion: Balancing AI Innovation with Ethical Responsibility

AI has tremendous potential to enhance education, but it must be implemented responsibly to avoid bias, privacy issues, and over-reliance on automation. The future of AI in education must focus on ethical transparency, fairness, and the balance between AI-driven learning and human mentorship.

By developing responsible AI policies, ensuring data privacy, and integrating AI with human educators, we can create an inclusive, fair, and effective AI-powered education system that benefits all learners. 🚀🎓

14. Next-Generation AI: Quantum AI & Explainable AI

As AI continues to evolve, cutting-edge advancements like Quantum AI and Explainable AI (XAI) are pushing the boundaries of what's possible. Quantum AI harnesses the power of quantum computing to solve complex problems exponentially faster than traditional AI, with applications in drug discovery, financial modeling, and materials science. Meanwhile, Explainable AI (XAI) is addressing the critical need for transparency in AI decision-making, ensuring that AI models are interpretable, accountable, and ethically aligned. This chapter explores how these next-generation AI technologies are shaping the future, their potential impact across industries, and the challenges of implementation, scalability, and ethical considerations.

14.1 Quantum Computing & Its Potential in Industry AI

As artificial intelligence (AI) continues to advance, traditional computing methods are approaching their limits in handling vast datasets and complex algorithms. Quantum computing, with its ability to process multiple possibilities simultaneously, is emerging as a revolutionary technology that could transform AI-driven applications across industries. By leveraging quantum mechanics, quantum computers have the potential to accelerate AI model training, optimize industrial processes, and solve computational problems that are currently infeasible for classical computers.

This chapter explores the fundamentals of quantum computing, its advantages over classical computing, and its potential applications in AI across industries such as healthcare, finance, and manufacturing. We also examine the challenges that must be overcome before quantum AI becomes mainstream.

1. Understanding Quantum Computing

1.1 How Quantum Computing Works

Unlike classical computers that use bits (which can be either 0 or 1), quantum computers use qubits (quantum bits), which can exist in superposition—meaning they can be both 0 and 1 simultaneously. This allows quantum computers to perform multiple calculations at once, exponentially increasing processing power.

Key principles of quantum computing:

✓ **Superposition** → Qubits can exist in multiple states at the same time, increasing computational power.

✓ **Entanglement** → Qubits can be linked together, allowing instantaneous communication and faster data processing.

✓ **Quantum Interference** → The ability to control quantum states to arrive at more accurate solutions.

☞ **Example**: Google's Quantum Supremacy Achievement

Google's Sycamore processor performed a calculation in 200 seconds that would take the world's most powerful supercomputer 10,000 years to complete.

2. How Quantum Computing Enhances AI

Traditional AI models rely on high-performance computing (HPC) and GPUs to process large amounts of data, but these systems are still limited by processing speed and energy consumption. Quantum AI, however, has the potential to:

2.1 Speed Up Machine Learning Training

✓ Quantum computing can process large datasets exponentially faster than classical computers.

✓ Algorithms like Quantum Support Vector Machines (QSVMs) and Quantum Neural Networks (QNNs) can enhance pattern recognition and deep learning.

☞ **Example**: IBM's Quantum AI Research

IBM is developing quantum-enhanced machine learning models to improve AI predictions and decision-making.

2.2 Solve Complex Optimization Problems

✓ Many industries rely on optimization algorithms, such as supply chain logistics, financial modeling, and healthcare resource allocation.

✓ Quantum computers can quickly identify optimal solutions in real time, reducing costs and inefficiencies.

☞ **Example**: Volkswagen's Quantum AI for Traffic Flow Optimization

Volkswagen is using quantum computing to optimize traffic patterns and reduce congestion in smart cities.

2.3 Enhance Natural Language Processing (NLP)

✓ Quantum AI can improve sentiment analysis, translation, and chatbot responses by handling linguistic complexities more effectively.

✓ Can significantly reduce training time for large language models (LLMs) like GPT.

☞ **Example**: Google's Quantum NLP Project

Google is exploring quantum-enhanced NLP algorithms to improve AI-driven customer support systems.

3. Industry-Specific Applications of Quantum AI

3.1 Healthcare: Drug Discovery & Genomics

✓ Quantum AI can simulate molecular interactions, accelerating drug discovery and reducing costs.

✓ Can analyze genomic data faster, enabling personalized medicine and disease prediction.

☞ **Example**: Quantum-Assisted Drug Discovery

D-Wave and Menten AI are using quantum computing to design new pharmaceutical drugs faster than traditional methods.

3.2 Finance: Risk Analysis & Fraud Detection

✓ Quantum algorithms can process massive financial datasets to detect fraud patterns in real-time.

✓ Can improve risk management models, helping banks and hedge funds make better investment decisions.

☞ **Example**: JPMorgan Chase's Quantum Finance Research

JPMorgan is developing quantum algorithms for portfolio optimization and high-frequency trading.

3.3 Manufacturing: Supply Chain Optimization

✓ Quantum AI can help predict and manage supply chain disruptions with better accuracy.

✓ Can optimize factory processes, reduce waste, and improve production efficiency.

☞ **Example**: Airbus' Quantum AI Research

Airbus is exploring quantum computing to improve aircraft design and streamline manufacturing.

4. Challenges & Limitations of Quantum AI

Despite its potential, quantum computing still faces several technical and practical challenges that must be addressed before it can be widely adopted.

⚠ **Hardware Limitations** → Quantum computers require extreme conditions (near absolute zero temperatures) to function properly.

⚠ **Error Rates & Stability** → Qubits are highly fragile and prone to quantum decoherence, leading to calculation errors.

⚠ **High Costs** → Developing and maintaining quantum systems is extremely expensive, limiting accessibility.

⚠ **Algorithm Development** → Quantum AI algorithms are still in their infancy and require new programming paradigms.

✔ **Solution:**

- Researchers are working on error-correcting quantum computers to improve stability.
- Companies like IBM, Google, and Rigetti are developing cloud-based quantum computing platforms to democratize access.

5. The Future of Quantum AI in Industry

🚀 **Quantum Cloud Computing** → Companies like IBM Quantum, Amazon Braket, and Microsoft Azure Quantum are making quantum computing accessible via the cloud.

🚀 **Hybrid Quantum-Classical AI** → Future AI models will integrate quantum and classical computing for enhanced efficiency.

🚀 **Quantum AI for Climate Modeling** → Scientists are exploring quantum-powered simulations to combat climate change.

🚀 **Mainstream Quantum Adoption** → By 2030, industries like pharmaceuticals, finance, and logistics may heavily rely on quantum AI for decision-making.

☞ **Example**: IBM's Quantum Roadmap

IBM plans to launch a 1,000-qubit quantum computer by 2026, pushing quantum AI closer to mainstream adoption.

6. Conclusion: A New Era of AI with Quantum Computing

Quantum computing has the potential to redefine industrial AI applications, unlocking new possibilities in machine learning, optimization, and predictive analytics. While challenges remain, ongoing advancements in quantum hardware, error correction, and hybrid quantum-classical computing are bringing us closer to practical, real-world applications.

As industries continue to explore the synergy between AI and quantum computing, businesses that invest in quantum AI research today will be the leaders of tomorrow's technological revolution. 🚀

14.2 Explainable AI (XAI) & Its Importance in Regulated Industries

Artificial Intelligence (AI) is transforming industries worldwide, but its decision-making processes often function as black boxes, making it difficult for users to understand how AI models arrive at their conclusions. In regulated industries such as healthcare, finance, and law, transparency and accountability are critical. This is where Explainable AI (XAI) comes into play.

XAI refers to a set of techniques and frameworks that make AI decision-making transparent, interpretable, and accountable. By ensuring that AI models provide clear explanations for their predictions, XAI helps build trust, ensures regulatory compliance, and enables businesses to make more informed decisions.

This chapter explores the importance of explainable AI in regulated industries, key XAI techniques, challenges, and real-world applications.

1. Why Explainability Matters in Regulated Industries

Many industries operate under strict regulations to protect consumers, ensure fairness, and maintain ethical standards. When AI-driven decisions impact people's health, finances, or legal rights, companies must explain those decisions clearly.

1.1 The Risks of Black-Box AI

✔ **Bias & Discrimination** → AI models may unintentionally discriminate based on race, gender, or socioeconomic status.

✔ **Lack of Trust** → Users may not trust AI-driven decisions without clear justifications.

✔ **Regulatory Non-Compliance** → Many governments now require AI transparency in decision-making.

☞ **Example**: The EU's GDPR & AI Transparency Requirements

The General Data Protection Regulation (GDPR) mandates that users have the right to explanation when AI systems make decisions about them.

1.2 Industries That Require Explainable AI

✓ **Healthcare** → AI-powered diagnoses and treatment recommendations must be transparent to doctors and patients.

✓ **Finance** → AI-driven loan approvals, credit scoring, and fraud detection require clear justifications.

✓ **Legal & Criminal Justice** → AI-based sentencing or parole decisions must be explainable to ensure fairness.

2. Key Explainable AI Techniques

XAI provides a variety of methods to make AI models interpretable while maintaining high performance. These techniques can be categorized into two main types:

2.1 Model-Specific Explainability

✓ **Decision Trees & Rule-Based Models** → Naturally interpretable models where each decision is based on explicit rules.

✓ **Linear Regression & Logistic Regression** → Simple models where feature weights show the impact of variables.

☞ **Example**: AI-Based Loan Approval Using Decision Trees

Banks use decision tree models to show why a customer was approved or denied a loan (e.g., income level, credit score, debt-to-income ratio).

2.2 Post-Hoc Explainability for Black-Box Models

For complex models like neural networks and deep learning, post-hoc methods are required:

✓ **LIME (Local Interpretable Model-agnostic Explanations)** → Creates interpretable approximations of black-box models.

✓ **SHAP (Shapley Additive Explanations)** → Assigns importance scores to each input feature, showing how they influenced predictions.

✓ **Grad-CAM (Gradient-weighted Class Activation Mapping)** → Highlights image areas that influenced a neural network's decision in computer vision models.

☞ **Example**: SHAP in AI-Based Medical Diagnosis

A healthcare AI system using SHAP can explain why it predicted a high risk of heart disease by showing key influencing factors like cholesterol levels, age, and BMI.

3. XAI in Regulated Industries: Use Cases

3.1 Explainable AI in Healthcare

- **Problem**: AI models assist in diagnosing diseases, but doctors need to understand how these models reach conclusions.
- **Solution**: XAI techniques like SHAP and LIME can show which factors led to a diagnosis, improving trust in AI-driven recommendations.

☞ **Real-World Example**: IBM Watson for Oncology

IBM Watson uses XAI techniques to provide interpretable cancer treatment recommendations based on patient data.

3.2 Explainable AI in Finance

- **Problem**: AI is used for credit scoring, loan approvals, and fraud detection, but customers and regulators demand transparency.
- **Solution**: Banks use decision trees and SHAP models to explain why a customer was approved or denied a loan.

☞ **Real-World Example**: FICO's Explainable AI Credit Scoring

FICO has integrated XAI techniques to explain credit scores and improve customer trust.

3.3 Explainable AI in Criminal Justice & Legal Systems

- **Problem**: AI-driven risk assessments influence bail decisions, sentencing, and parole approvals, but opaque models can lead to biased outcomes.
- **Solution**: XAI tools ensure that AI models are transparent and auditable, preventing discrimination.

☞ **Real-World Example**: COMPAS Algorithm for Criminal Risk Assessment

COMPAS, a criminal risk assessment AI, faced criticism for racial bias. Implementing XAI methods can help ensure fairness in legal decisions.

4. Challenges of Implementing Explainable AI

Despite its importance, integrating XAI into real-world systems presents several challenges:

⚠ **Trade-Off Between Accuracy & Explainability** → Highly explainable models (e.g., decision trees) are often less accurate than deep learning models.

⚠ **Scalability Issues** → XAI models may not scale efficiently for large datasets.

⚠ **Complexity in Neural Networks** → Making deep learning models interpretable remains a difficult challenge.

⚠ **Regulatory Uncertainty** → Global AI regulations are still evolving, making compliance complex.

✓ Solution:

- Develop hybrid AI models that balance performance and interpretability.
- Establish industry standards for AI transparency.
- Use XAI toolkits like IBM's AI Explainability 360 or Google's What-If Tool to simplify adoption.

5. The Future of Explainable AI in Regulated Industries

🚀 **XAI-Powered Healthcare AI** → Doctors will have access to detailed AI-driven diagnoses with clear explanations.

🚀 **AI Transparency in Finance** → Governments will require banks to provide AI-driven credit decisions with full disclosure.

🚀 **Regulatory Compliance AI Tools** → Companies will integrate automated XAI compliance systems to meet evolving regulations.

🚀 **AI Audits & Certifications** → AI systems will undergo third-party audits to verify fairness and transparency.

☞ **Example**: The U.S. National AI Initiative Act

The U.S. is investing in AI explainability research to ensure fairness and accountability in AI-driven industries.

6. Conclusion: The Growing Need for Explainable AI

Explainable AI is no longer an option—it is a necessity in regulated industries where transparency, fairness, and accountability are critical. As AI adoption grows in healthcare, finance, and legal sectors, the demand for interpretable, compliant, and trustworthy AI models will continue to rise.

By implementing XAI techniques, adhering to regulatory standards, and integrating AI-human collaboration, industries can unlock the full potential of AI while maintaining ethical and transparent practices. Businesses that prioritize explainable AI today will gain a competitive advantage in the AI-driven economy of tomorrow. 🚀

14.3 AI-Driven Automation & Future Jobs in AI Industries

Artificial Intelligence (AI) is rapidly transforming industries through automation, enhancing efficiency, reducing costs, and reshaping the workforce. While AI-driven automation offers significant benefits, it also raises concerns about job displacement, reskilling, and the future of human labor. Many industries—including healthcare, finance, manufacturing, and retail—are integrating AI into their daily operations, leading to a shift in job roles and the emergence of new career opportunities.

This chapter explores the impact of AI automation on jobs, the industries most affected, and the skills needed for the future AI-driven workforce.

1. How AI-Driven Automation is Reshaping Industries

AI-powered automation is transforming industries by enhancing productivity, reducing human error, and streamlining operations. However, it also challenges traditional job roles, requiring workers to adapt to new AI-powered environments.

1.1 Key Benefits of AI Automation

✓ **Increased Efficiency** → AI automates repetitive tasks, allowing businesses to operate faster.

✓ **Cost Savings** → Companies reduce labor costs while improving operational accuracy.

✓ **24/7 Availability** → AI-powered systems work continuously without fatigue.

✓ **Data-Driven Decision-Making** → AI provides insights that improve strategic planning.

☞ **Example**: AI in Customer Support

AI chatbots like ChatGPT and IBM Watson automate customer service, reducing the need for large call center teams.

1.2 Industries Most Affected by AI Automation

Several industries are seeing significant transformation due to AI-driven automation:

Industry	AI Automation Impact
Manufacturing	AI-driven robotics automate assembly lines.
Healthcare	AI-powered diagnostics and robotic surgeries enhance efficiency.
Finance	Algorithmic trading and AI fraud detection reduce manual intervention.
Retail	AI-driven inventory management and cashier-less stores.
Logistics	AI-powered supply chain optimization and self-driving trucks.

☞ **Example**: Amazon's AI-Powered Warehouses

Amazon uses AI robots to automate order fulfillment, reducing manual warehouse labor.

2. The Future of Jobs in an AI-Driven World

While AI automation will eliminate certain jobs, it will also create new roles that require AI-related skills. Workers must adapt by developing technical expertise and problem-solving abilities.

2.1 Jobs at Risk of AI Automation

Some jobs are more susceptible to automation due to their repetitive and rule-based nature.

✓ **Data Entry Clerks** → AI can quickly process and organize data.

✓ **Customer Service Representatives** → AI chatbots handle inquiries and support.

✓ **Telemarketers** → AI-driven voice assistants automate outbound calls.

✓ **Retail Cashiers** → Self-checkout and cashier-less stores reduce demand.

☞ **Example**: Self-Checkout Stores

Companies like Amazon Go use AI to eliminate the need for human cashiers.

2.2 Jobs That Will Grow Due to AI

AI is also creating new career opportunities in fields that require human creativity, critical thinking, and AI management skills.

✓ **AI & Machine Learning Engineers** → Develop and optimize AI models.

✓ **AI Ethics & Compliance Officers** → Ensure responsible AI usage.

✓ **Data Scientists** → Analyze and interpret AI-driven insights.

✓ **Cybersecurity Specialists** → Protect AI systems from cyber threats.

✓ **AI Trainers & Explainability Experts** → Train AI models and ensure transparency.

☞ **Example**: AI Ethics Officer Role Growth

With increasing AI regulations, companies are hiring AI ethics officers to ensure fairness and accountability.

3. Adapting to the AI-Driven Job Market

To stay competitive in an AI-powered world, professionals need to reskill and upskill in key AI-related domains.

3.1 Essential Skills for AI-Automated Industries

Workers should focus on skills that complement AI-driven automation:

✓ **Technical Skills** → AI, machine learning, Python, and cloud computing.

✓ **Critical Thinking & Problem-Solving** → AI cannot replace human intuition and ethical reasoning.

✓ **Data Literacy** → Understanding AI-generated insights.

✓ **Adaptability & Continuous Learning** → Staying up to date with emerging AI trends.

☞ **Example**: Google's AI Career Certificates

Google offers AI and data science courses to help professionals transition into AI-driven roles.

3.2 The Role of Governments & Companies in Reskilling

Governments and corporations must take responsibility for retraining workers affected by AI automation.

✓ **AI Training Programs** → Businesses invest in employee reskilling.

✓ **Public-Private Partnerships** → Governments collaborate with tech firms for AI workforce training.

✓ **AI Literacy in Education** → Schools integrate AI and coding into curriculums.

☞ **Example**: IBM's AI Training Initiative

IBM launched AI Skills Academy to train employees in AI-related fields.

4. The Ethical Considerations of AI Automation

As AI reshapes industries, it raises ethical concerns about job displacement and economic inequality.

⚠ **Job Loss & Unemployment** → Low-skill workers are at higher risk.

⚠ **Algorithmic Bias** → AI hiring tools may unintentionally discriminate.

⚠ **Unequal AI Access** → Developing nations may lag behind in AI adoption.

✔ Solution:

- Implement Universal Basic Income (UBI) to support displaced workers.
- Ensure AI fairness and diversity in hiring and automation practices.
- Promote AI accessibility for all socioeconomic groups.

☞ **Example**: AI-Powered Hiring Tools & Bias

Amazon's AI recruitment tool was scrapped due to gender bias in hiring recommendations.

5. The Future: Humans & AI Working Together

Despite automation concerns, AI will not replace humans entirely—instead, AI and humans will collaborate to create more efficient workplaces.

🔩 **Human-AI Collaboration** → AI enhances decision-making, while humans provide creativity and emotional intelligence.

🔩 **AI-Augmented Workplaces** → AI handles repetitive tasks, allowing employees to focus on strategic initiatives.

🔩 **New Business Models** → AI enables entirely new industries and professions.

☞ **Example**: AI-Assisted Surgeons

AI-powered robotic surgical assistants enhance precision, but human doctors make critical decisions.

6. Conclusion: Preparing for an AI-Driven Workforce

AI-driven automation is reshaping industries and job markets at an unprecedented rate. While some jobs will be automated, AI will also create new opportunities for workers with the right skills. The future workforce must adapt by reskilling, embracing AI technology, and collaborating with intelligent systems.

Companies, governments, and individuals must work together to ensure a smooth transition into an AI-powered economy. Those who invest in AI education and adaptability today will thrive in the workforce of tomorrow. 🚀

14.4 Challenges in Implementing Next-Gen AI

As Artificial Intelligence (AI) continues to evolve, next-generation AI technologies—including Quantum AI, Explainable AI (XAI), Autonomous AI, and AI-human collaboration systems—promise groundbreaking advancements across industries. However, implementing these cutting-edge AI models comes with significant technical, ethical, regulatory, and economic challenges. Businesses and governments must overcome these obstacles to fully unlock AI's potential while ensuring responsible and ethical deployment.

This chapter explores the key challenges in implementing next-gen AI, from computational complexity and data privacy concerns to regulatory hurdles and workforce transformation.

1. Technical & Infrastructure Challenges

Next-gen AI requires high-performance computing power, robust data ecosystems, and advanced algorithms, making deployment difficult for many organizations.

1.1 High Computational Costs & Energy Consumption

✓ AI models, especially deep learning and quantum AI, demand immense computing power.

✓ Training large-scale AI models is expensive and consumes vast amounts of energy.

✓ AI-driven data centers contribute significantly to carbon emissions, raising sustainability concerns.

☞ **Example**: GPT-4 Training Costs

Training large models like GPT-4 reportedly costs millions of dollars in compute resources, limiting accessibility to only large tech firms.

✓ Solution:

- Use efficient AI architectures like TinyML to reduce energy consumption.
- Develop quantum AI for faster computation with lower energy costs.

1.2 Lack of High-Quality Data & Data Bias

✓ AI models require massive, high-quality datasets for training.

✓ Poor-quality or biased data leads to inaccurate predictions and unfair outcomes.

✓ Data scarcity in certain industries (e.g., rare diseases in healthcare) limits AI effectiveness.

☞ **Example**: AI Bias in Facial Recognition

Studies found racial bias in facial recognition AI due to imbalanced training datasets, leading to discriminatory results.

✓ Solution:

- Develop diverse and representative datasets to eliminate bias.
- Use synthetic data to improve AI training where real-world data is scarce.

1.3 Lack of Generalization & AI's Black Box Problem

✓ Many AI models excel in narrow tasks but fail to generalize across different domains.

✓ Black-box AI models (e.g., deep learning) lack transparency, making it difficult to understand decision-making.

☞ **Example**: Explainability in Healthcare AI

Doctors may not trust AI-driven diagnoses if they cannot understand how the model reached a conclusion.

✓ **Solution:**

- Implement Explainable AI (XAI) techniques like SHAP & LIME to improve transparency.
- Develop hybrid AI systems combining symbolic AI with deep learning for better reasoning.

2. Ethical & Societal Challenges

The widespread adoption of next-gen AI raises ethical dilemmas, from job displacement to biased decision-making and the misuse of AI for harmful purposes.

2.1 AI and Job Displacement

✓ Automation threatens traditional jobs, especially in manufacturing, finance, and customer service.

✓ AI adoption requires reskilling the workforce, but education systems are slow to adapt.

☞ **Example**: AI in Banking

AI-powered chatbots and automation are replacing bank tellers and customer support roles, leading to workforce reductions.

✓ **Solution:**

- Governments and companies must invest in AI reskilling programs.
- Promote human-AI collaboration instead of full automation.

2.2 Bias & Fairness in AI Decision-Making

✓ AI models inherit bias from training data, leading to unfair and discriminatory decisions.

✓ Algorithmic bias in hiring, lending, and law enforcement can worsen social inequalities.

☞ **Example**: AI in Hiring

Amazon's AI hiring tool was scrapped after it was found to discriminate against women.

✓ Solution:

- Implement AI fairness audits to detect and eliminate bias.
- Use transparent AI models to ensure ethical decision-making.

2.3 The Risk of AI Weaponization & Misinformation

✓ AI can be misused for deepfake content, cyberattacks, and autonomous weapons.

✓ AI-generated misinformation and fake news threaten democracy and public trust.

☞ **Example**: Deepfake Threats

Political deepfakes have been used to spread misinformation during elections.

✓ Solution:

- Governments must enforce strict AI regulations to prevent misuse.
- Develop AI detection tools to identify deepfake content.

3. Regulatory & Legal Challenges

The rapid development of AI outpaces regulatory frameworks, making it difficult to enforce AI governance, ethical standards, and data protection laws.

3.1 Lack of Global AI Regulations

✓ AI policies vary across countries, leading to inconsistent regulations.

✓ Without proper regulations, companies can exploit AI for unethical purposes.

☞ **Example**: EU's AI Act vs. U.S. AI Policies

The EU AI Act enforces strict rules on AI transparency, while the U.S. has no unified AI regulation.

✓ **Solution:**

Establish global AI governance frameworks similar to GDPR for data privacy.

3.2 AI & Intellectual Property Rights

✓ AI-generated content raises legal questions about copyright and ownership.

✓ Who owns AI-generated art, code, or music? The AI developer or the user?

☞ **Example**: AI-Generated Art Legal Disputes

AI-created artworks have led to copyright lawsuits over intellectual property rights.

✓ **Solution:**

Governments must define AI-generated content ownership laws.

3.3 AI & Data Privacy Concerns

✓ AI collects and processes sensitive personal data, raising privacy risks.

✓ Companies often lack transparency about how AI models use customer data.

☞ **Example**: AI & GDPR Compliance

The GDPR law requires companies to provide explanations for AI-driven decisions impacting consumers.

✓ **Solution:**

Implement privacy-preserving AI techniques like federated learning.

4. Economic & Business Challenges

Businesses face challenges in adopting next-gen AI due to high costs, return on investment (ROI) concerns, and the need for AI talent.

4.1 High Implementation Costs

✓ AI infrastructure (e.g., cloud computing, GPUs, quantum computers) is expensive.

✓ Small and medium businesses (SMBs) struggle to afford AI adoption.

☞ **Example**: AI Adoption in Healthcare

Many hospitals cannot afford AI-powered diagnostics tools due to high costs.

✓ Solution:

Use AI-as-a-Service (AIaaS) to reduce costs for smaller businesses.

4.2 AI Talent Shortage

✓ There is a global shortage of AI engineers, data scientists, and ethicists.

✓ Many companies struggle to find AI experts to implement next-gen AI.

☞ **Example**: AI Skills Gap

The demand for AI engineers far exceeds the available workforce.

✓ Solution:

Invest in AI education programs and AI bootcamps.

5. Conclusion: Overcoming the Challenges of Next-Gen AI

While next-generation AI presents transformative opportunities, its adoption comes with technical, ethical, regulatory, and economic hurdles. Organizations must address these challenges through responsible AI development, workforce reskilling, ethical governance, and sustainable AI innovation.

By solving issues like bias, explainability, data privacy, and job displacement, businesses can harness AI's full potential while ensuring trustworthy and ethical AI deployment. The future of AI is not just about automation—it's about creating a human-centered AI ecosystem that benefits everyone. 🚀

15. The Ethical and Societal Impact of AI Across Industries

As AI continues to revolutionize industries, it raises critical ethical, social, and regulatory challenges that must be addressed. From bias in AI algorithms and job displacement due to automation to privacy concerns and the need for transparent decision-making, AI's impact extends beyond business efficiency. Governments, organizations, and researchers are working to establish ethical AI frameworks, fairness guidelines, and responsible AI governance to ensure AI benefits society as a whole. This chapter explores the ethical dilemmas, societal implications, and strategies for developing AI systems that are fair, unbiased, and aligned with human values.

15.1 Bias and Fairness in AI Decision-Making

Artificial Intelligence (AI) has become a powerful tool in industries ranging from healthcare and finance to hiring and law enforcement. However, as AI systems make critical decisions that impact people's lives, concerns over bias and fairness have gained significant attention. AI models are only as good as the data they are trained on, and if that data contains historical biases, AI can inadvertently reinforce discrimination and inequality.

This chapter explores how bias creeps into AI models, the consequences of unfair AI decisions, and strategies for ensuring fairness and accountability in AI-driven industries.

1. Understanding Bias in AI

AI bias occurs when an algorithm systematically produces prejudiced or unfair outcomes due to flawed data, improper model training, or lack of diversity in development. Bias can manifest in multiple ways, including:

1.1 Types of Bias in AI

✓ **Data Bias** – If AI is trained on unbalanced or incomplete datasets, it may reinforce existing societal biases.

✓ **Algorithmic Bias** – Some AI models favor certain groups over others due to inherent flaws in their design.

✓ **Human Bias** – Developers may unknowingly introduce their own biases while designing or training AI.

✓ **Selection Bias** – When training data does not accurately represent the entire population.

✓ **Confirmation Bias** – AI models may be unintentionally optimized to confirm existing beliefs, leading to biased results.

1.2 Real-World Examples of AI Bias

● **Racial Bias in Facial Recognition**

- Studies have shown that facial recognition AI has higher error rates for people of color compared to white individuals.
- In 2018, Amazon's Rekognition misidentified 28 U.S. Congress members as criminals, disproportionately affecting Black and Latino individuals.

● **Gender Bias in Hiring Algorithms**

- Amazon's AI hiring tool was scrapped after it was found to favor male applicants over female candidates.
- The AI model learned from historical hiring data that preferred male candidates, reinforcing workplace discrimination.

● **Bias in Credit Scoring**

- Some AI-driven credit scoring models unfairly lower the scores of minority groups due to biased financial data.
- In 2020, reports surfaced that Apple's credit card AI gave lower credit limits to women compared to men, despite similar financial backgrounds.

2. The Consequences of AI Bias

Bias in AI systems can lead to serious social, financial, and legal consequences:

✓ **Discrimination in Hiring** – AI may reject qualified candidates based on gender, race, or age.

✓ **Unfair Loan Approvals** – Biased AI can deny loans or charge higher interest rates to certain demographics.

✓ **Flawed Healthcare Diagnosis** – AI-driven medical tools may misdiagnose conditions in underrepresented patient groups.

✓ **Legal and Compliance Issues** – Companies using biased AI risk lawsuits, regulatory fines, and loss of public trust.

If left unchecked, biased AI reinforces existing inequalities and creates new forms of discrimination, making fairness a top priority for AI adoption.

3. Strategies to Ensure Fairness in AI

Organizations must actively detect, mitigate, and prevent AI bias to ensure ethical and fair decision-making.

3.1 Diverse and Representative Training Data

✓ AI models must be trained on inclusive datasets that represent all demographics, backgrounds, and perspectives.

✓ Developers should audit training data to identify and remove imbalances that could lead to bias.

☞ **Example**: The U.K.'s National Health Service (NHS) developed an AI-driven diagnostic tool that corrected racial biases by training it on diverse medical datasets.

3.2 Explainable AI (XAI) for Transparency

✓ Many AI models are black boxes, meaning their decisions are hard to understand.

✓ Explainable AI (XAI) techniques, such as SHAP (Shapley Additive Explanations) and LIME (Local Interpretable Model-Agnostic Explanations), help provide insights into how AI makes decisions.

☞ **Example**: The European Union (EU) has proposed AI regulations requiring "right to explanation" for AI-driven decisions affecting individuals.

3.3 Fair AI Algorithms & Bias Audits

✔ Developers should use fairness-aware algorithms that minimize biased predictions.

✔ Companies must conduct regular AI bias audits to ensure models remain fair over time.

☞ **Example**: Google and Microsoft have created Fairness Toolkits to help AI developers detect and remove bias in machine learning models.

3.4 Human Oversight & Ethical AI Teams

✔ AI should not be making critical decisions without human oversight.

✔ Organizations should establish Ethical AI Committees to review AI models before deployment.

☞ **Example**: Some hospitals now require human doctors to review AI-generated diagnoses before making treatment decisions.

4. Legal & Regulatory Frameworks for AI Fairness

Many governments and organizations are implementing AI fairness laws and regulations to prevent bias in automated decision-making.

4.1 Key AI Regulations on Fairness

✔ **EU AI Act (2024)** – Requires high-risk AI systems to be transparent, fair, and explainable.

✔ **GDPR (General Data Protection Regulation)** – Grants individuals the right to challenge AI-based decisions.

✔ **U.S. AI Bill of Rights (Proposed)** – Aims to regulate AI in hiring, finance, and healthcare.

☞ **Example**: The New York City Council passed a law requiring companies to audit AI hiring tools for bias before using them.

4.2 Ethical AI Frameworks from Tech Giants

✓ Google's AI Principles include commitments to fairness, transparency, and accountability.

✓ Microsoft's Responsible AI Guidelines require bias testing before deploying AI products.

5. The Future of Fair AI: A Call for Responsible Development

As AI adoption grows, ensuring fairness, transparency, and accountability must be a top priority. AI should not reinforce historical biases but rather be a tool for greater inclusivity and fairness.

✓ Organizations must proactively monitor AI models for bias and ensure they work equitably across all demographics.

✓ Governments must enforce strict AI fairness regulations to protect individuals from discrimination.

✓ Researchers must develop more robust, bias-resistant AI algorithms to ensure fair and ethical AI decisions.

The goal is not just to fix biased AI models but to build AI systems that promote fairness from the start. By working together—businesses, governments, and researchers—we can create an AI-powered future that is ethical, inclusive, and just for all. 🚀

15.2 AI and Data Privacy Regulations (GDPR, CCPA, etc.)

As Artificial Intelligence (AI) continues to integrate into industries such as healthcare, finance, retail, and government, concerns over data privacy and security have become more significant than ever. AI systems process massive amounts of personal and sensitive information, making them subject to various global privacy regulations designed to protect user rights. Laws like the General Data Protection Regulation (GDPR) in Europe and the California Consumer Privacy Act (CCPA) in the U.S. set strict rules for how companies collect, store, and use personal data.

This chapter explores how AI intersects with data privacy laws, the key regulations shaping AI-driven industries, and how businesses can ensure compliance while maintaining AI innovation.

1. The Intersection of AI and Data Privacy

AI thrives on big data, but with more data collection comes increased risks of privacy violations, security breaches, and unethical data usage. Many AI-driven applications, such as facial recognition, predictive analytics, and chatbots, require access to sensitive user data, raising questions about who owns the data, how it's used, and how it's protected.

1.1 How AI Collects and Uses Data

AI systems collect data through:

✓ **Online Activity** – Websites, social media, search engines, and e-commerce platforms track user behavior and preferences.

✓ **IoT Devices** – Smart assistants, fitness trackers, and connected home devices gather real-time user data.

✓ **Healthcare Systems** – AI in healthcare processes medical records, genetic data, and patient histories.

✓ **Finance & Retail** – AI-based recommendations in banking and shopping rely on transaction history and personal identifiers.

1.2 Data Privacy Risks in AI Systems

● **Unauthorized Data Collection** – AI may collect more personal data than necessary, violating privacy laws.

● **Data Breaches & Cyberattacks** – Hackers target AI-driven platforms to steal sensitive user information.

● **Bias in Data Usage** – AI systems may process personal data unfairly, leading to discrimination in hiring, credit approvals, or insurance rates.

● **Lack of Transparency** – Many AI algorithms do not disclose how they use data, violating regulatory requirements.

Due to these risks, governments worldwide have introduced strict privacy regulations to protect user rights and hold AI-driven businesses accountable.

2. Key Data Privacy Regulations Impacting AI

Several global privacy laws have been enacted to ensure that AI technologies handle data ethically and securely.

2.1 General Data Protection Regulation (GDPR) – Europe

✓ **Effective Date**: May 25, 2018

✓ **Scope**: Applies to any company that collects data from EU citizens, even if the business is outside Europe.

GDPR's Key Requirements for AI

✓ **User Consent** – Companies must get explicit permission before collecting or processing personal data.

✓ **Right to Explanation** – AI-driven decisions (e.g., credit approvals, job screenings) must be explainable to users.

✓ **Right to Erasure (Right to Be Forgotten)** – Users can request deletion of their personal data.

✓ **Data Protection Impact Assessments (DPIAs)** – Businesses must conduct privacy risk assessments for AI projects.

✓ **Strict Penalties** – Non-compliance can result in fines up to €20 million or 4% of annual revenue.

☞ **Example**: In 2021, Amazon was fined €746 million under GDPR for violating user data privacy in targeted advertising.

2.2 California Consumer Privacy Act (CCPA) – United States

✓ **Effective Date**: January 1, 2020

✓ **Scope**: Applies to companies with over $25 million in revenue or those that handle personal data of 50,000+ California residents.

CCPA's Key Requirements for AI

✓ **Right to Know** – Consumers can request details on how their data is collected and used.

✓ **Right to Opt-Out** – Users can stop companies from selling their personal data.

✓ **Right to Delete** – Consumers can demand companies erase their personal data.

✓ **Non-Discrimination Clause** – Companies cannot charge different prices or offer different services based on a consumer's privacy choices.

☞ **Example**: In 2022, Sephora was fined $1.2 million under CCPA for failing to disclose that it sold customer data to third parties.

2.3 China's Personal Information Protection Law (PIPL)

✓ **Effective Date**: November 1, 2021

✓ **Scope**: Governs how businesses process personal data of Chinese citizens.

PIPL's Key Requirements for AI

✓ **Strict Data Localization Rules** – Personal data must be stored within China.

✓ **Prohibition of Excessive Data Collection** – AI systems cannot collect unnecessary personal information.

✓ **Government Oversight** – Businesses must obtain government approval before transferring data internationally.

☞ **Example**: Didi (China's Uber) was fined $1.2 billion for violating PIPL's data security requirements.

2.4 Other AI-Impacting Privacy Regulations

✓ **Brazil's LGPD (Lei Geral de Proteção de Dados Pessoais)** – Brazil's GDPR-like law governing personal data processing.

✓ **India's Digital Personal Data Protection Act (DPDPA)** – Regulates AI and cross-border data transfers.

✓ **AI Act (Proposed by EU)** – Will enforce strict rules on high-risk AI applications like facial recognition and hiring algorithms.

3. How AI Companies Can Ensure Privacy Compliance

For AI-driven businesses, navigating global privacy regulations can be complex, but compliance is essential for maintaining trust and avoiding legal penalties.

3.1 Privacy-by-Design in AI Development

✔ AI models must be designed with built-in privacy safeguards.

✔ Data minimization – Only collect necessary personal data.

3.2 Explainable AI (XAI) for Transparency

✔ Users should understand how AI makes decisions affecting them.

✔ Businesses should implement explainability tools like SHAP and LIME.

3.3 Strong Data Security Measures

✔ Use encryption, anonymization, and access controls to protect sensitive data.

✔ Conduct regular audits to detect and fix vulnerabilities.

3.4 User-Centric Privacy Controls

✔ Offer users the ability to opt-out of data collection.

✔ Ensure clear privacy policies outlining how AI processes data.

☞ **Example**: Apple's App Tracking Transparency (ATT) requires apps to ask for user permission before tracking them.

4. The Future of AI and Data Privacy

AI and data privacy laws will continue evolving, with stricter regulations expected globally.

✔ The EU AI Act may become the world's first AI-specific regulation, requiring high-risk AI to undergo risk assessments.

✓ The U.S. is considering a federal privacy law similar to GDPR.

✓ AI must balance innovation with ethics, ensuring user trust while staying legally compliant.

AI businesses that prioritize privacy, transparency, and compliance will lead the future of responsible AI. By integrating ethical AI practices, companies can leverage AI's power while safeguarding user rights in an increasingly data-driven world. 🚀

15.3 AI's Role in Economic Inequality and Job Displacement

Artificial Intelligence (AI) is transforming industries, boosting efficiency, and driving innovation. However, its rapid adoption also raises concerns about economic inequality and job displacement. While AI creates new opportunities, it also threatens traditional jobs, disproportionately affecting low-skilled workers, widening wage gaps, and concentrating wealth among a few technology-driven entities. This chapter examines how AI contributes to economic inequality, its impact on employment, and potential strategies to ensure a more inclusive and balanced AI-driven economy.

1. The Double-Edged Sword: AI's Economic Impact

AI is both a wealth creator and a disruptor. On one hand, it increases productivity, reduces operational costs, and drives economic growth. On the other hand, automation and AI-driven decision-making replace human labor, leading to job losses and wage suppression in some sectors.

1.1 How AI is Reshaping the Global Economy

✓ **Automation of Repetitive Tasks** – AI replaces human workers in manufacturing, customer service, and data processing.

✓ **Job Polarization** – High-skill AI-related jobs increase, but low-skill jobs disappear, leaving a shrinking middle class.

✓ **Productivity Gains** – AI enhances efficiency, allowing businesses to do more with fewer employees.

✓ **Industry Disruption** – Sectors like finance, healthcare, retail, and logistics are adopting AI, changing workforce needs.

✓ **Wealth Concentration** – Tech companies and AI-driven enterprises capture a larger share of economic value, leaving others behind.

2. AI's Role in Job Displacement

2.1 Jobs Most at Risk from AI

● **Manufacturing & Industrial Jobs** – AI-driven robots and automated production lines replace human workers.
● **Retail & Customer Service** – AI-powered chatbots, virtual assistants, and cashier-less stores reduce demand for workers.
● **Transportation & Logistics** – Self-driving trucks, automated warehouses, and AI-powered logistics reshape the industry.
● **Data Entry & Administrative Jobs** – AI-driven document processing and automation tools eliminate clerical roles.
● **Financial Services** – AI handles risk assessments, fraud detection, and trading algorithms, reducing the need for human analysts.

2.2 Jobs Least Affected or Created by AI

☐ **AI & Data Science Roles** – Demand for AI engineers, data scientists, and machine learning experts is rising.
☐ **Creative & Strategic Jobs** – AI struggles with art, design, storytelling, and high-level decision-making.
☐ **Healthcare & Human-Centered Roles** – Doctors, therapists, and social workers require empathy and human interaction, making them harder to automate.
☐ **Skilled Trades & Repair Services** – Electricians, plumbers, and other skilled workers remain in demand due to hands-on work complexity.

3. AI's Contribution to Economic Inequality

3.1 Widening the Wealth Gap

AI benefits large corporations and highly skilled professionals while displacing workers in low-income jobs. The economic gains from AI are unevenly distributed, leading to:

✓ **Higher Profits for AI-Enabled Companies** – Tech giants like Google, Amazon, and Tesla dominate AI-driven innovation, accumulating massive wealth.

✓ **Job Market Polarization** – The gap between high-wage tech jobs and low-wage service jobs continues to grow.

✓ **Geographical Disparities** – AI investments are concentrated in developed economies, leaving developing nations struggling to keep up.

✓ **Decline in Labor's Share of Income** – As AI replaces workers, companies spend less on wages, benefiting shareholders more than employees.

3.2 AI and Wage Suppression

AI increases efficiency but reduces bargaining power for workers. With automation replacing many routine jobs, wages stagnate in fields where humans compete with AI-driven systems. Employers outsource tasks to AI, leading to:

● **Fewer Job Opportunities** – Businesses require fewer human workers to maintain operations.

● **Lower Wages for Non-AI Jobs** – AI drives down wages in jobs that remain, as fewer workers are needed.

● **Rise of the Gig Economy** – Many displaced workers turn to gig work and temporary contracts, which often lack stability and benefits.

4. Strategies to Address AI-Induced Inequality and Job Displacement

To ensure AI benefits everyone, governments, businesses, and educational institutions must take proactive steps to mitigate job displacement and reduce inequality.

4.1 Reskilling and Upskilling the Workforce

☐ **AI Education & Training** – Governments and companies should invest in AI-related skill development.

☐ **Lifelong Learning Programs** – Universities and online platforms should offer continuous education to help workers adapt.

☐ **Public-Private Partnerships** – Governments should collaborate with AI-driven companies to create retraining programs.

☞ **Example**: Amazon's "Upskilling 2025" program provides free AI and cloud computing training to employees.

4.2 AI-Driven Job Creation

While AI eliminates jobs, it also creates new employment opportunities. Policies should encourage:

✓ **AI in Human-Augmented Jobs** – AI should assist workers instead of replacing them (e.g., AI-assisted doctors or AI-powered teachers).

✓ **Growth in AI Ethics & Policy Roles** – Demand for professionals in AI ethics, governance, and compliance is rising.

✓ **AI-Supported Entrepreneurship** – Small businesses should leverage AI to increase productivity and create new markets.

☞ **Example**: The rise of AI has created millions of jobs in software development, cybersecurity, and AI ethics.

4.3 Universal Basic Income (UBI) and Social Safety Nets

Some experts propose Universal Basic Income (UBI) as a solution to AI-driven job loss. Governments could provide:

✓ **Guaranteed Income** – Monthly payments to citizens to offset AI-related job displacement.

✓ **Tax Reforms** – Companies benefiting from AI should contribute to worker retraining programs.

✓ **Shorter Work Weeks** – Reducing work hours while maintaining wages to distribute employment opportunities more fairly.

☞ **Example**: Finland tested UBI programs to support workers affected by automation, showing positive mental health and job-seeking outcomes.

4.4 Ethical AI Development & Policy Regulation

Governments must implement AI policies that prioritize fairness, transparency, and inclusivity. Policies should:

✓ **Mandate Ethical AI Use** – Ensure AI applications do not discriminate against workers.

✓ **Require AI Impact Assessments** – Companies should evaluate how AI affects jobs and economic inequality.

✓ **Encourage Responsible AI Innovation** – AI should enhance human potential rather than replace human labor.

☞ **Example**: The EU AI Act proposes regulations on high-risk AI applications to prevent discrimination in hiring and finance.

5. The Future of AI and the Workforce

AI will reshape the job market, but proactive policies and education can ensure a more equitable future. Instead of replacing humans entirely, AI should be leveraged to augment human capabilities, enhance job satisfaction, and create new economic opportunities.

✓ **Collaboration Between AI and Humans** – AI should serve as a co-pilot, not a replacement for human workers.

✓ **Fair AI Implementation** – Businesses must prioritize equity, transparency, and ethical AI development.

✓ **Investment in Human Capital** – By focusing on reskilling and innovation, AI can lead to a future where technology benefits all socioeconomic groups.

AI is a powerful tool that, when managed responsibly, can reduce inequality instead of exacerbating it. By investing in education, policy reform, and ethical AI, we can ensure a future where AI drives prosperity for all, not just a select few. 🚀

15.4 Building Trust and Transparency in AI-Driven Industries

Artificial intelligence (AI) is rapidly transforming industries, from healthcare and finance to manufacturing and retail. However, for AI to be fully embraced, it must be trusted by businesses, employees, and consumers alike. Transparency in AI decision-making is crucial to ensuring fairness, accountability, and ethical use. Without trust, AI adoption faces resistance due to concerns about bias, privacy, security, and lack of human oversight.

This chapter explores how organizations can build trust in AI by prioritizing transparency, explainability, fairness, and ethical governance to ensure responsible AI implementation.

1. The Importance of Trust in AI Adoption

Trust is the foundation of AI adoption across industries. Without it, businesses, regulators, and consumers may resist AI-driven solutions.

1.1 Why Trust in AI Matters

✓ **User Acceptance** – Employees and consumers must feel confident that AI systems are making fair and unbiased decisions.

✓ **Regulatory Compliance** – Industries with strict compliance requirements (e.g., finance, healthcare) need transparent AI to avoid legal risks.

✓ **Business Reputation** – Companies that fail to explain AI decisions may lose customers and face reputational damage.

✓ **Ethical AI Use** – AI should be aligned with human values, ensuring it does not harm or discriminate.

1.2 The Risks of Opaque AI Systems

🏛 **Algorithmic Bias** – AI trained on biased data can lead to discriminatory decisions in hiring, lending, and law enforcement.

🏛 **Black Box AI** – Many AI models, especially deep learning, lack explainability, making it difficult to understand why decisions are made.

🏛 **Data Privacy Concerns** – AI systems that collect and analyze user data raise security and privacy issues.

🏛 **Lack of Human Oversight** – Over-reliance on AI without human intervention can result in unintended consequences.

2. Key Pillars of AI Transparency

To build trust, AI systems must be transparent, explainable, and accountable.

2.1 Explainable AI (XAI): Making AI Decisions Understandable

📌 **What is Explainable AI (XAI)?**

Explainable AI (XAI) refers to AI models that provide clear reasoning behind their decisions, making them easier for humans to interpret and trust.

★ Benefits of XAI

✓ Helps regulators and auditors verify AI decisions.

✓ Allows users to challenge AI-based outcomes (e.g., loan approvals, medical diagnoses).

✓ Enhances consumer confidence in AI-powered services.

★ XAI Techniques

🔍 **Feature Importance Analysis** – Highlights which factors influenced the AI's decision.
🔍 **Decision Trees & Rule-Based Models** – Simpler AI models that provide clear, logical steps.
🔍 **Counterfactual Explanations** – Shows what changes would lead to a different AI decision.

☞ **Example**: In healthcare, AI predicting disease risks should explain which symptoms or patient history influenced its decision.

2.2 Fairness & Bias Mitigation in AI

★ How Bias Occurs in AI

AI can unintentionally learn biases from historical data, leading to unfair decisions in:

🖥 **Hiring & HR** – AI may favor certain demographics based on biased past hiring data.
🖥 **Banking & Lending** – AI-driven credit scoring may discriminate against minorities.
🖥 **Healthcare** – AI models trained on limited patient data may fail to provide accurate diagnoses for underrepresented groups.

★ Bias Mitigation Strategies

✓ **Diverse & Representative Training Data** – Ensure AI is trained on data from all demographics.
✓ **Bias Audits & Testing** – Regularly check AI systems for unintended discrimination.

✔ **Human Oversight in Decision-Making** – AI should assist, not replace, human experts in critical decisions.

☞ **Example**: IBM's AI Fairness 360 toolkit helps businesses detect and reduce bias in AI models.

2.3 Ethical AI Governance & Accountability

📌 **Why AI Needs Ethical Governance**

Organizations must have clear policies on how AI is used to prevent unethical practices.

📌 **Best Practices for AI Governance**

✔ **Ethical AI Guidelines** – Develop internal policies on how AI should be used responsibly.
✔ **AI Audits & Compliance Checks** – Regularly test AI systems for fairness, transparency, and security.
✔ **AI Ethics Committees** – Establish expert panels to oversee AI deployments in high-risk areas.

☞ **Example**: Google's AI Principles focus on fairness, privacy, and safety in AI development.

3. Strategies for Building Trust in AI

3.1 Human-Centered AI Design

AI should be designed to support human decision-making, not replace it.

✔ **Keep Humans in the Loop (HITL)** – AI should assist rather than fully automate high-stakes decisions.
✔ **User-Friendly AI Interfaces** – AI systems should present decisions in a way that non-experts can understand.
✔ **Customizable AI Controls** – Users should be able to adjust AI settings based on their preferences and needs.

☞ **Example**: Tesla's Autopilot system includes driver monitoring to ensure humans remain engaged while AI assists.

3.2 Transparency in AI Development & Deployment

✔ **Disclose How AI Works** – Companies should publicly explain how their AI models function and make decisions.

✔ **Provide AI Explainability Reports** – Organizations should document data sources, model design, and potential biases.

✔ **Allow User Appeals** – Consumers should have a way to challenge AI-driven decisions (e.g., credit scores, job applications).

☞ **Example**: Microsoft's AI Transparency Initiative publishes detailed reports on how its AI models operate.

3.3 Regulatory Compliance & Global AI Standards

📌 **AI Regulations to Watch**

✔ **EU AI Act** – Classifies AI systems by risk levels and mandates strict transparency for high-risk applications.

✔ **GDPR & CCPA** – Enforce data privacy rights, requiring companies to explain how AI handles user data.

✔ **NIST AI Risk Framework** – Provides guidelines for responsible AI use in businesses.

📌 **How Companies Can Stay Compliant**

✔ Follow local and global AI regulations to ensure ethical deployment.

✔ Conduct independent audits of AI systems for fairness and security.

✔ Maintain clear documentation on AI decision-making processes.

☞ **Example**: Financial institutions using AI for credit scoring must comply with Fair Lending Laws to prevent discrimination.

4. The Future of Trustworthy AI

To unlock AI's full potential, organizations must make transparency and accountability core principles of AI development. The future of AI will depend on:

✓ **Stronger AI Governance** – Governments and businesses will collaborate on ethical AI frameworks.

✓ **Advancements in Explainability** – More research will focus on interpretable AI models.

✓ **Greater Consumer Awareness** – Users will demand more transparency in AI-powered services.

✓ **Responsible AI Innovation** – Businesses that prioritize trust will gain a competitive advantage.

By making AI more transparent, fair, and accountable, industries can build the trust needed for sustainable AI adoption. The key is to create AI that not only enhances efficiency but also respects human values and ethical standards. 🚀

16. Conclusion: The Road Ahead for AI in Industry

AI has already transformed industries, but its journey is far from over. As advancements in machine learning, automation, quantum computing, and ethical AI continue to evolve, businesses must stay adaptable and forward-thinking. The future of AI in industry will be shaped by regulatory developments, ethical considerations, and the integration of AI with emerging technologies such as the metaverse, blockchain, and augmented intelligence. This final chapter reflects on the key takeaways from AI's impact across industries, the challenges that lie ahead, and the exciting possibilities for businesses, professionals, and society in the AI-driven future.

16.1 Lessons from Industry AI Implementation

As artificial intelligence (AI) continues to transform industries, businesses and organizations have learned valuable lessons from both successful and failed implementations. While AI offers immense potential for efficiency, automation, and data-driven decision-making, its adoption is not without challenges. Companies that integrate AI effectively must navigate technical, ethical, operational, and regulatory hurdles to maximize benefits while mitigating risks.

This chapter explores key takeaways from AI deployments across industries, highlighting best practices, common pitfalls, and real-world insights to help organizations develop scalable, transparent, and effective AI solutions.

1. Understanding the Reality vs. Hype of AI

1.1 AI is Not a Magic Solution

One of the most common misconceptions is that AI can instantly solve complex industry challenges. In reality, AI is only as good as:

✓ The quality of data it learns from.

✓ The clarity of business objectives it is designed for.

✓ The human expertise guiding its implementation.

📖 **Lesson Learned**: Companies that adopt AI without a clear strategy often fail to see meaningful ROI. Instead of adopting AI for the sake of "innovation," organizations should align AI solutions with real business needs.

1.2 The AI Hype Cycle: Managing Expectations

AI adoption follows a hype cycle, where excitement about AI's capabilities often leads to overpromises and under-delivery.

📌 **Phases of AI Adoption:**

1️ **Initial Excitement** – AI is seen as a game-changer, leading to high investments.

2️ **Reality Check** – Early challenges appear, such as data limitations, ethical concerns, and system inefficiencies.

3️ **Maturity & Real Value** – Organizations refine AI applications for long-term success.

📖 **Lesson Learned**: Organizations that successfully implement AI focus on gradual, scalable deployment rather than expecting immediate transformation.

2. Key Factors for Successful AI Implementation

2.1 Data Quality and Management is Critical

📌 AI is only as good as the data it is trained on. Poor data quality leads to biased models, inaccurate predictions, and operational failures.

✓ **Lesson**: Companies must prioritize data collection, cleaning, and governance to improve AI accuracy.

✓ **Example**: In healthcare, AI models trained on incomplete patient records have failed to provide reliable diagnoses.

2.2 Human Oversight is Essential

📌 AI should augment, not replace, human decision-making. AI-powered automation is powerful, but full automation without human oversight can be dangerous.

✓ **Lesson**: AI should be deployed as a decision-support tool, ensuring humans remain in control of critical decisions.

✓ **Example**: In finance, algorithmic trading systems without human supervision have led to flash crashes, causing market instability.

2.3 Ethics & Transparency Drive AI Trust

📌 Trust is a major factor in AI adoption. If customers, employees, or regulators do not trust an AI system, its adoption will face resistance.

✓ **Lesson**: Companies should prioritize explainability, fairness, and bias detection in AI models.

✓ **Example**: In hiring, AI-driven recruitment tools have been scrapped after being found to discriminate against women and minorities.

3. Common Pitfalls and How to Avoid Them

3.1 Over-Automation Without Testing

📖 **Mistake**: Some companies rush to automate processes without proper testing, leading to failures.

✓ **Solution**: Pilot AI solutions on a small scale before full implementation.

3.2 Ignoring Regulatory Compliance

📖 **Mistake**: Some organizations deploy AI without considering data privacy laws (e.g., GDPR, CCPA).

✓ **Solution**: Ensure AI models comply with legal and ethical guidelines before deployment.

3.3 Underestimating Change Management

📖 **Mistake**: Employees resist AI adoption when they feel threatened by automation.

✓ **Solution**: Provide proper AI training and involve employees in AI strategy discussions.

4. Case Studies: Lessons from Industry AI Deployments

✦ **Healthcare**: AI-powered diagnostics in radiology led to higher efficiency, but early models lacked transparency, causing regulatory delays.

✦ **Finance**: AI-driven fraud detection reduced financial crime, but black-box models raised concerns about bias and explainability.

✦ **Retail**: Personalized AI recommendations increased sales, but early implementations had privacy concerns, requiring stronger data protections.

5. Final Thoughts: Building a Future-Ready AI Strategy

AI's future in industries depends on responsible implementation, continuous learning, and ethical alignment. Companies that succeed with AI focus on transparency, human-AI collaboration, and long-term value creation.

By learning from past implementations, organizations can build AI solutions that drive innovation, efficiency, and trust across industries. 🚀

16.2 The Future of AI Regulation & Compliance

As artificial intelligence (AI) continues to revolutionize industries, governments and regulatory bodies worldwide are working to establish legal frameworks and compliance standards that ensure AI is deployed ethically, fairly, and safely. While AI offers immense benefits in healthcare, finance, manufacturing, and beyond, its rapid advancement raises concerns about bias, data privacy, security, accountability, and transparency.

This chapter explores the future of AI regulation and compliance, examining current regulatory trends, challenges in enforcement, and how businesses can proactively adapt to evolving AI laws.

1. The Need for AI Regulation

1.1 Why AI Needs Governance

AI-driven decisions now influence hiring, medical diagnoses, financial transactions, and legal judgments. Without clear regulations, AI can:

🏛 **Reinforce Bias** – AI trained on biased data can lead to discriminatory hiring, lending, or law enforcement.

🏛 **Lack Transparency** – Many AI models (especially deep learning) operate as black boxes, making their decisions hard to interpret.

🏛 **Threaten Privacy** – AI-powered surveillance and data analysis raise serious privacy concerns.

🏛 **Cause Security Risks** – AI can be manipulated or exploited, leading to fraud, cyberattacks, or misinformation spread.

✔ Regulation ensures that AI serves society fairly, ethically, and securely while fostering innovation.

2. Current AI Regulations & Global Compliance Standards

2.1 Major AI Regulations Around the World

📌 **European Union – AI Act (2024 & Beyond)**

✔ The first comprehensive AI law, classifying AI systems into risk categories:

- **Unacceptable Risk AI (banned)** – Examples: Social scoring (like China's system), AI-driven mass surveillance.
- **High-Risk AI (strict regulation)** – Examples: AI in hiring, healthcare, finance, and law enforcement.
- **Limited & Minimal Risk AI** – Examples: AI chatbots, recommendation systems, where transparency is required.

📌 **United States – AI Executive Orders & State Laws**

✔ No federal AI law yet, but:

- AI Bill of Rights (2022) provides ethical guidelines.
- SEC & FTC regulate AI in finance, advertising, and consumer protection.
- California Privacy Rights Act (CPRA) enforces AI transparency in data collection.

📌 **China – AI Regulation Focused on Government Oversight**

✓ Strict AI rules on:

- **Deepfake & facial recognition** AI – Requires government approval.
- **Algorithmic recommendation transparency** – Platforms must disclose AI-driven decisions.

📌 **Canada, UK, India & Others**

✓ Countries are drafting AI-specific regulations to balance innovation and ethical concerns.

📖 **Lesson**: Businesses operating internationally must ensure their AI systems comply with different regional laws.

3. Key Areas of AI Compliance & Future Regulations

3.1 AI Transparency & Explainability (XAI)

✓ **Future Requirement**: AI models must explain their decisions in high-stakes sectors like healthcare and finance.

✓ **Regulatory Trend: Explainable AI** (XAI) will become mandatory for hiring, lending, and medical AI tools.

☞ **Example**: If AI denies a loan, companies must provide a clear explanation instead of just an automated rejection.

3.2 Bias & Fairness in AI

✓ **Future Requirement**: AI systems must be tested for bias before deployment.

✓ **Regulatory Trend**: Companies will need bias audits & fairness reports.

☞ **Example**: AI-powered HR software must not favor certain demographics in hiring decisions.

3.3 AI & Data Privacy Compliance

✓ **Future Requirement**: AI systems must comply with data privacy laws (GDPR, CCPA, etc.) and allow users to opt out of AI processing.

✓ **Regulatory Trend**: More laws will limit AI's ability to track, store, and analyze personal data without consent.

☞ **Example**: AI-driven targeted advertising may face stricter consent laws to protect user privacy.

3.4 Cybersecurity & AI Risk Management

✓ **Future Requirement**: AI must be designed with built-in security features to prevent hacking and data breaches.

✓ **Regulatory Trend**: Governments will require companies to disclose AI vulnerabilities and conduct security audits.

☞ **Example**: AI-driven financial fraud detection systems must be secured against adversarial AI attacks.

3.5 AI in Autonomous Systems (Self-Driving Cars, Robotics, Drones, etc.)

✓ **Future Requirement**: AI-powered machines must meet safety, liability, and ethical standards before public deployment.

✓ **Regulatory Trend**: Strict safety testing will be required for self-driving vehicles, AI drones, and industrial robots.

☞ **Example**: Tesla's Autopilot system is under scrutiny for accidents linked to AI decision-making errors.

4. How Businesses Can Prepare for Future AI Regulations

📌 4.1 Build Ethical & Transparent AI Frameworks

✓ Adopt explainable AI models (XAI) for high-risk applications.

✓ Conduct AI fairness & bias audits before deployment.

📌 4.2 Strengthen Data Privacy & Security

✓ Ensure AI complies with GDPR, CCPA, and upcoming global laws.

✓ Implement data minimization techniques to reduce privacy risks.

📌 4.3 Monitor Global AI Regulatory Changes

✓ Stay updated on AI compliance laws in different countries.

✓ Appoint AI governance teams within organizations to manage compliance.

📌 4.4 Engage with Policymakers & Industry Leaders

✓ Companies should collaborate with regulators to shape future AI laws.

✓ Participate in AI ethics boards & industry consortia to stay ahead.

5. The Future of AI Regulation: What to Expect

✓ **Stronger AI Auditing Requirements** – Companies will need third-party audits for AI fairness and transparency.

✓ **Standardized Global AI Compliance Laws** – Efforts will increase to harmonize AI regulations worldwide.

✓ **Stricter AI Liability & Accountability Laws** – Companies will be held legally responsible for AI errors and bias.

✓ **More Ethical AI Guidelines from Governments** – Nations will balance innovation with responsible AI governance.

☞ **Final Thought**: The future of AI regulation will focus on protecting users, ensuring fairness, and maintaining transparency while fostering innovation. Businesses that prepare for these changes today will be well-positioned for AI success tomorrow. 🚀

16.3 What's Next for AI in the Coming Decades?

Artificial intelligence (AI) is advancing at an unprecedented pace, transforming industries and reshaping the way humans interact with technology. Over the next few decades, AI will become more powerful, more autonomous, and more integrated into daily life. From general AI and human-AI collaboration to breakthroughs in quantum computing and ethical AI governance, the future promises revolutionary developments.

This chapter explores the next frontiers of AI, the challenges that lie ahead, and how societies and businesses must prepare for the AI-driven world of tomorrow.

1. The Rise of Artificial General Intelligence (AGI)

1.1 From Narrow AI to General AI

Today's AI is narrow AI, meaning it is task-specific—designed for things like speech recognition, recommendation systems, and medical diagnostics. However, researchers are working toward Artificial General Intelligence (AGI), an AI capable of performing any intellectual task a human can do.

📌 **AGI Characteristics:**

✓ Can learn and adapt to new situations without retraining

✓ Can perform multiple complex tasks simultaneously

✓ Can exhibit reasoning, creativity, and problem-solving abilities

🚀 **Potential Impact:**

✓ AGI could automate most cognitive tasks, leading to a new industrial revolution.

✓ It could outperform humans in research, engineering, and decision-making, accelerating technological progress.

🔔 **Challenges:**

✓ **Ethical concerns** – Who controls AGI, and how do we prevent misuse?

✓ **Economic disruption** – How do we handle job displacement as AGI takes over complex work?

2. AI & Human Collaboration: The Future of Work

2.1 AI as an Augmentative Force

Rather than replacing humans entirely, AI will increasingly work alongside people, augmenting their skills and automating repetitive tasks.

📌 **Future AI-Human Work Scenarios:**

✓ AI-powered virtual assistants will handle most administrative tasks.

✓ AI-driven medical diagnostics will enhance doctors' ability to treat patients.

✓ AI co-pilots will assist software engineers, artists, and writers in content creation.

☞ **Example**: Tools like ChatGPT and GitHub Copilot already help professionals work faster.

📢 **Challenges:**

✓ **Workforce reskilling** – People must learn to work alongside AI rather than be replaced by it.

✓ **Ethical oversight** – Ensuring AI supports human creativity and decision-making rather than controlling it.

3. The Integration of AI with Emerging Technologies

3.1 AI + Quantum Computing

📌 **What to Expect?**

✓ Quantum computing will exponentially increase AI's processing power, enabling hyper-advanced problem-solving.

✓ AI models will be trained in minutes instead of weeks, revolutionizing scientific research.

🚀 **Potential Breakthroughs:**

✓ **Drug discovery** – AI + quantum computing could simulate molecules in real-time, speeding up medical innovations.

✓ **Cryptography & security** – AI-powered quantum encryption will make data nearly unbreakable.

🔒 Challenges:

✓ Quantum computing is still in its infancy—widespread applications may take decades.

3.2 AI + Robotics

📌 What to Expect?

✓ AI-powered humanoid robots will assist in factories, homes, and healthcare.

✓ Fully autonomous robot workers will handle dangerous tasks in construction, mining, and space exploration.

🚀 Potential Breakthroughs:

✓ AI-driven elderly care robots could support aging populations.

✓ AI-enabled space exploration will push the boundaries of deep-space travel.

🔒 Challenges:

✓ Ethical concerns about robot rights, autonomy, and accountability.

3.3 AI + Biotechnology & Brain-Computer Interfaces (BCI)

📌 What to Expect?

✓ AI-powered brain chips (like Elon Musk's Neuralink) could allow direct communication between humans and machines.

✓ AI will decode thoughts, enabling paralyzed individuals to control devices with their minds.

🚀 **Potential Breakthroughs:**

✓ AI-enhanced gene editing could eliminate genetic diseases.

✓ AI-driven bioengineering could lead to longer human lifespans.

🔔 **Challenges:**

✓ Who owns brain-data privacy?

✓ What happens when AI starts altering human biology?

4. The Ethical & Societal Impact of Future AI

4.1 AI Governance & Global Cooperation

As AI becomes more powerful, international collaboration will be necessary to set ethical guidelines and prevent AI misuse.

📌 **Key Future Regulations May Include:**

✓ **AI accountability laws** – Holding companies and governments responsible for AI mistakes.

✓ **AI warfare treaties** – Preventing autonomous weapons from making life-and-death decisions.

✓ **Global AI Ethics Boards** – Ensuring AI benefits all of humanity, not just corporations or governments.

🔔 **Challenges:**

✓ Different countries have competing AI agendas, making regulation difficult.

✓ AI regulations must balance innovation with responsibility.

4.2 AI & Economic Inequality

While AI will create new jobs and industries, it will also widen the wealth gap if access remains unequal.

📌 **Future AI-Driven Economic Trends:**

✓ AI-driven automation will eliminate repetitive jobs while creating new AI-related careers.

✓ Universal Basic Income (UBI) could be implemented to counter job displacement.

🔊 **Challenges:**

✓ If AI is controlled by a few tech giants, it could lead to economic monopolization.

✓ Workers must be reskilled for AI-powered industries.

5. The Next 50 Years: AI's Ultimate Potential

5.1 AI & The Search for Extraterrestrial Intelligence (SETI)

🚀 AI may help us analyze vast amounts of cosmic data, accelerating the search for alien life.

5.2 AI-Generated Creativity & Consciousness

📌 **Could AI become self-aware?**

✓ Some researchers believe AI will develop consciousness, raising ethical and philosophical debates.

✓ AI artists, composers, and writers will create entirely new forms of creative expression.

🔊 **Challenges:**

✓ What rights would a sentient AI have?

✓ Should AI be considered "alive" if it gains self-awareness?

6. Final Thoughts: The Future is AI-Driven

Artificial intelligence is poised to reshape the world in ways we are only beginning to understand. While the coming decades will bring unimaginable advancements, they will also introduce new risks, ethical dilemmas, and societal challenges. The responsibility falls on governments, businesses, researchers, and individuals to ensure AI is developed and used ethically, safely, and inclusively.

The future of AI is not just about technology—it's about the future of humanity itself. 🚀

16.4 Final Thoughts: AI as a Partner, Not a Replacement

As we reach the conclusion of this book—and indeed, the final chapter of the AI from Scratch series—it's important to reflect on the true role of AI in our world. Throughout history, technological advancements have often been met with fear and uncertainty, as humans worry about machines replacing their work, creativity, and even their sense of purpose. However, AI should not be viewed as a threat but rather as a partner—an assistant that enhances human capabilities rather than replaces them.

In this chapter, we will explore how AI can be ethically and responsibly integrated into industries, ensuring that it serves as a collaborative tool rather than a substitute for human intelligence. By embracing AI as a partner rather than a replacement, businesses, workers, and society as a whole can harness its power to drive innovation while maintaining the human touch that makes industries thrive.

1. AI as an Augmentative Force, Not a Job Killer

One of the biggest concerns surrounding AI is its impact on jobs. While automation will undoubtedly change the nature of work, AI should be seen as a tool for augmentation rather than a means for replacement.

📌 How AI Enhances Human Work:

✔ **Automation of repetitive tasks** – AI can handle data entry, scheduling, and customer inquiries, freeing humans for more creative and strategic work.

✔ **Decision-making support** – AI-driven analytics can process vast amounts of information to assist professionals in healthcare, finance, and education.

✓ **Enhanced productivity** – AI-powered tools like chatbots, virtual assistants, and predictive analytics help employees work smarter and faster.

🚀 **Real-World Example:**

♦ **In healthcare, AI doesn't replace doctors**—it assists them in diagnosing diseases faster and more accurately.
♦ **In finance**, AI-driven robo-advisors help human analysts by sorting data and detecting trends, allowing for more informed financial decisions.

Rather than taking jobs away, AI is changing job roles and creating new opportunities that require human oversight, creativity, and ethical judgment.

2. The Power of Human-AI Collaboration

AI alone is not perfect—it requires human intuition, emotional intelligence, and moral judgment to function effectively. The future lies in a collaborative partnership between humans and AI.

📌 **Industries Benefiting from Human-AI Collaboration:**

✓ **Healthcare**: AI-powered imaging helps radiologists, but human doctors make the final diagnosis.
✓ **Finance**: AI detects fraud, but human analysts review and confirm suspicious transactions.
✓ **Education**: AI personalizes learning, but teachers provide mentorship, emotional support, and ethical guidance.

🚀 **Case Study: Human-AI Partnership in Creative Work**

♦ In the music industry, AI can generate melodies, but artists still compose and refine songs to give them emotional depth.
♦ In journalism, AI can assist in drafting reports, but human writers ensure storytelling, analysis, and ethics remain intact.

Rather than replacing human expertise, AI empowers professionals to make better decisions, focus on high-value tasks, and solve complex problems more efficiently.

3. Ethical AI: The Need for Responsible AI Development

For AI to truly serve as a partner and not a threat, it must be developed and deployed responsibly. Ethical AI ensures that AI systems are fair, unbiased, transparent, and accountable.

📌 **Key Principles for Ethical AI Development:**

✔ **Transparency**: AI decisions should be explainable and understandable.

✔ **Fairness**: AI should not reinforce biases in hiring, lending, or law enforcement.

✔ **Accountability**: Companies and governments must take responsibility for AI mistakes and biases.

🚀 **Future of Ethical AI:**

◆ Explainable AI (XAI) will become a standard, ensuring that AI-driven decisions are not "black boxes."
◆ AI ethics boards will monitor and regulate AI deployment across industries.
◆ Diversity in AI development will help reduce algorithmic bias.

By building AI with human values at its core, we ensure it enhances lives rather than causing harm.

4. AI as a Partner in the Future of Humanity

As we look ahead, it's clear that AI will become even more integrated into our daily lives—from smart assistants and self-driving cars to AI-driven healthcare and education. But rather than fearing AI, we must embrace it as a powerful tool for human progress.

📌 **How to Approach AI in the Future:**

✔ **Invest in AI literacy** – Understanding AI's capabilities and limitations will help individuals and businesses adapt.
✔ **Encourage human-AI collaboration** – Industries should develop AI solutions that support and amplify human expertise.

✓ **Prioritize ethical AI** – Governments, businesses, and researchers must work together to ensure AI serves the greater good.

🚀 **Final Thought:**

AI is not here to replace us—it is here to help us solve problems, improve efficiency, and unlock new possibilities. By working alongside AI rather than against it, humanity can achieve remarkable advancements while keeping human values, creativity, and ethics at the forefront.

Artificial Intelligence is no longer confined to research labs and tech giants—it is now a fundamental driver of change across every major industry. In **Industry AI: Applications in Healthcare, Finance, and Beyond**, the final volume of the *AI from Scratch series*, we explored how AI is shaping the future of business, medicine, finance, manufacturing, and beyond.

From AI-powered medical diagnostics that detect diseases with greater accuracy to algorithmic trading systems that process financial data in milliseconds, this book has showcased the real-world applications of AI that are revolutionizing industries today. We've examined the challenges, opportunities, and ethical considerations that come with integrating AI into business processes and discussed the future of AI in industry, from quantum AI to Explainable AI (XAI).

As we close this journey, one thing is clear: AI is no longer just a tool—it is a partner in progress. Whether enhancing efficiency, improving decision-making, or unlocking new business models, AI is here to stay. The future belongs to those who embrace its potential responsibly and strategically.

This book serves as both a guide and a reflection on AI's transformative power. As AI continues to evolve, so must our understanding, ethics, and approach to its implementation. The AI revolution is far from over—this is just the beginning.

Thank you for joining this journey through the AI from Scratch series. Now, it's time to build the future with AI. 🚀

Dear Reader,

As I close the final pages of **Industry AI: Applications in Healthcare, Finance, and Beyond**, I want to take a moment to express my deepest gratitude to you—the reader. Whether this is your first book from the *AI from Scratch series* or you've been with me from the very beginning, your curiosity, passion, and commitment to learning have made this journey truly meaningful.

Writing this series has been more than just a professional endeavor; it has been a journey of discovery, growth, and a shared vision for the future of AI. With each book, I have aimed to break down complex AI concepts into accessible, practical knowledge, and it is your engagement—your desire to learn and innovate—that has kept me inspired.

To all the students, AI enthusiasts, professionals, researchers, entrepreneurs, and visionaries who have embarked on this journey with me—thank you. Your support, feedback, and enthusiasm have made this series possible. AI is not just about algorithms and data; it's about people, about how we use technology to create a smarter, more efficient, and ethical world.

This book may mark the end of the AI from Scratch series, but it is only the beginning of what AI can achieve. As you move forward, I encourage you to keep exploring, keep questioning, and most importantly, keep building. The future of AI is in your hands.

With gratitude and excitement for what's to come,

Gilbert Gutiérrez

✸ *The Future is Not AI*

vs.

✸ *Humans—It's AI with Humans.*